On the Methodology of ARCHITECTURAL HISTORY

Guest Editor
Demetri Porphyrios

Demetri Porphyrios Introduction 2
Ernst Gombrich Hegel and Art History 3
Joseph Rykwert Gottfried Semper and the Problem of Style 11
Arturo Carlo Quintavalle The Philosophical Context of Riegl's *Stilfragen* 17
Spiro Kostof Paul Frankl's Principles of Architectural History 21
Georges Teyssot Neoclassic and 'Autonomous' Architecture: the Formalism of Emil Kaufmann 25
Guido Neri The Artistic Theory of Erwin Panofsky 31
Alan Colquhoun Gombrich and Cultural History 37
Cesare de Seta Benevolo's *Storia* 41
Kenneth Frampton Giedion in America: Reflections in a Mirror 45
Robert Maxwell Reyner Banham: the Plenitude of Presence 53
Yves Alain Bois Francastel's Interdisciplinary History of Art 59
Stefan Morawski Marxist Historicism and the Philosophy of Art 61
Kurt Forster Walter Benjamin: Residues of a Dream World 69
Manfredo Tafuri The Uncertainties of Formalism: Victor Sklovskij and the Denuding of Art 73
Maurice Culot and **Philippe Lefèbvre** Argan: the State of Defiance 79
Tomas Llorens Manfredo Tafuri: Neo-Avant-Garde and History 83
Demetri Porphyrios Notes on a Method 95

A.D. Architectural Design Profile

INTRODUCTION

Architectural history has been taught and studied in a manner that has generally avoided the questioning of its methodological tools, never exposing, therefore, its own ideological assumptions. It is true that architectural history has always had tools of analysis, yet, by avoiding the systematic discussion of these tools, it has blurred its epistemological foundations.

My intention to edit a volume that would attempt to fill this gap—at least provisionally and as a collective working paper—dates back to 1975, when, while at Princeton University, I had ample opportunity to discuss these and related issues with Professors A Vidler, C Schorske, K Frampton, D Coffin, S Morawski, A Colquhoun, and J Rykwert, to all of whom I am greatly indebted. Since then the project was discussed many times with Cristian F Otto, editor of the *Journal of the Society of Architectural Historians*, who, after a long and time-consuming search, had to give up the idea '*...saddened that the discipline is so uninterested in itself...*'

This experience led me to a growing realisation of the need to raise the level of consciousness of the epistemological foundations of the various architectural histories; especially in a period like ours, burdened as it is with ephemeral, ad hoc and surreptitious 'theory-hunting'. Bearing this in mind, it becomes clear that the study of the methodology of architectural history is as important for the non-theoretically orientated designer as it is for the student of history himself. For it is only through a familiarity with the ideological presuppositions which underly the various methods of historical analysis that the designer can pass judgment on the otherwise seemingly 'objective' texts which form his own historical consciousness.

This *Architectural Design* profile on the methodology of architectural history is a small but significant move in this direction. The reader will, of course, gain by referring to certain important recent contributions to the subject, to which I am equally indebted. I would mention particularly the following: the papers of the seminar on *The History, Theory and Criticism of Architecture* held at MIT and edited by M Whiffen, 1964-65; the relevant chapters in M Tafuri's *Theories and History of Architecture*, (1968), 1976; N Pevsner's *Some Architectural Writers of the 19th Century*, 1972; the papers of the symposium on *Architectural History and Social Sciences* held at the Kunsthistorisch Institut der Rijksuniversiteit, Utrecht, 1978; and D Watkin's *The Rise of Architectural History*, 1980. This issue, however, does not aim to present the historiographic contributions of art historical research—important as these may be; rather, it focuses on a number of significant art and architectural historians in an attempt to analyse their particular modes of historical thinking: their philosophical conceptions of history, their categories of historical classification, their categories of chronological or stylistic periodisation, the way in which they have understood the concepts of form and style, their view of the relationship between form and social life, etc.

I have organised the issue, therefore, in the manner of a comparative anthology. Each contributor has been asked (a) to choose from the writings of the historian/critic he comments upon an excerpt which reveals—to the extent that this is possible—its underlying methodological assumptions; (b) to comment critically on these assumptions and their philosophical affiliations. Three texts—those by Professor Gombrich, Professor Morawski, and myself—differ in format from the others, in that they attempt to map the problematic of three major historiographic traditions: Hegelianism, Marxism, and Structuralism.

This issue, however, is not a comprehensive account, tidily weaved and confidently signposted. I have seen my editorial task as that of collating certain significant texts on method previously not translated into English, as well as commissioning new texts from a number of authoritative contemporary historians and critics. My aim has been to compose, not a definitive manual, but a stimulating anthology of distinct but mutually reinforcing accounts. I can by no means claim total objectivity either in the choice of subjects discussed or in the choice of the contributors. This is partly, no doubt, due to the unavoidable theoretical bias; but it is also the result of the difficulties of programming that are encountered in the course of undertaking such an ambitious project.

I would like to thank all those who have collaborated in this issue, for their patience and forbearance, and for their ready and generous response to my editorial promptings during the three years of the volume's growth. I would also like to thank the publisher Dr Andreas Papadakis for his unfailing encouragement, and extend my special thanks to Miss Penelope Farrant and Mr Ian Latham for their technical and editorial assistance.

Demetri Porphyrios

Acknowledgements Our sincere thanks are due to all those publishers who have given permission to reprint essays, extracts and illustrations from their publications—their contributions are acknowledged on the appropriate pages. The extracts on page 20 and page 82 are reprinted respectively from *Principles of Architectural History* by Paul Frankl, and *Architecture and Utopia, Design and Capitalist Development* by Manfredo Tafuri, by permission of The MIT Press, Cambridge, Massachusetts, copyright Massachusetts Institute of Technology. The essay by Spiro Kostof on page 21 'Paul Frankl's Principles of Architectural History' is reprinted by permission of the Society of Architectural Historians, copyright December 1971 by the Society of Architectural Historians (all rights reserved).
Manfredo Tafuri's essay 'The uncertainties of Formalism: Victor Sklovskij and the denuding of art' was translated from the original Italian by Judith Landry. Ernst Gombrich's essay 'Hegel and art history' was translated by Angela Wilkes and the author. Other translations from the Italian and German were carried out by Jacqueline Gargus and Eileen Martin. We are grateful to Maxine Pollack for editorial assistance.

© **Copyright Architectural Design, 1981.** All rights reserved. The contents of this publication are copyright. Reproduction in part or in full without written permission from the publisher is strictly forbidden.

Editor and Publisher: Dr Andreas C Papadakis
Technical Editor: Ian Latham
Production Editor: Penelope Farrant

Published in Great Britain by Architectural Design, 7 Holland Street, London W8. Phototypeset by Tradespools Ltd, Frome, Somerset. Printed by Headley Bros, Ashford, Kent.

Front cover 'Historia' from Cesare Ripa, *Historiae et Allegoriae*, Augsburg, Hertel, c 1758–1760
Inside front and back covers Illustrations from *Historiae et Allegoriae*

ARCHITECTURAL DESIGN SUBSCRIPTIONS

	UK & O'seas	USA & N America
Full annual subscription	£29.50	US$65.00
Special annual student rate	£25.00	US$55.00

NOTE Subscriptions can be backdated and include *AD News*.

AD 'AGENTS' collect five new subscriptions to get their own free - enclose five subscription orders with payments, we will send one year free.

To start your subscription now, please complete the panel on the right and send this form together with your payment/credit card authority/bank draft, direct to:-

**Subscription Department,
ARCHITECTURAL DESIGN,
7/8 Holland Street,
London, W.8.**

☐ I wish to subscribe to *AD* at the full rate.
☐ I wish to subscribe to *AD* at the student rate, and enclose proof of student status. (College . . . . Year . . . .)
☐ I claim a free subscription to *AD*, and enclose five new subscription orders (please attach names and addresses) and payments. Starting date: Issue No . . . . Year . . . . . .
☐ Payment enclosed by: cheque/postal order/draft, VALUE £ . . . . . .
☐ Please charge £ . . . . to my credit card.
Account No.

☐ AMERICAN EXPRESS
☐ DINERS CLUB   ☐ BARCLAYCARD / VISA
☐ ACCESS/MASTER CHARGE/EUROCARD

Signature . . . .
Name . . . .
Address . . . .
. . . .

Hegel and Art History
ERNST GOMBRICH
b 1909

It is my belief that Hegel is the father of the history of art, or at any rate of the history of art as I have always understood it. We are of course accustomed to the idea that sons rebel against their fathers, and if we are to believe psychologists, they do this because they want, and indeed need, to break away from the overpowering influence of paternal authority. I still believe that the history of art should free itself of Hegel's authority, but I am convinced that this will only be possible once it has learned to understand Hegel's overwhelming influence.

I described Hegel as the father of the history of art. This is a role normally attributed to Johann Joachim Winckelmann, but it seems to me that rather than Winckelmann's *Kunstgeschichte des Altertums* (History of Ancient Art) of 1764, it is Hegel's *Lectures on Aesthetics* (1820–29) which should be regarded as the founding document of the modern study of art, as they contain the first attempt ever made to survey and systematise the entire universal history of art, indeed of all the arts. Hegel himself looked up to Winckelmann as one of the men who, in his words, *'in the field of art was able to awaken a new organ and to open up totally new methods of approach to the human mind'*.[1] (A1 p 92) But Winckelmann's concept of art was quite different from Hegel's. For him the essence of art lay in the Greek ideal and so, as his predecessor Vasari had written about the rebirth of this artistic ideal, so Winckelmann was concerned with the development of this exemplary art into absolute perfection. At the same time he saw his work as a *Lehrgebaüde*, a theoretical treatise, aiming to demonstrate, through the example of Greek art, what beauty was. Hegel, if I may simplify for a moment, incorporated this theory into his philosophical system, but restricted its range of validity. The credit for having given classical shape to sensuous beauty still went indisputably to the Greeks, but Classicism itself only represents one phase of art, as the history of art can no more stand still than history itself.

I would like to try and formulate briefly what Hegel appropriated from Winckelmann and how he broadened the scope of the static system to form a universal history of art as we know it today. He found three fundamental ideas in Winckelmann which he incorporated into his own structure of ideas. The most important among them is the firm belief in the divine dignity of art. Just as Winckelmann is really celebrating the visible presence of the divine in a work of man in his famous hymn to the beauty of the Apollo of Belvedere, so too Hegel ultimately saw in all art a manifestation of transcendent values. It is a point of view which Plato consciously rejected, but which neo-platonism brought back into circulation in European intellectual life, for it credits the artist with the ability to look at the Idea itself and to reveal it to others. I may perhaps call this metaphysical faith in art *aesthetic transcendentalism*, with the warning that it is not of course to be confused with Kant's transcendental aesthetics. This aesthetic transcendentalism tinged with neo-platonism certainly appears less pronounced in Winckelmann than it perhaps does in the philosophy of his friend and rival, Anton Raphael Mengs, yet Winckelmann's cult of beauty nevertheless draws its justification from there. The second fundamental idea that Hegel took over can be described as *historical collectivism*. By this I mean the role that is assigned to the collective, to the nation. For Winckelmann, Greek art is not so much the work of individual masters as the expression or the reflection of the Greek spirit, with the concept of spirit not yet quite containing the metaphysical overtones that it has in Hegel of course, but being much closer to Montesquieu's *Esprit des Nations*. Thirdly, even in Winckelmann this consummate expression is the end result of a development, and in fact of a development whose intrinsic necessity is intelligible. The stages of Greek art, the progression of style, led quite logically to what Winckelmann calls the 'beautiful style', passing through the phase of the noble or austere style, and leading inevitably, by making concessions to sensual pleasure, to decline. In this third instance we can talk of a *historical determinism* which explains why, for all its perfection, Greek art had already to bear within it the seeds of its own decline.[2]

It is clear that this determinism is to some extent incompatible with what Winckelmann felt to be his mission: the call to emulate Greek works and to return to the Golden Age of art. This flaw in Winckelmann's doctrine was naturally all the more evident to his contemporaries as they were struggling to gain awareness of the independent identity of their national art. Here I am thinking primarily of Herder, but also of Schiller, whose essay, 'Über Naive und Sentimentalische Dichtung' aims to do justice to the Golden Age of Classical Greece, without regarding it as an absolute.

After all, those were the years in which this ancient dream of a Golden Age became unexpectedly topical. It seemed as if human reason only needed to take control of the reins to make the dream come true. I am talking of course about the French Revolution, which Hegel also regarded as virtually a cosmic event:

'For as long as the sun has shone in the firmament and the planets have revolved about it,' he says in the *Philosophy of*

History, '*man has not been seen to stand on his head, that is on his thoughts, and to construct reality accordingly ... All thinking beings have celebrated this era ... an enthusiasm of the spirit has filled the world with awe, as though the divine has at last come to a true reconciliation with the world.*' (p 529)

I am convinced that Hegel's philosophy, which I would like to describe as *metaphysical optimism*, can only really be understood in relation to this event. Like many of his contemporaries, he looked at the developments preceding the triumph of reason from the standpoint of this climactic event and, even in the stages of natural evolution, from dead matter through plants and the animal kingdom to man, he found confirmation of his theory that the entire historical process was a necessary development leading to the evolution of the self-knowing spirit.

Like other ideas, Hegel had certainly adopted the belief that art plays an important role in this cosmic process from his boyhood friend Schelling. The three passages on the religion of art in Hegel's difficult early work *The Phenomenology* (1806) are on the whole couched in such abstract terms that the actual history of art plays no part in them, yet it seems to me that even here, as in the subsequent *Encyclopaedia* (1817), Winckelmann's three fundamental ideas lie behind the abstractions. For here too art is essentially theophany, the unveiling of the divine, and here too it is bound to a historical collective. In Hegel's words,

'*the work of art can only be an expression of the God if ... it takes and extracts ... without adulteration ... the indwelling spirit of the nation.*' (*Encyclopaedia* p 462)

Thus, just as aesthetic transcendentalism and collectivism are raised to the status of dynamic principles, so the logic of development in Winckelmann is elevated into logical determinism. For art also has a part to play in the self-creation of the spirit, which takes place with all the compelling force of a syllogism. Likewise with the history of art it is a question of '*revealing the truth ... which is manifest in the history of the world.*' (A III 573)

The metaphysical optimism proclaimed in these words now also necessarily carries with it a further principle, which is no less fundamental to Hegel's conception of the history of art than it is to his interpretation of all other historical events: I am talking about the principle of *relativism*, which in Hegel's work is a result of the dialectic. As far as the history of art is concerned, this *dialectic relativism*, which is itself again relative, only really first becomes important in the *Lectures on Aesthetics*.

These lectures, which Hegel gave four times in Berlin, are known to us through the loving reconstruction of his student Hotho, who used Hegel's notes for his lectures as well as the notes that his students took. For this reason perhaps one ought not to weigh each word too carefully, but on the whole they bear the stamp of indisputable authenticity. Like other works of Hegel, they are hardly an easy read. The abstract presentation, of which I do not need to give examples, often becomes abstruse, but when the reader is about to lose patience he is occasionally placated by a passage that appears to be rooted in living experience.

Hegel had a genuine feeling for painting, and incidentally for music too, but his knowledge of the actual history of art was so scarce that he let himself be hoaxed into believing that the tomb of Count Engelbert II von Nassau in Breda was the work of Michelangelo. Nevertheless, Hegel had a clear notion of what he called the requirements of scholarship, '*the precise familiarity with the wide realm of individual works of art, both ancient and modern*'. According to him scholarship in the field of art also demands,

'*a vast wealth of historical, and also very detailed knowledge, as the individuality of a work of art is related to something individual and thus requires detailed knowledge if it is to be understood and explained.*' (A I 30) He speaks with gratitude of the achievement of connoisseurs, yet rightly recalls that they occasionally limit their knowledge of a work of art to its purely external aspects and '*have little notion*' of the true nature of the work of art ... '*not knowing the value of deeper studies ... they dismiss them.*' (A I 56) Naturally these deeper studies were what mattered to Hegel. His aim was to prove the validity of what to him was an essential, comforting belief in universal reason, by showing that the history of art could be perceived in the terms of those steadily evolving principles which in his philosophy determine all events. Even where such an undertaking appears misguided, the reader cannot fail to be struck by the consistency with which Hegel sets about extracting the meaning allotted to every art form, to every age and to every style. This very consistency was necessary in order to help emphasise the very heart of his doctrine, namely the dialectic, which firmly established the metaphysical optimism in relativism.

This relationship can most easily be explained by again referring to the Classicism of antiquity, which for Hegel culminated in Greek sculpture. For as an art form sculpture stands somewhere between architecture, which is still inextricably bound to matter, and painting, which represents the more advanced process of spiritualisation, as its real subject is light – a thought which perhaps stems from Herder.[3]

Of course for Hegel even painting represents only a phase to be passed through before coming to music, which is an almost completely dematerialised art form, and music must in turn give way to poetry, which deals with pure meaning. The value of all the arts is again, however, relative, as '*art is far ... from being the highest form of expression of the spirit*'; it is dissolved by reflection and replaced by pure thought, by philosophy, as a result of which art belongs to the past. (A I 24–25)

For Hegel, therefore, the art of antiquity, as Winckelmann had looked at it, certainly forms the pivot of the true history of art, but its perfection was only possible for a limited spiritual phase of time, for just as long as it was still possible to represent the gods as visible beings. What precedes the art of antiquity is a less aware phase: Oriental art. Hegel calls this pre-art (*Vorkunst*) and, following the neo-platonist, Creuzer, he attributes to it a particular form of symbolism which is not yet adequate to the spirit.[4] Hegel had the fortune, or the misfortune, to write about Ancient Egyptian art just before the hieroglyphs were deciphered, and thus before the picture of Egyptian civilisation was radically altered. For Hegel, Egypt

'*is the land of the symbol and sets itself the spiritual task of the self-deciphering of the spirit, without really attaining its end. The problems remain unsolved and the solution which we are able to provide consists therefore merely of interpreting the riddles of Egyptian art and its symbolic works as a problem that*

Above The Sphinx and Great Pyramid of Memphis (Flaxmann, *Lectures on Sculpture*, pl XI)
Right Apollo Belvedere

Above Hans Holbein, *Georg Gisze, a German Merchant in London*, 1532

the Egyptians themselves left undeciphered' (A I 456–57). '*As a symbol for this proper meaning of the Egyptian spirit, we may mention the Sphinx. It is, as it were, the symbol of the symbolic itself . . . They are recumbent animal bodies out of which the human body struggles, thus forming the upper part of the body . . . The human spirit is trying to force its way forward out of the dumb strength and power of the animal, without coming to a perfect portrayal of its own freedom and animated shape.*' (A I 465)

Thus an unexplained monument of art becomes for Hegel a metaphor for the spirit of the entire age. And once firm in his opinion that at that time the spirit, like the sphinx, remained shackled to the animal, he was also able to state that, '*the Egyptians constructed their towering religious buildings in the same instinctive way in which bees build their cells . . . Self-awareness has not yet come to fruition and is not yet complete in itself, but pushes on, searching, conjecturing, continually producing, without attaining absolute satisfaction and therefore always restless.*' (A II 286)

It is not difficult to see how much this dramatic picture of the struggling spirit owes to the principle of the dialectic, for it essentially represents a negation of the Classical ideal which Hegel, as well as Winckelmann, saw translated into reality in the art of Ancient Greece. Yet no matter how often Hegel refers to Winckelmann in the passages concerned, he still saw, with remarkable lucidity, that the sixty years which separated him from his master had radically transformed the image of Greek sculpture. The discovery of the sculpture of Aegina, and above all of the Parthenon, inevitably altered the emphasis. In fact Hegel is one of the first virtually to dismiss the Belvedere Apollo with a joke taken from an English journal describing it as a 'theatrical coxcomb' (A II 431), and to describe the Laokoon as a late work already declining into mannerism (A II 434). It may be that Hegel did not care much for these works. He had never been to Italy and looked for reasons to explain '*why the sculpture of antiquity leaves us somewhat cold . . . we feel at once more at home with painting . . . in paintings we see something that works and is active within ourselves.*' (A III 17)

A crucial point in Hegel's view of history was the idea that sculpture belonged to pagan antiquity and painting to the Christian era, which Hegel called the Romantic era. This was naturally aided by the coincidence that marble statues survive more easily than paintings. Hegel knew of course that the ancient Greeks held their painters, such as Zeuxis and Apelles, in no less esteem than they did their sculptors, and he was not entirely happy with this interpretation of painting as a subjective, romantic art form. But since, as he cautiously says, the inmost heart of the Greek outlook corresponds more closely '*with the principle of sculpture than with any other art . . . the backwardness of painting in relation to sculpture is only "to be expected."*' (A III 20) Whatever the case may be, Hegel's efforts to examine each art form according to its ability to express certain spiritual values led him to describe the painter's medium with a clarity that has rarely been equalled, before or since, in the history of art.

For us, the notion of 'painterliness' is linked with the name of Heinrich Wölfflin, who in his *Principles of Art History* so articulately described the development of style from sculpture to painting. We should recall that Hegel too believed that the sculptural necessarily precedes the 'painterly'. Thus Hegel talks of the plastic-sculptural element in painting and describes the problems of composition in painting in a passage which could almost have been written by Wölfflin: '*The next type of arrangement still remains entirely architectural, a homogenous juxtaposition of the figures, or a regular opposition and symmetrical conjunction both of the figures themselves and of their attitudes and movements. The pyramidal form of the group is very popular here . . . In the Sistine Madonna too this type of grouping is still retained as decisive. In general it is restful to the eye because the pyramid draws together by its apex what would otherwise be a scattered juxtaposition, and gives the group an external unity.*' (A III 98)

But the painter who, as Hegel says, uses all the means

available to him in his art (A III 99), the 'painterly' painter, finds still more possibilities of development and thus, in the course of artistic evolution that Hegel exhaustively describes, Dutch 17th-century painting virtually becomes an end in itself.

It would indeed be worthwhile to assemble a small anthology of the passages in which, tired of adopting a dry tone, Hegel gives us his spontaneous reaction to painting. The grinding noise of his conceptual mill is silenced, giving way to a real love of the work of art. A brief example must again suffice: *'While classical art essentially gives shape in its presentation of its ideal only to what is solid, here we have, arrested and brought before our eyes, the fleeting expressions of changing Nature – a stream, a waterfall, the foaming waves of the ocean, a still life with random flashes of glasses and plates etc, the external shape of spiritual reality in the most specific situations: a woman threading a needle by the light, a band of robbers frozen in movement, the most momentary aspect of a gesture, which quickly passes, the laughing and guffawing of a peasant; in all this Ostade, Teniers and Steen are masters ...'* (A II 227) *'But even though heart and thought remain unsatisfied, closer inspection reconciles us to them. For it is the art of painting and the painter that should delight and transport us. And in fact if we want to know what painting is, we must look at these small pictures in order to say of this or of that master: now he can really paint ...'* (A II 226)

Hegel had been to the Netherlands and was obviously filled with enthusiasm for Dutch paintings. Whereas his description of Italian art is largely based on the fundamental work by Rumohr, which had just been published, his writing here is based entirely on his own observations. There is still perhaps an ideological element in this. The catholicising of the Nazarenes had spoiled for many the pleasure in the recently discovered, so-called 'primitive' Italian painters, whereas in Holland Hegel could enjoy the triumph of protestantism both in and through the paintings. *'It would not have occurred to any other people, under any other circumstances, to portray subjects like those that confront us in Dutch paintings as the principal content of a work of art.'* Hegel finds the justification for their choice of subjects in, *'their sense of a self-earned freedom, through which they have attained well-being, comfort, integrity, spirit, gaiety and even a pride in their cheerful daily life.'* (A II 226)

If we like, we can still see even in this glorification of the Dutch people a reflection of Winckelmann's idealising of the Greeks. And just as in Winckelmann, a result of the Hegelian system is that this blossoming of an art form bears within it its inner dissolution. The 'colour magic' of painting brings an inevitable transition to music. When analysing this art form too, Hegel surprises us by showing a lively enthusiasm for Mozart and Rossini which contrasts strangely with his somewhat laboured attempts at a purely conceptual edifice.

One thing is certain in any case. As far as Hegel was concerned, his aesthetic theory of categories formed an integral part of his total system of philosophy for, as is stated in the *Aesthetics*, *'only the whole of philosophy can be equated with the knowledge of the universe as the* one *organic totality in itself ... within the crowning circle of this scientific necessity each single part is on the one hand a circle turning in on itself, while on the other hand, it has a simultaneous and necessary connection with other parts – a backwards from which it is derived and a forwards towards which it drives itself, in so far as it fruitfully engenders an "other" out of itself again, making it accessible for scientific knowledge.'* (A I 42–43)

There is obviously something extremely tempting about a system like this, in which every conceivable natural, spiritual or historical phenomenon has its place, and precisely because Hegel was the last and the most consistent person to construct such a system, his philosophy did not lose its effect when the influence of his metaphysics dwindled. A spiritual succession is therefore not confined only to philosophers who had subscribed to every definition in his *Encyclopaedia*. It is indeed well known that Karl Marx, for example, opposed to Hegel's thesis of the primacy of the spirit the antithesis of the primacy of matter, in order, to use the famous double meaning of the dialectic, both to cancel and to keep the system (*aufheben*). His is the most influential but by no means the only attempt to secularise, as it were, the Hegelian metaphysics, without thereby sacrificing the synopsis of at least all the historical events. In my book *In Search of Cultural History*,[5] I tried to show the great extent to which the leading champions of culture and aesthetics in the German-speaking countries come under the spell of Hegel. The striving to 'reconstruct' the spirit of the age in art runs from Carl Schnaase, through Jacob Burckhardt, Heinrich Wölfflin, Karl Lamprecht, Alois Riegl and Max Dvořák to Ervin Panofsky. Brief as my analysis was, I neither want to nor can repeat it here. One matter however is close to my heart. I do not wish to create the impression that I lack respect for these masters. It cannot be too often repeated that the best tribute that one can pay a scholar is to take him seriously and to reappraise his lines of argument constantly. I would be the very last to demand that art and cultural history should give up seeking relationships between things and content themselves with cataloguing. If that had been my aim, I would certainly not have concerned myself with Hegel. What gave me pause was not the belief that it is hard to establish relationships between things but, paradoxically, that it often seems all too easy. The gigantic structure of Hegel's aesthetic can itself serve as proof for this thesis. Although his virtuosity is evident, we have already seen how, in his interpretation of Egyptian art, he tried to slip from the metaphorical into the factual, or how he relegated a figure like Apelles to the verge of Greek art, to fit in with his construction of the historical sequence of the arts.

Even the professional historian succumbs easily to the temptation to *corriger la fortune*. Ultimately every historical portrayal is, and indeed must be, selective. It is thus natural to confine oneself to what appears to be significant and to neglect that which appears less essential. My friend, Sir Karl Popper, the great methodologist of science, has made me sensitive to the dangerous allures of these siren songs.[6] The true scientist does not seek confirmation for his hypotheses; he is primarily on the look-out for contrary examples. A theory which cannot conflict with anything has no scientific content. The danger of the Hegelian heritage lies precisely in its temptingly easy applicability. After all, the dialectic makes it all too easy for us to find a way out of every contradiction. Because it seems to us as though everything in life is really inter-connected, every method of interpretation is easily accepted. Here it depends above all on a plausible point of departure. *'The artist must eat'* we read in Lessing, and since artists cannot indeed paint without eating, it is certainly possible to base a credible system of art history on this universal need.

All these attempts at interpretations often make me think of the old anecdote about the farmer who had sold a pig for 300 crowns. He is sitting comfortably in the inn with his sack of coins in front of him. He empties it onto the table and begins to count, *'One, two, three,'* He gets to ten, then fifty, then a hundred and begins to yawn – 150, 180, 181. Suddenly he sweeps the money together and shoves it back into the sack. *'But what on earth are you doing?'* his companions ask him. *'It's been right up to now, so the rest will be right,'* the farmer replies.

I do not imagine of course that I am the first or indeed the only art historian who likes to count again. On the contrary I have often asked myself whether today, nearly one and a half centuries after Hegel's death, my polemic against certain interpretations of history is not perhaps a case of tilting at windmills. And yet I have found often enough that it is not windmills that one is charging, but real giants. I have already mentioned five of these giants by their weird names. They are *aesthetic transcendentalism, historical collectivism, historical determinism, metaphysical optimism* and *relativism*. They are all related to the giant Proteus, since they remain constant in every metamorphosis.

The idea of the transcendency of art becomes transparency in the secularised form. Though no longer the manifestation of the self-realising spirit, the work of art is still seen as the expression of the spirit of the age, which, as it were, remains visible across its surface. The word 'expression', with its elusive ambiguity, facilitates this transition, enabling the historian to disclose the philosophy of an age, or its economic conditions, behind the work of art. What is common to both methods is naturally the connection with collectivism, for the way leads from the individual work of art via the style, which should now be interpreted as a symptom, a manifestation of class, race, culture or the age.

Determinism now assumes an explicit, or at least implicit, key role in this method. Therein, indeed, lies the Hegelian heritage: in claiming to show that the Gothic style is a necessary result of feudalism or of scholasticism, or that all three phenomena are merely different manifestations of the same underlying principle. Now, it may well be conceded that both direct and indirect connections exist between these disparate phenomena. The question is merely to find the point at which, to use a variation on one of Hegel's favourite expressions, triviality is converted into absurdity. Certainly historical determinism has found so many opponents that the question would appear to be settled, if ever a question could be settled. There is no need to make any decision here about the problem of causality, of the validity of natural laws or of free will, in order to refute the idea that the course of history follows a necessary development. Thus the Nobel Prize winner from Göttingen, Manfred Eigen, emphasised recently that we can accept the validity of the laws of nature without this being a sufficient reason to conclude that history follows an irrevocable and pre-determined course. I often like to compare the multifarious influences that lie behind artistic creation with the influence that climate has on vegetation. No-one will deny that this dependency exists, and the fact that the vegetation in turn influences the climate may also recommend the comparison to partisans of the dialectic. It is even possible to learn of variations in the climate from looking at the annual rings of an old tree. And yet the calculation is only of limited validity, for the mutual effect is not confined to these two factors alone; numerous other factors, which cannot be calculated in advance or reconstructed, come into play. It is worth remembering that the chance importation of a couple of rabbits into Australia nearly led to the entire land being completely stripped of vegetation. You can't get around the reality of chance.

I know of course that in the second edition of the *Encyclopaedia* Hegel explained the famous sentence taken from his Philosophy of Law, *'Whatever is rational* (vernünftig) *is real and whatever is real is rational'*, to the effect that what he understood by reality was *'not the merely empirical … existence mingled with chance but the existence that is inseparable from the concept of reason'*.[7] Ultimately however this attempt at salvage is based on a circular argument, for if chance has nothing to do with philosophy, then history certainly has nothing to do with it either. For time and time again history bears out the old proverb, *'Kleine Ursachen, grosse Wirkungen'* (Important developments have small beginnings) – a veritable spell which banishes once and for all the ghost of historical determinism.

This really appears so obvious that we have to ask ourselves why people so often resist this insight. Maybe the power of chance hurts our self-esteem. We talk about blind, senseless or stupid coincidence and even find misfortune, both in life and history, easier to bear, if we can regard it as unavoidable fate. How much easier it would be if we shared Hegel's metaphysical optimism, which tries to convince us that ultimately everything is for the best. The wish gives birth to the thought, in whatever way faith in a pre-determined happy ending to the cosmic play may be formulated. Granted that not all determinists are also optimists. Oswald Spengler, for example, who had so much in common with Hegel, prophesied the inevitable decline of the Western world. On the other hand of course the essential factor in metaphysical optimism is that there cannot and ought not to be any decline or deterioration which does not pave the way for a higher form of development.

I do not think I am too far wrong if I also describe this relativism as the official dogma, so to speak, of contemporary art historical teaching, in so far as it has pledged itself to determinism. One cannot condemn that which is unavoidable, any more than a geologist can condemn the Ice Age. Certainly it was some time before art historians came to adopt this attitude, which goes far beyond Hegel in its levelling tendency. According to Hegel there is naturally a decline, even if it does serve progress. Today it is considered scientific to eradicate the concept of decline from the art historian's vocabulary wherever possible, so as to allot every era that was once condemned, its rightful place in the chain of development. The vindication of Gothic art in the 18th century was accepted even by Hegel. Later, following in the tracks of Burckhardt, Wölfflin reinstated Baroque art, Wickhoff defended Roman art, Riegl the art of late antiquity and Max Dvořàk the catacomb paintings and El Greco. Walter Friedlander completely freed mannerist art from the stigma of decline, and Millard Meiss undertook a positive evaluation of the painting of the late trecento. At the moment we are even witnessing a revival of respect for French 19th-century Salon painting, which until recently was still considered to be the ultimate in kitsch.

I will by no means dispute that we have profited a good deal from all these efforts: we have cast off prejudices and have learnt to look more closely.

I am a peace-loving man and am quite prepared to let each of the five giants have his plaything as long as he limits his territorial claims. I will even concede to metaphysical optimism the reality of a form of progress which links nature with history. We have understood since Darwin that there is no need here for a teleology; only for the cruel mechanism which eliminates the unadapted. Perhaps in the field of art too a chance mutation occasionally leads to a highly promising solution, which in turn leads to further selection. The history of art has been presented along such lines of development first in antiquity, then in the Renaissance and also by Winckelmann, and what at the time was seen as decline can admittedly also be interpreted in the relativist sense as yet another process of adaptation. But adaptation to what? After all, not every collective, not every group, makes identical demands on artists and on their standards. In connection with this, my revered Julius von Schlosser quite rightly insisted that one should not confuse the real history of art with the history of artistic idioms or styles.[8] Certainly the history of style lends itself rather better to attempts at hypothetical reconstruction than does the phenomenon of artistic mastery. Even the masterpiece is not independent of a favourable constellation of circumstances, but here I will willingly concede to aesthetic transcendentalism that the highest artistic achievement soars into a sphere which even in principle defies scientific analysis.[9]

The continued topicality of the issues raised by Hegel seems to me unquestionable. But they become burning problems only in connection with the present situation in art. It is necessary here to recall the intrinsic ambiguity of the word 'history' which has also crept into the title of this lecture. 'Hegel and Art History' may be taken to refer to Hegel's relations to the historiography of art, such as I have discussed them here; but these words may also imply that Hegel influenced the development of art itself, and this, no doubt, is a much weightier question.

We must never forget that the writing of history can in its turn effect the further course of events and it is this feed-back – which Hegel would probably have described as 'dialectic' – which accounts for the decisive influence of the philosophy of history. Let us recall that Hegel saw in art not only a reflection of the Divine but also an aspect of the continuous process of creation which passes through the artist (A I 50). The role which classical antiquity assigned most of all to the poet is therefore attributed to every true artist; he is a seer, a prophet, who is not only the mouthpiece of God but also helps God to achieve His own self-awareness.

Hegel's lectures on the philosophy of history tell us even more explicitly than do those on aesthetics how Hegel conceived the historical role of such a divine mission. It is true that his reflections on what he called *'world historical individuals'* refer more immediately to political leaders. He had, most of all, Napoleon in mind, who had overcome and yet preserved the achievements of the French Revolution and whom, in a famous letter written after the battle of Jena, he described as *'this world-soul'*.[10] But when Hegel speaks of great men we are entitled also to include artists; in any case artists would not allow themselves to be excluded. According to Hegel it is the task of what he calls *'these business managers of the World Spirit to be aware of the necessary next step to be taken by their world, to make this step their aim and to devote their energy to this'* ... *'They represent, as it were, the next species which had already been prefigured internally.'* (p 46)

It is obvious that it is not granted to ordinary mortals to recognise and understand this anticipation of the future in the present. There is only one conclusion, therefore, that one can draw from Hegel's philosophy: whatever the World Spirit may be aiming at, it must be something new. Thus the old is being devalued while the unknown and untried at least carries within itself the possibility of harbouring the seeds of the future. To be rejected by his age becomes the very hallmark of genius. The great masters must be ahead of their time, for if they were not they would not be great masters.

Those of us who do not regard the changes of styles, of trends, and of fashions as a revelation of higher purposes must ask ourselves how we can really know what the future will appreciate; indeed we may even wonder why we must assume that the next generation will necessarily have a better taste than our own. But for those who endorse Hegel's metaphysical optimism, the process of selection has been shifted from the present to the future. It is only future success which counts as valid, as a true verdict, the test of the Divine Will. Criticism of contemporary events becomes theoretically impossible because such criticism always incurs the danger of turning out as blasphemy in the future. All that remains for the critic in the end is to try and see which way the wind blows. As Popper has shown an even more dangerous giant looms up behind metaphysical optimism: metaphysical opportunism.

Neither Popper nor I have ever wished to assert that the philosophy of progress in art, the theory of the avant-garde,[11] was exclusively inspired and nourished by Hegel's philosophy. And yet I believe that it could be shown what an essential contribution was made by the Hegelian tradition. I have drawn attention elsewhere to a remark by Heinrich Heine who explicitly derived this consequence for art criticism from Hegel's philosophy. Heine, who regarded Hegel as the greatest German philosopher since Leibniz, placing him above Kant, took issue in his Paris Salons of 1831 – the year of Hegel's death – with the critics who had censured a painting by Descamps because it was badly drawn. He insisted that *'every original artist, and even more so every artistic genius, must be judged by his own aesthetic standards ... Colours and shapes ... are no more than symbols of the Idea, symbols which rise in the mind of the artist when the sacred World Spirit moves it'*. Heine speaks of the *'mystical bondage'* of the artist, and in view of this lack of freedom any criticism becomes arrogant pedantry.

It is true that in the field of art criticism it took a good deal of time for the critics to admit defeat and thus to arrive at what Hegel would have called the self-abrogation of art criticism. But every successive wave of the artistic revolution of the 19th century gave a fresh uplift to optimistic relativism. The belief in progress polarised not only the political world but also the world of art; all that was left was the impetus of the advance and the inertia of the reactionaries. In this constellation it was no longer the task of the critic to criticise, his mission was to assist the good fight of the movement; he became the herald of the new epoch and did his best to turn these prophesies into reality. Remember with what relish the artistic manifestoes of the early 20th century indulged in apocalyptic rhetoric announcing the new dawn, the new era, the new dispensation. Here too Hegel provided the direct inspiration. Eckart von Sydow, in a pamphlet of 1920 on *German Expressionist Culture and Painting*, wrote: '*We may say, with but a few qualifications, that the German Spirit has once more found immediate contact with the World Soul, as in the days of the Middle Ages.*' (p 73)

I do not want to be misunderstood. Such utterance does not speak against Expressionism, merely against its metaphysical underpinning in aesthetic transcendentalism. I would even go further and admit that a metaphysical faith can indeed inspire an artist or an artistic movement. Nearly all great art is religious and the religious element in Hegel's philosophy also had its inspiring effect. I believe that the historian of the art of our century has to study Hegel much as a student of the ecclesiastical art of the Middle Ages must get to know the Bible. Only in this way can he, for instance, learn to understand the triumphant rise of modern architecture and its present crisis.

Take the words Walter Gropius wrote in 1923 in his article on 'The Idea and the Structure of the National Bauhaus': '*The attitude of a period to the world becomes crystallised in its buildings, for in these both the spiritual and material resources of the age find their simultaneous expression*'.[12] Of what kind of expression he dreamt we know from the beautiful speech which he made at the opening of the first exhibition of students' work at the Bauhaus: '*Instead of sprawling academic organisations, we shall witness the rise of small, secret, and self-contained leagues, lodges, workshops, conspiracies, intent on guarding the mystery which is the core of the faith and on giving artistic shape to it until the time when these isolated groups will be fused once more by an all embracing and vigorous spiritual vision which must eventually achieve its manifestation in a great Gesamtkunstwerk, combining all the arts. This great communal creation, this cathedral, of the future, will in its turn illuminate with its radiance even the smallest objects of everyday life.*'[13]

I hope you too sense the intoxicating sweep of these words of a great architect. Intoxication, however, is so often followed by a hangover and you know we did not have to wait for this very long. A few months ago, Sir John Summerson, one of the most outstanding critics and historians of architecture in England, on the occasion of his being awarded the Gold Medal of the Royal Institute of British Architects, spoke of his beginnings as an enthusiastic champion of Modern architecture in England and remarked that he finds the naive optimism of his early articles downright repellent.[14] Another of the leading English critics made the frank confession in front of the same forum that during the struggle for Modern architecture he had occasionally praised works which he did not really find so very good, simply because they were modern not reactionary.[15] These confessions are worthy of the highest respect and indeed we must warmly welcome all the debates which take place today wherever architecture is being taught and practised. For it is through the encountering of arguments and counter-arguments that we shall learn from the mistakes of the last few decades.

In the visual arts of painting and sculpture such a return to a critical debate will not be quite so easy, for, after all, they lack the practical criteria to which such a work has to do justice. Here the critic is entirely thrown back on himself. Naturally, we must not demand that the critic should have no prejudices and no dreams of the future. But theoretically, he never has the right to operate with the slogans of 'Our Age' and even less of 'Future Ages'.

It was Immanuel Kant who insisted on the stern and frightening doctrine that nobody and nothing can relieve us of the burden of moral responsibility for our judgment; not even a theophany, such as Hegel saw in history. '*For*' – he writes – '*in whatever way a Being might be described as Divine . . . and indeed appear so*', this cannot absolve anyone of the duty '*to judge for himself whether he is entitled to regard such a Being as a God and to worship it as such*'.[16] It may well be that Kant here demands more than is humanly possible, and yet much would be achieved if the insight that Kant was right gained ground in the world of art.

Notes

1 I quote from the edition *Hegels Werken in zwanzig Bänden*, Suhrkamp Verlag, Frankfurt-Main, 1970. The abbreviation A1 refers to the first volume of the lectures on aesthetics.
2 In my lecture series *The Ideas of Progress and their Impact on Art* published by Cooper Union, New York, 1971 (not commercially available), I go further back to Winckelmann's sources.
3 I am grateful to my student Alex Potts for information on Herder's *Plastik* (1778).
4 Cf my essay 'Vom Wert der Kunstwissenschaft für die Symbolforschung' in *Wandlungen des Paradiesischen und Utopischen (Problem der Kunstwissenschaft, II)*, Berlin, 1966.
5 Oxford, 1969.
6 K R Popper, *Logik der Forschung*, Wien, 1935; *Die offene Gesellschaft und ihre Feinde*, Bern, 1957; *Das Elend des Historizismus*, Tübingen, 1965.
7 I quote from Karl Rosenkranz, *Georg Wilhelm Friedrich Hegels Leben*, Berlin, 1844, p 335.
8 Julius von Schlosser, ' "Stilgeschichte" und "Sprachgeschichte" der bildenden Kunst'; in *Sitzungsberichte der Bayr. Akademie der Wissenschaften, Phil-Hist Abt*, 1935, I. See also my *Art History and the Social Sciences*, Oxford, 1975.
9 Cf my lecture 'Art History and the Social Sciences', Oxford, 1975.
10 Karl Rosenkranz, *op cit* p 229.
11 Renato Poggioli, *Teoria dell'Arte d'Avanguardia*, Bologna, 1962. Poggioli does not refer to Hegel in this context.
12 Printed in *Manifeste*, 1905–1933, Diether Schmidt, Dresden, 1964, p 290.
13 *Ibid*, p 238.
14 Cf 'The Hollow Victory, 1932–1972', *Journal of the Royal Institute of British Architects*, December 1976.
15 J M Richards, in the *RIBA Journal* May 1972.
16 *Die Religion innerhalb der Grenzen der blossen Vernunft*, II Abschn, II Teil, 4 Stück, par I, Werke, Berlin, 1914, Bd VI p 318.

Editorial Note: This lecture was delivered by the author in February 1977 on the occasion of his being awarded the Hegel Prize of the City of Stuttgart. In his opening words the author thanked the spokesman of the prizegiving body for his kind words and for having made it easier for him to explain why the honour of this great award had also caused him some embarrassment; '*To some extent,*' he continued, '*this applies to all public honours, since the recipient usually knows full well that he is not all that praiseworthy, but I am quite particularly conscious of not being Hegelprize-worthy. After all criticism of the Hegelian heritage plays no minor part in my writings. Heinrich Heine once spoke of himself as of a "run-away Romantic". Maybe I am also something like a run-away Hegelian.*'

GOTTFRIED SEMPER
Der Stil
1803–1879

Surrounded by a world full of wonder and vigour, whose laws man will never understand (though he may sense their existence and long to know them), a world which reaches him in a few interrupted chords that leave his soul unsatisfied, man conjures into being the perfection he lacks, and, creating a miniature world where the cosmic laws, though restricted, may appear complete in themselves, he gratifies the cosmogonic instinct within him.

If man's imagination creates these images by presenting him with particular scenes from nature, expanded and adapted to his mood so that he believes he perceives in the individual image the harmony of the whole and is torn from reality for moments through this illusion, then this enjoyment of nature – which on principle is no different to the enjoyment of art – may, like the beauty of nature itself, be assigned to a lower category than that of the general aesthetic (as it only exists where a receptivity to beauty coincides with the power of the observers' imagination to complete and perfect).

But this aesthetic enjoyment of the beauty of nature is by no means the most primitive or original manifestation of the artistic urge; on the contrary this sense is undeveloped in simple people. The simple savage will be delighted to recognise the formative powers of nature as they are manifest in reality – in the regularity of certain periodic divisions of space and time, in a wreath, a string of beads, a decorative flourish, a dance, the rhythm of the lute as it accompanies the dance, the stroke of an oar and so on. Music and architecture, the highest purely cosmic (and not imitative) arts, developed from these beginnings, and no other art can do without their legislative support.

But beside that general natural phenomenon with its sublime fear, its confusion of charms and its incomprehensible laws, there are even more active elements which arouse our spirits and render them susceptible to the illusions of art. An endless struggle, the fearful law of the survival of the fittest, according to which one consumes the other only to be consumed in turn may be present throughout nature, but it is manifest to us in all its cruelty and harshness in the world of animals, that which is closest to us, forming the mirror of our own earthly existence and that of our history. The endless process of destruction through life has no conclusion or general direction, the spirit varies between hatred and pity and may well mourn over the dictate that the individual is created only to serve as fodder for the whole.

Then there is the element of chance, the illogical, the absurd, which we encounter on every step of our earthly progress, and the law which we believed we had grasped, is rudely affronted. There is the deep and incomprehensible storm-ridden world of our own emotions; passions at war with each other and with fate, chance, morals and laws; imagination opposing reality; foolishness at war with itself and the cosmos; nothing but confusion. The arts, by bringing these struggles and conflicts to a conclusion, can group them into a narrow framework, thereby drawing us out of our torment into brief moments of eternal conciliation. It is these moods which have given rise to lyrical, subjective and dramatic manifestations in art.[1]

The enchantment, which captivates the spirit through art in all its different forms and manifestations, is *beauty*. It is not so much a quality of art as one of its effects, in which the most varied elements both within and without the 'beautiful' object are active at once. These elements, insofar as they do not proceed from the beautiful object itself, must be reflected in it and condition its particular form.

GOTTFRIED SEMPER was born in Hamburg in 1803. His architecture is distinct from the romantic classicism of his friend Schinkel, and his adaptions of Romanesque, Gothic and Renaissance features represent typical examples of 19th-century historicism. His renovations at the Dresden Opera House in 1878 and at the Burgtheater in Vienna reveal an original approach to massing, with prominence given to the functions of the buildings. His written contributions to the theory of architecture emphasise the influence of structure on style and seek to encourage a greater use of colour.

Moreover the elements must proceed from the laws of nature and correspond to these, for although art is only concerned with the form and the appearance and not the essence of things, it can nevertheless do no other than follow the dictates of natural phenomena and create its form even if only through following the eternal law which moves through all the realm of nature, emerging here undeveloped, there in completed form. This analogy between the general formative powers of nature and those of art will be clearest and most readily understood by a consideration of what speculative aesthetics regards as the formal elements of pure beauty.

A phenomenon can only appear as such by cutting itself off, by separating itself as an individual phenomenon from the general. But this separation from the general is only absolute in the initial stages of formation. The more highly developed forms of plants and animals are distinguished by the fact that they reflect both the relation to the general, from which they came and in which they are rooted or stand, and to the particular, which appears as an objective or subjective contrast to them. Their creation and form are determined by these relations.

But since the principle of individualisation is sharply and clearly symbolised in any phenomenon which claims to be complete, we see three formative elements emerging. These may be active in the creation of forms, but often in lower formations their activities converge, or one will slumber. These formative elements, where all three are active at once, correspond to the three spatial dimensions of height, width and depth. Now insofar as the multiplicity of form must gather itself into unity in three ways corresponding to the three formative elements, the following three conditions are necessary components of formal beauty: 1) symmetry, 2) proportion, 3) direction.

It is hardly possible to imagine a fourth spatial dimension, and no less inconceivable is the idea of a homogeneous fourth to the attributes of beauty either.

Note

1 Hence art has the same aim as religion, namely to lift man out of the imperfect element of existence, to let him forget his earthly sufferings and struggles in the contemplation of the perfect. But the two are contradictory in that faith will immerse itself, driven by the sense of mystery and wonder, in the incomprehensible and sometimes formless, while art gives form to the formless and naturally, indeed inevitably, gives wonder expression in works of art. In the same way the desire for knowledge and the desire for truth are a third form of the same desire for perfection. But the ultimate goal is unattainable, the realm of the unknown is in contrast to what is known so that no formal support or quantitative standard can emerge which might form a part of the artistic whole. So science will always remain incomplete and inconclusive as a form. It is not knowledge but only the effort to acquire knowledge which gives satisfaction. But in art the highest, as long as it betrays inadequate ability and unsatisfied aims, will have to submit to limits if the highest goal which can be achieved is artistic striving for a concept of perfection which should form the basis of every work of art. Both religion and philosophy leave their proper spheres, indeed they renounce their true essence, when they take on artistic forms which illustrate the interaction of the three manifestations of spiritual desire and display that combination which is most favourable to artistic creation, as we find in the Greeks.

Gottfried Semper, *Der Stil in den technischen und tektonischen Künsten oder Praktische Aesthetik*, 2nd revised edition, F Bruckmann Verlag, Munich, 1978, pp XXI–XXIV.

Gottfried Semper and the Problem of Style
JOSEPH RYKWERT
b 1926

I shall only consider here Gottfried Semper's theory of style which he presents in *Der Stil*,[1] a presentation which begins with the abrupt offer of the wreath as the archetypal work of art.[2] For Semper, a wreath is the prime example of a textile object. The functions which led the first man to connect pieces of material, were *first* the desire to order and to bind and *second*, that to cover and to shelter, to delimit. Semper describes the details of textile materials at some length before he returns to the conceptual process which the making of textiles involves: fibre leads to thread and twine, thread and twine suggest knots. The knot is *'perhaps the oldest technical symbol and the expression of the first cosmogonic ideas which arose among the peoples'*.[3] [...]

By a curious use of word-play, Semper foreshadows his later reference to the knot as the essential work of art quite early in the textile chapter, when he considers the term *Naht*: the seam, the joining. It is, he says, an expedient, a *Nothbehelf* for the joining of two planes of similar or dissimilar material. But the very juxtaposition of *Noth* and *Naht* suggests a connection. The seam is an analogue and symbol which has archaic roots, for the usage of joining orginally separated planes. Here he presents the reader with a primary and most important rule of art in its simplest form: to make a virtue of necessity.[4]

In a footnote, Semper confesses that the word-play might have seemed so facile as to be meaningless; though the connection between *Naht* and knot (*Knoten, nœud, nodus*) seemed to him in some way related to the Greek ἀνάγκη, force, necessity. Presumably he had made himself familiar with the articles *Knoten, Naht* etc, in Jakob and Wilhelm Grimm's German dictionary.[5] However, he found the answer to his problem after he had written this passage in the work on linguistics by Albert Höfer, a disciple of von Humboldt.[6] Höfer justified the word-play, and pointed out the relation of such words to the Indo-European root *noc*, Latin *nec-o, nexus, necessitas, nectere,* νέω (to spin).[7]

The linguistic details apart, the making of virtue of necessity is advanced by Semper at the beginning of the book.[8] It is in fact the first of the two essential rules which govern all human fabrication; which is always the result of a need, whether physically experienced or raised to a symbolic plane.[9] The second rule is that it is conditioned by the material used in its fabrication, as well as the actual process by which it is made. Only the use of colour is not bound by these two fundamental rules. But this materialist law is prefaced by the categoric statement that the work of art can only be understood as a whole and cannot be analysed into a series of stimuli to be

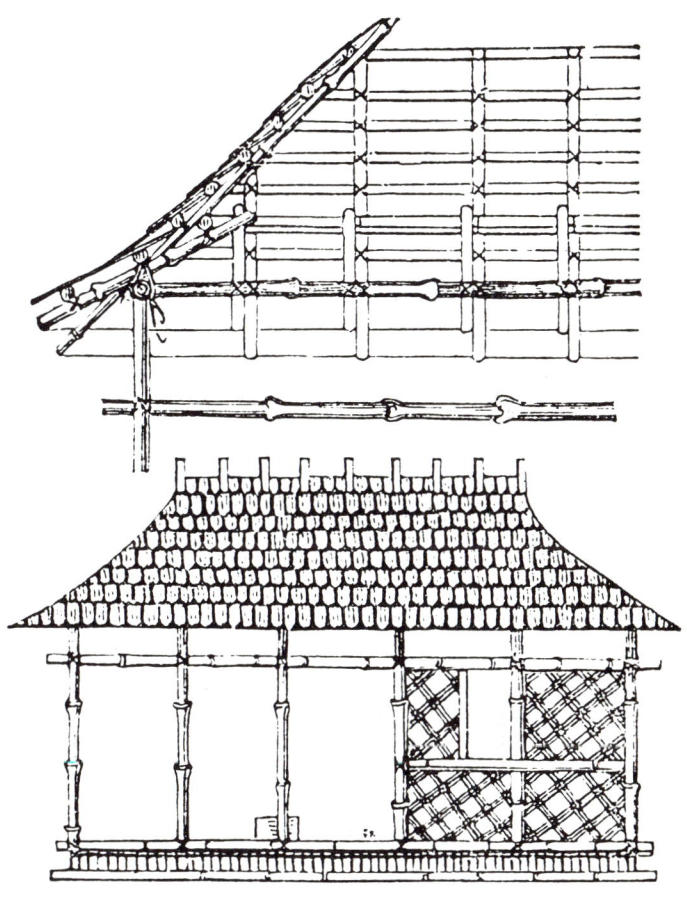

The primitive house at the exhibition of 1851 (G Semper, *Der Stil*, vol II p 263)

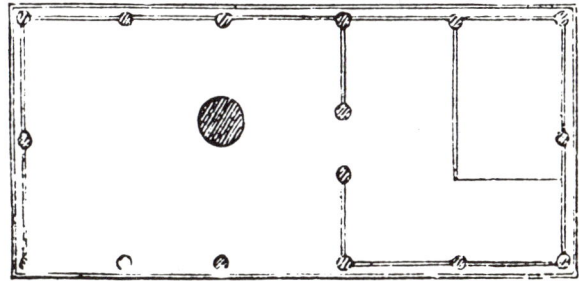

JOSEPH RYKWERT, Professor of Art at the University of Essex, has lectured and taught at all major Western European and American universities and is currently Slade Professor of Fine Arts at the University of Cambridge. His many publications include an edition of Alberti's *Ten Books of Architecture* (1955), *The Idea of a Town* (1963; second edition 1976), *Church Building* (1966), *On Adam's House in Paradise* (1972), an edition of the writings of Adolf Loos (1972), and *The First Moderns* (1980).

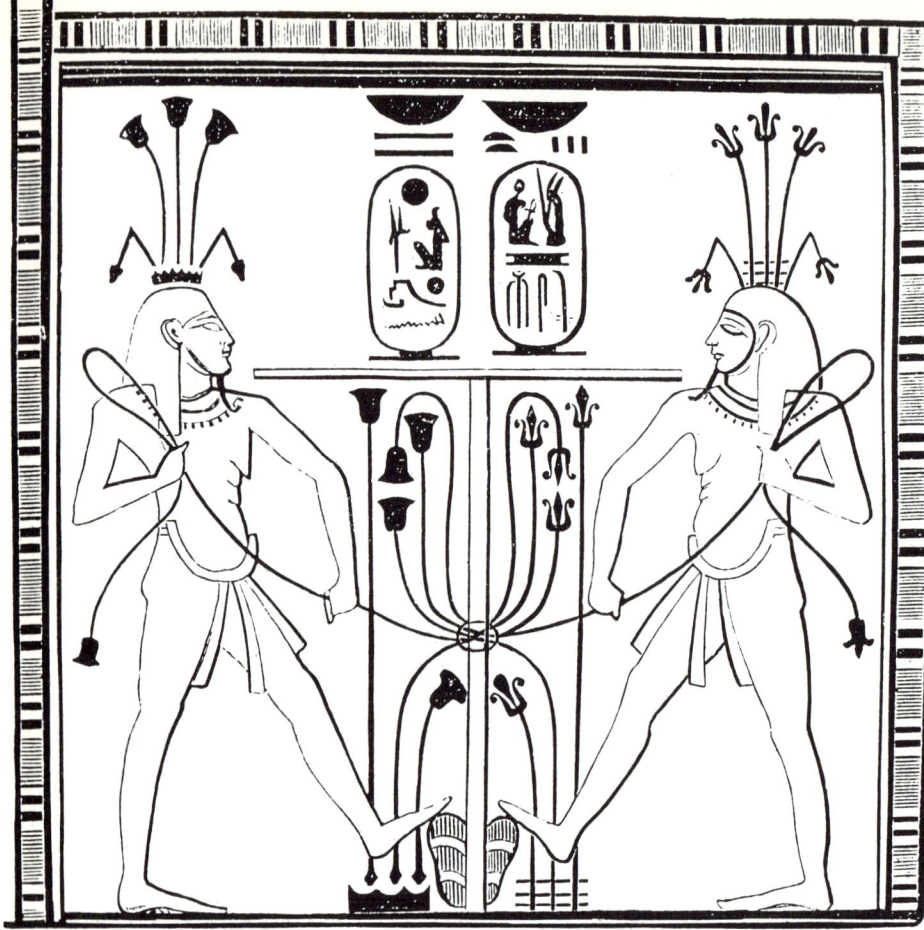

Above Example of proportional laws in radial forms (G Semper, *Der Stil*, vol I p xxv)

Left Egyptian plant design (G Semper, *Der Stil*, vol I p 79)

considered under laboratory conditions, an attitude which Semper condemns even more severely than he does the older idealist speculations to which, after all, he owes his debt.

The work of art, he says succinctly in the Prolegomena, is man's response to the world which is full of wonder and mysterious powers, whose laws man thinks he might understand but whose riddle he never resolves, so that he remains forever in unsatisfied tension. The unattained completeness he conjures into play by building a miniature universe for himself. [...]

This teleological structure of the beautiful introduces the exposition of the 'three moments' through which (in Semper's notion) forms are seen as unified and beautiful. These are symmetry, proportionality, and unity of movement. He examines them in relation to natural phenomena, to snow-flakes, flowers, astronomical movement, and briefly alludes to their reference to human works. But the application of this conceptual framework is never made explicit in the book. [...]

The difficulty in reading Semper now is inherent in his method: we are used to a historic ordering of such material, and his is classificatory. [...] His first interest was in an interpretative taxonomy in establishing the conditions under which style is generated. It is a problem with which von Rumohr had wrestled at some length.[10] [...] The model which Semper followed was not offered by any connoisseur or philologist: his aim was to emulate the great formal classificatory system of Georges Cuvier. Semper had come across Cuvier's work when he was in Paris for the first time and held him, throughout his life, in the greatest reverence.[11] [...] Within Semper's lifetime, Cuvier's system was both emulated and attacked, although it was to be overtaken by the evolutionary biology of Darwin, Wallace and Huxley.[12]

The great innovation which Cuvier had introduced was to shift the emphasis from description by the identifiable members of an organism, and classification by description, to classification by the function performed: so that resemblance was no longer the principal criterion of classification, but the working of the member within the organism.[13] The old taxonomies, based on resemblance, are broken by Cuvier's new principle. Function (and its hierarchical disposition of the organism from within) is the dominant principle of classification. This hierarchical disposition of the functions: breathing, digestion, circulation and locomotion, common to most animals (he later added that of the nervous system, to which he was in the end to attribute the determining role) was hierarchically attenuated on a descending scale, from man to the amoeba which does not have nervous, circulatory, locomotion organs, and only functions for ingestion.[14] Such a view of the planned and purposive organisation of the functions of organs implied a new kind of classification in biology based on the principle of the community of function rather than on resemblance; which further implied a discontinuous view of organic development. Species, in this view, were fixed and developed by their particular inherent formal laws, never by some transformation from one to another. This condition, this discontinuity, allowed Cuvier to construct a *history of nature*, a history which he saw in terms of cataclysmic change, as against the *natural history* of the 18th century biologists, for whom natural development was always continuous. It is this fixity of the species which made Cuvier appear so old-

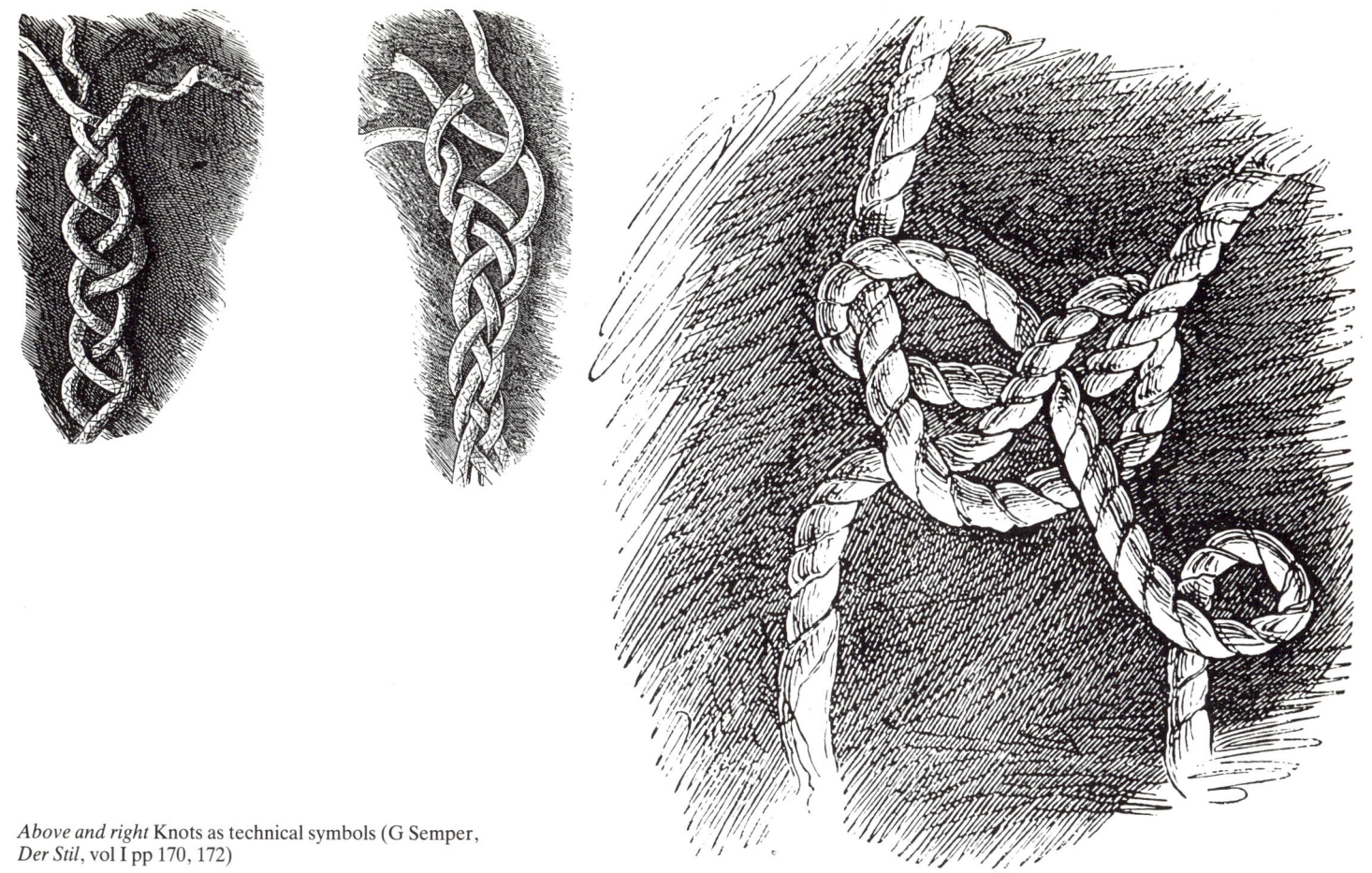

Above and right Knots as technical symbols (G Semper, *Der Stil*, vol I pp 170, 172)

fashioned to the post-Darwinian scientists; it is this same discontinuity which so marked Semper's thinking.[15] He had come to admire Cuvier first as the arranger, according to the idea just outlined, of the great collection of natural specimens at the Jardin des Plantes, which we know him to have visited assiduously.[16] [...] And again he was struck by the confusion of the material in the Great Exposition, and the inability of the Jury system, as it was organised there, to cope with the mass of evidence. His own reaction to it was set out in the paper *Wissenschaft, Industrie, Kunst*, in which he proposed a quadruple organisation of human artefacts, and in which the primitive hut provided a model of articulation. This hut is made up of four radical, irreducible elements: the hearth, which is the *'moral foundation of settlement'*,[17] the walls, the terrace, the roof. These four radicals correspond to four ways of operating (not, as is often said, to four materials): moulding for the hearth, which produces ceramics; weaving and platting to the walls, which produces textile; carpentry and joinery to the terrace and the roof; to which is added stereotomy, or masonry which replaces joinery in the making of substructures and later even textile in walls; but stereotomy also displays a radical action, that of heaping up which cannot be reduced to any of the others. Metalworking was added as a fifth element to the book. [...]

Semper was also a contemporary of many great philologists: Franz Bopp was ten years his senior, the Grimms 15; as the curious *excursus* on *Noth* and *Naht* has already indicated, Semper had a very considerable interest in linguistic speculation. [...] Thus, if Cuvier attributed a dynamic coherence to organisms, and demonstrated it through the purposive organisation of their functions, analogously, the linguists of Humboldt's and Bopp's generation saw speech in all its architectural development, displaying the will of a people to maintain itself, through the power or ability to speak the language which is its own.[18] [...] In that memorable phrase of von Humboldt's: '*Language is not an act* (Ergon), *but an activity* (Energia) ... *it is the ever-recurring work of the spirit to make articulated sound able to utter or express thought.*'[19] [...] Hence the interest of these scholars for the oral traditions which provide a history of language more archaic than that of the written word: the traditions enshrined in the fairy-tale and the epic myth. [...] The internal character of each epoch, the interdependence of the form and the material within it, was to be treated by Semper in his third volume. [...]

The works of man [...] mirror the laws of nature: but they do so to satisfy both maker and user; the do not follow natural laws as if in obedience to some blind necessity. [...] They are the products of the collective, of society exactly in the same way as the springs of language were collective in the new comparative linguistics. As linguistics also followed the example of Cuverian articulation and broke the 18th-century idea of a progressive history of language within which older and younger languages could be distinguished, Semper wanted, analogously, to break the organisation of the history of art, as it had been set up by Winkelmann in the first place, with its insistence on the priority of one people over another, with its hieratic attention to the individual artists; Semper's scheme was to concentrate on the unity of making, whether courtly or popular, and the growth of the arts and crafts from certain root processes, which were part of the universal human experiences: settlement and partition.[20] There are therefore, in Semper's system, two primary archetypes: the hearth and the cloth, the *Urherd* and the *Urtuch*. They were the first marks of settlement and fabrication. [...]

The enormous intellectual effort which the creation of Semper's great work involved has not been fully appreciated, I submit. The importance which Semper gave to the priority of textile arts is still underestimated, even though Heinz Quitzsch has devoted a chapter to this very matter in his recent monograph of Semper's theories.[21] If you take a look at the contents page of *Der Stil*, you will find that Semper gives almost as much space to textiles as he does to the other three arts put together.[22] And this was no accident. For the principle of *Bekleidung* allowed him to posit a unitary origin for all the arts; to give logical priority, paradoxical though it may seem, to ornament over structure, and so attempt to reconcile the ancient structure-ornament opposition which had dogged classical architectural theory. He did so, what is more, by appealing to the underlying laws of nature. This priority also meant another thing: that architecture, as queen of the arts—Semper, of course, like all of us architects, was afflicted by a certain justified professional chauvinism—was of its very nature *bedeckt*. And that part of its proper decking-out was painting and sculpture.

The major arts, as I have insisted, partake of the same nature and obey the same formative laws as *Kunstgewerbe* in the Semperian system. The proper mediator of these laws is architecture, and they are embodied in an exemplary and seminal manner in the first man-made objects. There is therefore no major category distinction between the major and the minor arts, between arts and crafts, between *Kunst* and *Kunstgewerbe*, to use these German terms which were to assume the character of slogans at the break of the century. Indeed in his whole conception of the link between necessity and beauty, Semper departed radically from the historians of art on whom he draws, as well as from his contemporaries.

Although the break between art and craft is inherent in the development of 19th-century 'arts and manufactures', to use a phrase familiar to Semper, yet another, and perhaps more decisive break between man the tool-maker and man the image-maker was made by social anthropologists.[23] The caves of Altamira were unacceptable to the social scientists as well as to the historians of art who were Semper's contemporaries and immediate juniors. The progress of man from the shaping of rough tools to the making of beautiful images seemed as natural as any part of the evolutionary process, and the continuity which this implied did not admit of the abrupt and integrated view of the making process which Semper held. Which is why so many dismissed the paintings at Altamira, if they took any notice of them at all, as the work of rustics or even as forgeries. They were only described accurately and given a tentative dating at the beginning of the 20th century.[24]

When that happened, the great beauty of the prehistoric paintings and bold carvings appeared much more impressive than the clumsy and repetitive Paleolithic cutting tools. The changed view of prehistoric man was contemporary with a more radical shift in the intellectual climate. Of this, Alois Riegl's attack on what he called the materialistic structure of Semper's system was symptomatic. In Riegl's view, the artist could not be thought of as conditioned by his materials and methods of manufacture. Riegl saw him as bound only by an intellectual horizon exemplified by the concept of *Kunstwollen*, which I do not wish to discuss here. Enough to say that Riegl's rejection of what seemed to him a straightforward materialist account of the genesis of art has been the screen through which many art historians have looked at Semper.[25] It is difficult otherwise to justify such a description of *Der Stil* as you may find in Lionello Venturi's *History of Art Criticism*. 'Repulsive as it is,' says Venturi, '*such a materialistic conception of art as Semper's has had its use: it has recalled the attention of the historian to the way in which the spirit is realised in matter, to the way in which material has been sensitised by art.*'[26]

Such a gross caricature misses the fine ambiguity of Semper's system. [...] The great lesson of *Der Stil*, that of adapting a comparative morphology to the history of art, has however foundered. On the one hand, was the Scylla of the discovery of man, the first image-maker: a discovery with which even Riegl found it so difficult to come to terms.[27] On the other, was the Charybdis of the decisive division between arts and crafts. In the first decade of our century, the division had become acute and contentious. The Deutsche Werkstätte were founded just before the century turned, at the time when Alfred Lichtwark first popularised the notion of *Sachlichkeit* as an aesthetic criterion.[28] In 1907, at the foundation of the Werkbund, the division was institutionalised.[29] And in the next year, you have Loos' resounding attack on the very notion of ornament.[30] [...]

The divergence between the work of art and the craft or industrial product, between *Kunst* and *Kunstgewerbe* is as clearly, as emphatically stated, as it ever was in the great debate between Hermann Muthesius and Henry van de Velde which was to shake the Werkbund in 1914.[31]

In conclusion, let me return to Semper and the problem of Style. Familiar as he was with 'the styles' as a cant phrase of his time, his view of style as a concept was, like that of his contemporary, Viollet-le-Duc, quite free of the taint that 'styles' were ornamental vocabularies, to be applied at random, or even with some associational overtones. [...] Semper was passionately involved in the construction of a theory of style, to resolve the many conflicts which the academic tradition had left in question. He did so while the horizon of historical knowledge extended immeasurably and the pressure of new functions and new materials made unprecedented demands on the designer's ingenuity. It is perhaps hardly surprising therefore that Semper adopted the primitive hut as the organisational principle of all artistic phenomena, and provided an analogue of it in his ideal four-fold museum, in which the unity the hut represented could be reconstructed by the visitor through his re-experience of the four ways of making come together. It is easy to understand his scheme; and yet it had a powerful influence on such diverse matters in the teaching of art in Great Britain;[32] on the development of ethnology, particularly on Franz Boas and his school;[33] and most surprising of all, on the architects of the Chicago School. The notion of the curtain-wall is said to have been formulated with reference to Semper's insistence on the conceptual priority of textile art.[34]

But it is the whole structure of Semper's system which now

looks more interesting, yes, and more relevant than it ever did since its publication. We have lost the cheerful certainties of the Werkbund. We do not read Ruskin and Morris again simply as historical documents: their views have acquired a new urgency. In this climate, Semper's concern to trace all artistic activity to a transformational morphology, based on four root ways of the willing hand's working of inert material, acquires fascinating possibilities. [...]

It is Semper's great insight into the way in which the artist and the craftsman relate what they think to what they do [...] which seems to me invaluable and urgent. Conceived at the moment when thinking and doing were to be disastrously divorced, it may well contain a hint for their new reconciliation.

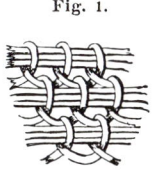 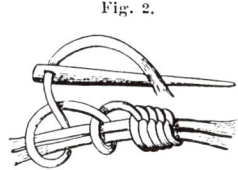 

Elementary forms of sewing and weaving (G Semper, *Der Stil*, vol I p 174)

Notes

1 *Der Stil in den technischen und tektonischen Künsten oder Praktische Ästhetik. Ein Hanbuch für Techniker, Künstler and Kunstfreunde von Gottfried Semper*, München, 1863. The second edition, which is quoted, appeared in München in 1878 and 1879, with a preface by the author's son, Hans Semper.
2 Semper, *Der Stil*, Vol 1, 1978, p 12.
3 *Ibidem*, p 169.
4 '... *Das Gesetz nähmlich aus der Noth eine Tugend zi Machen.*' The proverb seems to have been coined by St Jerome, but is a fairly universal proverb, which Semper proposes as the first rule of art. *Der Stil*, Vol 1, p 73 & note 1.
5 J & W Grimm, *Deutsches Wörterbuch*, svv.
6 Semper gives the reference to Höfer's *Sprachwissenschaftliche Untersuchungen*, pp 223f.
7 Semper's further reference is to L Diefenbach, *Vergleichendes Wörterbuch der Gothischen Sprache*, Frankfurt A/M, 1851, sv Nauths, and to J Grimm, *Deutsche Grammatik*, Berlin, 1822.
8 Semper, *Der Stil*, Vol 1, p 7.
9 The word symbol was very much under discussion since Kant's rethinking of the term; but it had been given very close attention by the students of language. (Georg) Friederich Creuzer's *Symbolik und mythologie der alten Völker, besonders der Griechen* (Leipzig & Darmstadt, 1810 and 1812) was widely known. But Semper knew also Karl Otfried Müller's rather different views of the matter, since he heard his lectures when a student at Göttingen. Müller sets out his difference from Creuzer in the *Prolegomena zu einer Wissenschaftlichen Mythologie*, Göttingen, 1825, pp 331ff.
10 Cf von Rumohr, *Italienische Forschungen*, Berlin & Stettin, 1828, Vol 1, pp 48ff. In the same place, von Rumohr also concerns himself briefly with the notion of Type. Semper was very familiar with von Rumohr and his work, indeed designed his tomb in Dresden. The passage in question is in Vol 1, pp 103ff.
11 H Semper, *Gottfried Semper, Ein Bild seines Lebens und Wissens*, Berlin, 1880. See also Semper, *Kleine Schriften* (ed M & H Semper), Berlin and Stuttgart, 1884, pp 7ff.
12 It was, of course, attacked earlier, and Goethe was much involved in the controversy. See L W Goethe, *Werke*, ed E Beutler, Zürich and Stuttgart, 1966, Vol XVII, pp 380ff; these essays were first published in the *Jahrbuch für Wissenschaftliche Kritik*, Berlin, 1830 and 1832.
13 The place of Cuvier in the history of biology, and the importance of his theories, as well as their relationship to economic theory and linguistics is discussed by Michel Foucault in *Les Mots et les Choses*, Paris 1966, pp 229ff. Cuvier, while not maintaining an active interest in contemporary German philosophy, knew of the earlier linguistic speculations, as is clear from the *Histoire des Sciences Naturelles, depuis leurs Origines jusqu'à nos Jours*, edited from Cuvier's lectures by M Magdaleine de Saint-Agy, Paris 1841, whose conception of the place of the Indians in world history and their relation to other cultures, the Egyptians in particular, owes much to Friederich von Schlegel's *Über die Sprache und Weisheit der Indier*, Heidelberg 1808, to which he makes specific acknowledgement in Vol 1, p 30.
14 M Foucault, *op cit*, p 276f.
15 The catastrophic theory of biological development is set out in his *Recherches sur les Ossements Fossiles ... par M le Baron G Cuvier* (2nd ed), Paris, 1821, Vol I, pp iii ff. On the recent appearance of homo as a species, *ibid*, pp LXIV ff.
16 H Semper in *Kleine Schriften*, *op cit*, and G Semper, *ibid*, pp 259ff.
17 Semper, *Der Stil*, Vol II, pp 335f; cf *Kleine Schriften*.
18 M Foucault, *op cit*, p 303. On Humboldt and Bopp, see Pieter A Verburg, 'The Background to the Linguistic Conceptions of Franz Bopp', in Thomas E Sebok, *Portraits of Linguistics*, Bloomington, 1966, Vol I, p 226ff and further on his differences from Humboldt, pp 234ff.
19 Wilhem von Humboldt, *Über die Verschiedenheit des Menschlichen Sprachbaues und ihren Einfluss auf die geistige Entwicklung des Menschengeschlechts*, Berlin, 1836, plvii. '*Sie (die Sprache) ist kein Werk (Ergon), sondern eine Tätigkeit (Energia) ... Sie ist nähmlich die sich ewig wiederhollende Arbeit des Geistes, den articulierten Laut zum Ausdruck des Gedanken fähig zu machen.*'
20 On the human skin as the primary ornamented surface, Semper, *Der Stil*, Vol I, p 92f. On the archaic, even archetypical nature of the platted screen, see Vol I, pp 27f, 213ff, in which the nature of the Urtuch is described, while the Heerd is given a special section in Vol II, pp 335ff. Semper, *Die Vier Elemente der Baukunst, ein Beitrag zur Vergleichenden Baukunde*, Braunschweig, 1851, pp 55ff.
21 H Quitzsch, *Die Ästhetischen Anschauungen Gottfried Sempers*, Berlin, 1962, pp 65ff.
22 Textiles, p 468; Ceramics, p 198; Carpentry, p 314; Masonry, p 124; Metals, p 106.
23 See, for instance, R Munro, *Paleolithic Man*, Edinburgh, 1912, pp 203ff; cf A Leroi-Gourhan, *op cit*, pp 28ff.
24 E Cartailhac and E Breuil, *La Caverne d'Altamira à Santillane, près de Santander (Espagne)*, Monaco, 1906.
25 A Riegl, *Stilfragen*, Berlin, 1893, p 17ff. His insistence on the priority of reprsentational art over ornament, and in particular of carving over any form of weaving or platting, pp 26ff.
26 Lionello Venturi, *Storia della Critica d'Arte*, Turin, 1964, p 231.
27 Riegl found it difficult to explain why the first artists did not model plants which are still, and therefore easier to observe, in preference to animals, pp 51ff.
28 Through the review *Pan*, and his books: *Makartbouquet und Blumenstrauss*, München, 1894, and *Palastfenster und Flügeltür*, Berlin, 1899, and his patronage as director of the Hamburg Kunsthalle. C Gurlitt, *Die Deutsche Kunst seit 1800*, Berlin, 1924, pp 464f. Also N Pevsner, *Pioneers of Modern Design*, Harmondsworth, 1960, pp 33, 108.
29 In October 1907. See P Bruckmann, 'Die Gründung des Deutschen Werkbundes 6.10.1907', in *Form X*, 1932, reprinted in 'Die Form', *Stimme des Deutschen Werkbundes, 1925–1934*, pp 82ff.
30 Adolf Loos, *Ornament und Verbrechen*, 1908, reprinted in Trotzdem, Innsbruck, 1931, pp 79ff.
31 On this incident, see Julius Posener, *Anfänge des Funktionalismus*, Frankfurt a/M, 1964, pp 199ff.
32 See, R Redgrave, *Manual of Design*, 1875, pp 15ff.
33 See Gene Weltfish, *The Origins of Art*, Indianapolis, 1953, pp 25ff.
34 Semper, *Der Stil*, Vol I, pp 8f. On the American translation of Semper, see N Pevsner, *Some Architectural Writers of the Nineteenth Century*, Oxford 1972, p 252, n 3. I owe the suggestion of the origin of the term, and perhaps in some part also the concept of curtain-wall in Semper's thinking, to Mrs Rosemary Bletter.

Stilfragen
ALOIS RIEGL
1858–1905

Let us now consider what might have caused the conditions which, for the last 25 years, have so frequently exercised a paralysing effect on art historical research. Perhaps, the main reason is the materialistic concept of the origins of all artistic creation, as formulated since the sixties of our century, a concept which instantly won over artists, connoisseurs and scholars. It is customary to attribute the new theory of the technical and material origin of ornamental and artistic forms to Gottfried Semper, though this is as unjust as to identify modern Darwinism with Darwin. The parallel between Darwinism and materialism in art seems to me appropriate, especially since there is a close causal connection between them, in so far as the concept of the materialistic influence on the origins of art [...] is but the transposition, so to speak, of Darwinism onto the plane of the life of the spirit. But, as one must distinguish between Darwin and the Darwinists, so one should draw a clear distinction between Semper and the Semperians. Semper claimed that material and technique should also be taken into consideration in the development of artistic form, whereas the Semperians oversimplify and claim that every artistic form is the product of material and technique. [...] Gottfried Semper [...] would have disliked the idea of a purely mechanical and material imitative impulse taking the place of the artist's free creative will. But by now the confusion which made this concept appear as the very idea of the great art historian Semper has been well established. [...]

Amidst such a mental climate, this book puts forward its own fundamental principles for a history of ornamental art. The fact that it deals only with basic principles [...] needs no justification. In a field whose terrain is fought over inch by inch, and indeed whose very basis is in doubt, the most important thing is to ensure oneself of some solid positions [...] so that one can then proceed to attempt a general, systematic elaboration. [... In the first] chapter—the very title of which announces the discussion of the essence and origins of the geometric style—I hope I have succeeded in explaining not only that there is nothing to make us suppose *a priori* that the oldest geometric decorations are linked to particular techniques, and especially to those of the art of weaving, but also that the oldest historically verifiable remains contradict this hypothesis. We are also brought to the same conclusion by other reflections of a more general nature. In fact, the need to adorn the body appeared to us far more primary than the need to protect it with woven products. Decorations which serve no other purpose than that of fulfilling the desire for ornament, including linear and geometric forms, appear long before the art of weaving originates. Thus the principle which for 25 years, has dominated the study of art is eliminated; namely that of identifying simplistically textile ornament with all other two-dimensional decoration. Once one disputes that the oldest two-dimensional decoration was carried out on textiles and with weaving techniques, the concept of the identity of the two forms of art loses all validity. *Two dimensional ornament becomes the superior unity of which textile ornament is but a subordinate part, just like any other decoration on a flat surface.* [...]

Every religious symbol is destined, with time, if it has any artistic features at all, to become fundamentally and indeed exclusively an ornamental motif. Its continued and widespread use, the outward form to which consecration imparts a stereo-typed character, its execution in various materials, all this means that the symbol is made ever more familiar to man until it becomes almost a necessity for him to see it reproduced. The simple faith of the ancients has made a very special contribution to this process of development. The symbol was worn on clothes, it was carved on tools and on numerous objects which were constantly in front of people's eyes. There was hardly an object in the houses of the ancient Egyptians on which the lotus flower was not reproduced in one form or another. The people to whom that symbol was transmitted were no longer—judging from the free use they usually made of it—subject to the hieratical sense of the Egyptians. For the Assyrians, the Phoenicians and the Greeks the symbolic meaning of the lotus had been eclipsed. Hellenistic and Roman art seems to sum up this whole process: its decorative apparatus is formally derived largely from ancient oriental symbolism, while rejecting the latter's essence. With their sophisticated sense of the beautiful in art, the Greeks chose only those motifs which actually lent themselves to aesthetic perfection, such as palms, sphinxes, centaurs, but not divinities with heads of animals, scarabs and the like.

In fact ancient Egyptian art had already concentrated on the artistic perfection of most of the plant motifs which it had dealt with. And even in this first period of artistic representation, the floral themes underwent a stylisation necessitated by the reproduction techniques of *en creux* negative relief and of painting. Once again the basic postulate was symmetry. In fact, the motif was represented for its objective meaning, but the representation was carried out with a close observance of those early artistic postulates which had already been at the heart of artistic creation during the strictly geometric phase, when representation corresponded to the pure need for ornament. [...] If, as we may suppose, [other less developed civilisations] did not possess their own ornamental floral motifs until their encounter with Egyptian civilisation, they were now introduced to a tradition that they could subsequently reproduce by borrowing its models or by copying them in some way or another. Apparently no-one thought of stylising a motif taken from the flora of their own country, since they now had ready-made ones from different origins. For the same reason today, we still use mainly the ancient motifs which have been handed down to us, even though we have designers far more skilled than those of antiquity.

Capital decoration at Erechtheum (A Riegl, *Stilfragen*, fig 113)

> **ALOIS RIEGL** was born in Linz in 1858. He studied under Sickel and from 1881 to 1883 he was a member of the Institut für Geschichtsforschungen in Vienna. He also studied under Thausing and Eitelberger, and one of his research colleagues was the art historian Wickhoff. After the resignation of Wickhoff from the Österreichisches Museum in 1886, Riegl took the directorship of the department of textiles until 1897, when he became professor at the University of Vienna. He lectured on late Roman and Baroque art until 1902. From then onwards he devoted himself to the study of the preservation of monuments and in 1905, the year of his death, he drew up a legislative proposal on the subject. His book *Stilfragen* (1893) remains his most seminal study; he also published *Die spätrömische Kunstindustrie* (1901) and, posthumously, *Die Entstehung der Barockkunst in Rom* (1908).

Excerpt from Alois Riegl, *Stilfragen*, first published by Verlag von Georg Siemens, Berlin, 1893. This extract is taken from the Italian edition entitled *Problemi di Stile*, Feltrinelli, Milan, 1963, pp 2–4, 53–54.

The Philosophical Context of *Stilfragen*
ARTURO CARLO QUINTAVALLE
b 1936

Alois Riegl's *Stilfragen* (*The Problems of Style*) was published in 1893.[1] This book is particularly characteristic of the Viennese school of art history in that it attempts a universal history of art, following the contemporary tradition of comparative philological university studies. The book traces the history of decoration from the Egyptian to the Arab and Late Byzantine periods, both in the east and the west. Its importance, however, lies in the methodological risk it took: it attempted to reconcile the contemporary debate between the philosophies of Herbart and Taine; that is, between the traditions of positivism and evolutionism.

Late 19th-century Vienna—as Schlosser has pointed out in his essay on the Viennese School—was a stronghold of Herbartism. The Prussian centralised and conservative empire had its own philosophy; one that has little to do with Hegel. Indeed Herbart's position[2] (cf, his *Manual for an Introduction to Philosophy* Königsberg, 1813) stressed the Kantian *thing in itself*. For Herbart philosophy is conceptual thinking directed away from the subject. Everything becomes reduced to the Kantian categories of space and time. In his writings on psychology,[3] Herbart insists on the influence of external substances on the thinking subject; an influence which he claims to be mathematically measurable. The same external stimuli always effect similar psychological behaviour and thus can be scientifically determined by them.

Clearly such a theory, postulating the metaphysical entities of the *subject* and of the *thing in itself* (metaphysical in that they are conceived in the abstract and not in a dialectical relationship), when brought to bear on art, could not fail to produce an aesthetic dominated by the laws of cause and effect. Hegel's dialectic of beauty in the real world is abandoned: instead, Herbart follows the Kantian theme of 'free' beauty abstracted from the real. For Herbart beauty is 'free' and so it can only exist as beauty form. There follows a formalism which classifies the works of art on the basis of their specific qualitative and quantitative characteristics that give rise to the artistic genres.

For Zimmermann (cf his *Geschichte der Aesthetik*, 1858)—a pupil of Herbart who greatly influenced Riegl—beauty is understood in the Herbartian formalistic categories, now, however, set in motion by historical evolution. In his *Aesthetic* (*Allgemeine Aesthetik als Formwissenschaft*, 1865) the works of art are divided into two kinds: those linked to the modes of perception, and thus figurative; and those linked to the modes of thinking, and thus lyrical. In fact, Zimmermann following Herbart, makes a clear distinction between two kinds of

The lotus motif in decoration (A Riegl, *Stilfragen*, fig 26)

ARTURO CARLO QUINTAVALLE, born in 1936, is Director of the Institute of Art History at Parma University, where he founded and directs the Centre of Communications Studies. Amongst the most noted of Italian specialists in medieval history, he has, over the last ten years, developed an interest in contemporary art and mass communication, promoting the semiotic study of the different codes and communications systems in society. Quintavalle is the author of numerous publications on photography and contemporary art.

perception: the sensuous and the intellectual, producing accordingly two genres of artistic production.

Were these aesthetic theories the only ones spread by the Viennese School of Art History? Concerning the theory of *Einfühlung*,[4] Herbart's theory, if nothing else, at least gave back to the work of art its psychological dimension; a dimension that was against any materialist interpretation of art. For Darwin's theories and the popularity that the law of causality had been enjoying in German artistic culture had produced a materialist tradition, the prime advocate of which was Semper.[5] According to that tradition, the material substance itself was thought to be the determining factor of the form of a work of art. Semper's greatest work, based on the studies of Chevreul and Brücke on the physiology and psychology of vision, had appeared in 1863 under the title *Der Stil in den technischen und tektonischen Künsten*; a work which Riegl, in his *Stilfragen*, was to attack several times.

There is still another school of historiography which must be examined in connection to Riegl: the advocates of the theory of 'pure visibility', of whom the sharpest theoretician was Fiedler.[6] Fiedler is indebted both to Herbart's formalism and to certain aspects of the idealistic aesthetic of Hegel and the Romantics, which make him value the artist as divine creator and individual. Fiedler's theories had a great impact on Riegl's thinking: in 1893, the year of *Stilfragen*, Adolf von Hilderbrand published *The Problem of Form in Figurative Art*. In this book, many aspects of Fiedler's theories were carried to the extreme; something which Riegl was to repeat in his *Spätrömische Kunstindustrie*.

At the same time, the positivist tradition had an illustrious representative in the Viennese school, namely senator Giovanni Morelli, also known as Ivan Lermolieff, who was the author of various volumes on some of the greatest collections of paintings in Europe (Berlin, Munich, Dresden, and the Borghese in Rome). In his writings, Lermolieff stressed a 'scientific' method for the analysis of paintings: the task of the historian was by no means to address the creative individuality of the artist, singling out his personal *maniera*—as had been the case with the aesthetics of Idealism from Hegel to Schelling and the French artists of the 19th century.

This rough outline of the thought of the most prominent Viennese thinkers on art gives us an understanding of the late 19th-century break away from the aesthetics of Romanticism. Hegel's 'dialectic of becoming' and the problem of the artist as creator, have no place in the new social and cultural climate of late 19th-century Vienna, despite Schelling's irrationalist proclamations. [...] A glance through the most diverse manuals—from the middle of the century onwards—suffices to show the esteem that positivism was securing for itself. The law of causality between object and art was particularly stressed by Kugler (1842) and Springer (1855) until it finds its apotheosis in the brilliant schematisation of Charles Blanc's *Grammaire des arts du dessin* (1880). Beyond Semper's theories, the theses of Taine and those of Comte (cf his *Cours de philosophie positive*, 1830–42) enjoyed remarkable popularity: both Taine and Comte affirmed once again the law of cause and effect, this time between art and the historical-social environment. In France as well as in Germany, the rejection of Hegel's dialectic and the acceptance of the positivist theories had occasioned the great inventories of classical and Christian antiquity, like the *Pauli Wissowa* and the *Kraus* respectively, which accompanied the publication of the great inventories of the origins, from the *Migne* to the *Monumenta Germaniae Historica*.

Further the works of Rumohr, and Passavant here also related to the erudite culture and the philological tradition; but these, along with Bartsch's work on engraving, were now to be superseded by the positivist culture of Morelli: namely the emerging historian-expert who, from Bode, to Berenson, to Suida, to Friedlander, was to weigh heavily on the subsequent progress of art history. Wickhoff's *Wiener Genesis* came out in 1895, that is just two years after the publication of *Stilfragen*. This book practically laid the foundations of the history of Roman art. What is more important, the book opened up a new area of investigation, one which had hitherto been excluded by the evolutionist tradition of historiography since, from Winckelmann onwards, anything outside Graeco-classical art was by definition not art.

On what basis, then, is the historical vision of Wickhoff, and even more so of Riegl, founded? They address neither the exemplary classical texts nor classical art itself: instead they both attempt to map the historiographic problems of artistic periods hitherto excluded from debate and research. But while the accent of Austrian culture in general might be placed on the diffusion of positivism, something should be said of the cultural historicism of Burckhardt whose major works had all antedated those of Wickhoff and Riegl.

Burckhardt saw history as the dialectical relationship between politics, church and culture; his central interest, however, was not political but cultural history, the latter being conceived in a cyclical sense (cf, for example, his work on *The Era of Constantine the Great*). It is certainly in cultural history that Burckhardt found the driving force of historical events, borrowing a lot from both Mommsen and Ranke. Hegel's teleological conception of history did not appeal to Burckhardt; his idea of history being one of constant evolution, development in which individual creations play a determinant role. In Burckhardt, there is also a vein of Semper's culture, but certainly his history was intended to suggest a lot more to contemporary academics than, say, a pragmatic methodology such as Droysen's. That his interest was directed towards the recuperation of the creative artistic individuality while emphasising the cyclical evolution of society in its complex entirety, made Burckhardt stand in direct contrast to positivist versions of art history such as that of Taine.[7] It is from Burckhardt, then, that the recuperation started: a recuperation of the positive values of the philosophy of Hegel, whose historical dialectic had been mislaid.

Burckhardt's conception of history seems to have been very important for Riegl. Riegl's decision to make the typification of figurative schemes the subject matter of his historical analysis (cf for example, the lotus leaf from the Egyptians onwards, the vine decoration from the Greeks onwards, the acanthus, etc) should perhaps be accounted for by his eagerness to give a historical synthesis to the disparate series of historical relationships. Even in the field of contemporary archaeological finds, his principles of typification had a remarkable weight; the link between the Egyptian and Mycenaean cultures was, for example, foreshadowed in his work well before the discoveries made by Evans on Crete, which officially allowed archaeologists to link the two civilisations. Furthermore Riegl established the relationship between Mycenae and the pre-Hellenic civilisation, while he demonstrated the significance of the latter as regards the artistic experiments of the various Aegean islands. Finally, he traced the links between Greek and Roman art through the elaboration and development of the Hellenic vine decoration. Riegl outlined many other aspects of cultural history which were to become important to future historiography, as for example the naturalistic origins of the Ravenna cestus capitals, the development of vine decoration in Arab regions, etc.

But we are not interested here in making a list of the specialised contributions made by Riegl in his *Stilfragen*. Instead, it is important to note the repercussions such findings have had. From the very beginning of this book, Riegl takes up the polemic with Semper, stating explicitly that the technical-materialist conception of art is but *'the displacement of Darwinism onto the level of the life of the spirit'*. Against Semper, Riegl proclaimed that the creative inventiveness which a work of art exhibits betrays *'an imminent artistic impulse'* in man; it is such artistic impulse which, for Riegl, discredits the Semperian theory of the material origins of all geometric decoration in weaving. Standing the materialist argument on its head, Riegl states categorically that *'the need for decoration is . . . one of the most elementary needs of man; indeed, more elementary than the need to protect his body.'*

Riegl's conception of 'artistic impulse' prepared the ground for his later concept of *Kunstwollen*; the 'Will to Form', or 'Aesthetic Urge'. For once Riegl has denied the material and technical derivation of decoration; in his conclusion to the chapter on the 'Geometric Style', he states that *'there is something in man which makes him feel pleasure in the beauty of form, something which neither we nor the followers of the theory of the technical-material origin of art are able to define; and . . . this something has freely and independently given rise to the geometric combinations of lines'*. [. . .]

Surely we can find in Riegl themes of Burckhardt's or Taine's historiography, that is a certain historical fatalism, as for example when he discusses the decline of the Egyptians and their supersession by *'new forces . . . by peoples whose energy was not yet exploited'*; but these are very rare passages. The true method of *Stilfragen* is one which articulates a rich historical fabric on the basis of well chosen motifs or 'types', outlining in this way a series of cultural connections between middle-eastern and western civilisations, from the Egyptians, Persians or Phoenicians to the Mycenaeans, Hellenes, Romans, Arabs and Late Byzantines. [. . .]

Riegl's position was clear as regards Semper: Semper's theory, Riegl writes, is one *'according to which the work of art is nothing more than the mechanical product of three factors: (a) the use for which it is intended, (b) what it is made out of and, (c) the technique used to make it . . . In contrast to this mechanical conception of the nature of the work of art'*, Riegl continues, *'I am the first—as far as I know—to have proposed a hypothesis according to which the work of art is the result of a determined and conscious artistic will which, after a hard struggle, overpowers both the sensuousness of material and technique.'* [. . .]

To re-read *Stilfragen*, to understand it, as I have attempted, in the context of Austrian culture[8] at the end of the 19th century and in connection with Hegel's thought, the philosophy of Herbart, positivism and evolutionism, and in particular in connection with the universal histories of the time as well as with Burckhardt's seminal work, enables us to recognise the real origins of today's historiography of art and architecture in Europe.

Notes

1 Alois Riegl was born in Linz on January 14, 1858. He became a pupil of Sickel's historical-philological school and from 1881 to 1883 he was a member of the Institut für Geschichtsforschungen (Institute for Historical Research) in Vienna, then under the direction of Sickel.

2 Herbart was born in Oldenburg in 1776. He was a professor in Königsberg from 1809 until 1833 and subsequently professor in Göttingen, where he died in 1841. His position in both his *Einleitung zur allgemeine praktischen Philosophie* (1808) and his *Lehrbuch zur Einleitung in die Philosophie* (1813) was against the empiricist school of philosophy.

3 Cf his *Manual of Psychology* (1816) and his *Psychology as a Science; newly founded on experiment, metaphysics and mathematics* (1824–25).

4 By Robert Vischer, see *Drei Schriften zum Aesthetischen Formproblem* (1872–90). By Worringer, who with Vischer popularised the theory of *Einfühlung*, see *Abstraktion und Einfühlung* (1908), translated into English as *Abstraction and Empathy* (1953).

5 Semper was a Darwinist, but knew also of the research on the physiology of vision, particularly that of Chevreul, author of *Loi du contraste simultané des couleurs* (1838), and similar studies by Helmholtz and Brücke. Semper was an architect and maintained that a work of art is fundamentally determined by the properties of the material and the technique used for its shaping. His best known work is *Der Stil in den technischen und tektonischen Künsten* (1861–63, 1st edition; 1878–79, 2nd edition). His other works are *Bauten, Entwürfe und Skizzen* (1881), and *Kleine Schriften* (1884).

6 Conrad Fiedler (1841–95); see his *Schriften über Kunst* (1913–14); translated into Italian as *Aforismi sull'arte* (1945), ed Antonio Banfi.

7 In the field of art history, concerning his connections with Taine, see Müntz, *Storia dell'Arte durante il Rinascimento* which was originally published in 1888–1895.

8 Among the studies on the work of Riegl we note: M Dvořák, in *Mitteilungen der Zentralkommission für Erforschung und Erhaltung der Denkmäler* (1905), pp 255–275; E Heindrich, *Beiträge zur Geschichte und Methode der Kunstgeschichte* (1917), pp 87–109; W Waetzold, *Deutsche Kunsthistorischer* (1924); E Wind, in *Zeitschrift für Aesthetik und allgemeine Kunstwissenschaft*, (1924), pp 129–169; E Panofsky, 'Über das Verhältnis der Kunstgeschichte zur Kunsttheorie', *ibid*, pp 129ff; E Panofsky, 'Der Begriff des Kunstwollens', *ibid*, 1920; H Sedlmayr, 'Introduction' to the collection of Riegl's articles edited by K M Swoboda, Munich, 1928; J von Schlosser, *La scuola viennese di storia dell'arte*, Bari, 1936. Of the Italian studies we note: L Venturi, *Storia della critica d'arte* (1945); C L Ragghianti, in *Commenti di Critica d'Arte* (1946) and in *Profilo della Critica d'Arte in Italia*, (1947); Ranuccio Bianchi Bandinelli, *Storicita dell'Arte classica* (1943) and *Archeologia e cultura* (1961); A Banfi, 'Introduction' to Fiedler's *Aforismi sull'arte* (1945); S Bettini, 'Introduction' to *Industria artistica tardoromana* (1953).

Principles of Architectual History
PAUL FRANKL
1879–1962

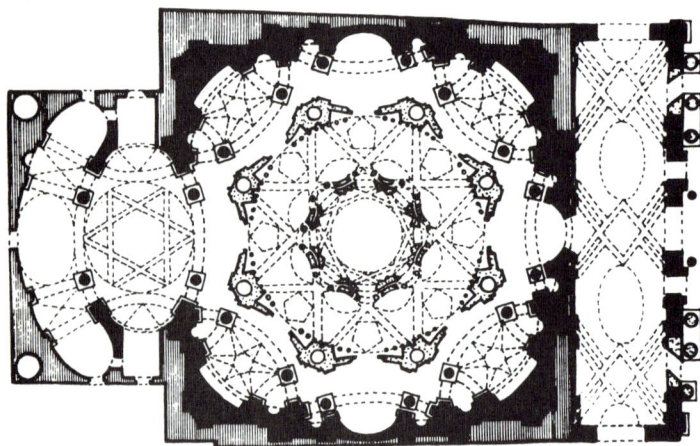

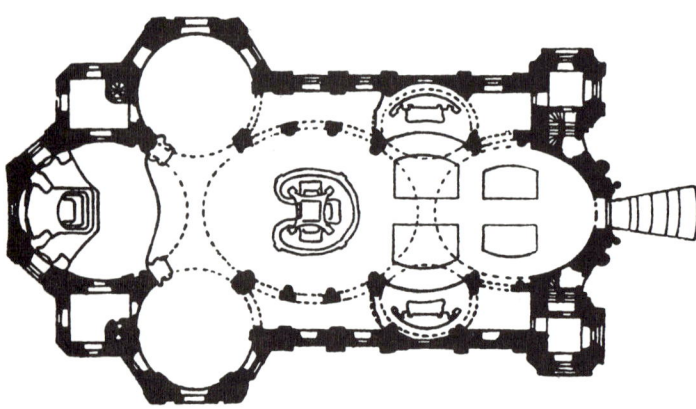

Spatial Form
Turin, S Lorenzo, 1668, plan (top), and Vierzehnheiligen, Pilgrimage Church, 1743, plan (*Principles of Architectural History*, figs 40, 50)

PAUL FRANKL was born in Prague in 1879 and died in Princeton, New Jersey in 1962. He took his doctoral degree in Munich in 1910, and in 1914 he presented his *Die Entwicklungsphasen der neueren Baukunst* (translated as *Principles of Architectural History*, 1968) as his *Habitationsschrift* to Professor Heinrich Wölfflin. In 1921 he was appointed professor at Halle University, but was dismissed by the Nazis in 1934. He went to the United states in 1938 and two years later became Research Fellow at the Institute for Advanced Study at Princeton, a position which he held until his death. His major books include *Principles of Architectural History* (1914, translated 1968); *Diefrühmittel alteriche und romanische Baukunst* (1926); *Das System der Kunstwissenschaft* (1938); *The Gothic: Literary Sources and Interpretations Through Eight Centuries* (1960); and *Gothic Architecture* (1962).

Buildings may last mechanically and chemically longer than pictures, but their life span as living works of art is often much shorter.

It has frequently been said that the theatre of the Residenz in Munich, filled with the court society of 1753, was not the same then as it is today. People are part of architecture. This too distinguishes architecture from both paintings and sculpture, for we do not stand in front of a building but are surrounded by it. Architecture and people interact. The general purpose of the theatre in the Munich Residenz has at least remained the same; it is still in constant use as a theatre. But the convent in Kempten is now a courthouse. Legal proceedings are now held in the Fürstensaal (about 1740), and the equipment necessary for these proceedings has been installed. The convent at Ebrach has become a prison. But even when an 18th-century palace retains some or all of its furnishings and tourists are guided round its rooms, it is still a mummy. Such a palace is incomplete because festivals are no longer celebrated in it. There are no more theatre and ballet performances held before a tipsy audience, which has been driven up to the door in light carriages, with liveried servants, and which has amused itself in the evening with a splendid fireworks display in the park. The one integrating element in all these palaces was destroyed forever in the French Revolution. A painting can be interpreted and brought to life again, because the figures remain in it always. A building dies as soon as the life within it has vanished, even if we know the customs of the people who once belonged to it.

Nevertheless, a trace of this vanished life remains behind in a building to the extent that the purpose is incarnated in the form of the space. This is purpose in a very general sense and does not include specific incidents. It is unnecessary to know what sort of compliments were paid at those festivals or how people laughed and lied, for these are details that never affect architecture. More influential are the meaning of the festival in the life of the patron and the predominance of artistically decorated state rooms over work spaces. Detailed knowledge of the course of such festivities will deepen our appreciation of a palace, just as an understanding of the conduct of war will deepen our appreciation of a castle. We must know how a society entertained itself, whether it favoured tournaments or tilting at the ring on horseback, whether the court included jesters and dwarfs, whether music and dance were more common than conversation and cards, and how people dined. Each of these aspects of life forms part of the building programme and, indeed, modifies that programme according to the significance that each enjoys.

A history of building programmes is therefore part of cultural history, and my task would be easier if studies in cultural history were more advanced, although I am concerned only with a *part* of these studies. It has long since been observed that a connection exists between the two disciplines; only the nature of this connection has been disputed. It was once customary to sketch a picture of a civilisation as a grand backdrop for the period of artistic development under consideration. But the fault of this method was that the background contained a great deal that had no influence upon artistic development, or that the influential factors were either lacking or were not brought into sharp relief. The bridge between art and life remained undiscovered. This bridge is nothing other than the building programme, the purpose in general, and for that reason it is difficult to begin with the cultural image, to go from the infinite number of bridges to all aspects of life. The opposite path is easier. We must begin with art itself and there seek the threads that bind it to civilisation in general. Cultural history is not to be understood as a mere collection of data from public and private life. It is, rather, the ordering of these data round centres of thought that implies change in social expression.

Paul Frankl, *Principles of Architectural History* (Cambridge, Mass, MIT Press 1968), pp 159–60.

Paul Frankl's Principles of Architectural History
SPIRO KOSTOF
b 1936

Principles of Architectural History is an important book. Published in Leipzig in 1914, under the title *Entwicklungsphasen der neueren Baukunst*, it holds a creditable position in that constellation of theoretical writings by German scholars that has formed the basis of modern art history. Of these men, Heinrich Wölfflin, Frankl's professor at Munich, is the best known, thanks to early translations of his major works; *Principles of Art History* became available in English in 1932, and the paperback version made it a regular feature of the reading lists for art history courses. August Schmarsow, on the other hand, is practically unknown and for the seminal thought of Alois Riegl, Anglo-Saxon readers have only an Italian version of *Die Spätromische Kunstindustrie* to fall back on. The lack may be due to *'an antagonism toward theory and abstraction that developed in the second generation of art historians',* as pointed out by James Ackerman.[1]

In his Preface to the original edition, Frankl cites this illustrious German trinity—Wölfflin, Schmarsow, and Riegl—as 'godfathers', along with Jacob Burckhardt, Heinrich von Geymüller, and Cornelius Gurlitt. [...] To the extent that the reader is familiar with Frankl's predecessors and immediate contemporaries, his book today will appear dated. But even with due allowance for the fertile context in which it was written, *Principles of Architectural History* remains fresh. And it could only be due to the snaillike progress in art historical method that the book contains parts that are, in fact, quite topical today, if not perhaps revolutionary. In his *Principles of Architectural History*, Frankl considers the historical span of the post-medieval period; 1420 to 1900. He divides it into four phases, corresponding approximately to the Renaissance (1420–1550), the Baroque (1550–1700), the Rococo (18th century), and the modern. Subdivisions within these phases, increasingly isolated since his day (Early, and High Renaissance Mannerism, etc), are here ignored. Actually, the third phase is characterised principally as an aggravated reading of the second, and for the modern period Frankl has no clear formulation except to insist that it partakes of the first two phases but is independent of either. In essence, therefore, the book is a study of the classical ground covered by Wölfflin and other godfathers, and in Wölfflinian manner it is studied in terms of stylistic polarities. But whereas Wölfflin developed his five polarities from an analysis of painting and sculpture primarily, Frankl is concerned only with architecture. Partly as a result of this and partly as a conscious attempt to improve on his mentors, Frankl views the buildings of each phase under four categories of his own: spatial form; corporeal form;

Corporeal Form
Haarlem, Vleeshal, 1602, facade (*Principles of Architectural History*, fig 80)

SPIRO KOSTOF, Professor of Architectural History at the University of California, Berkeley, previously taught at Yale University and was a visiting professor at the Massachusetts Institute of Technology. A former president of the Society of Architectural Historians, he received the Christian Research Foundation Award for his first book, *The Orthodox Baptistry of Ravenna* (1965). His other books include *Caves of God* (1972), *The Third Rome: 1870–1950* (1973), and *The Architect: Chapters in the History of the Profession* (1977).

Visible Form
Rome, S Carlo alle Quattro Fontane, facade, 1665 (*Principles of Architectural History*, fig 87)

Munich, St John Nepomuk, 1731, facade (*Principles of Architectural History*, fig 85)

visible form; and purposive intention.

The first two are, in a sense, the least original. Space as a central concern for the study of art and architecture may be said to be largely the invention of German theoreticians in the decades before the appearance of Frankl's *Principles*. But Frankl avoids both the dry abstraction of *Raumgestaltung* theories and also the Schmarsovian identification of architecture chiefly with space, in contrast to corporeality as the prime element of sculpture, and light, of painting. Although with Frankl we are still far from Bruno Zevi's 'creative personality of spaces', there is in the separate discussion of Protestant churches at least an admission that architectural space within the same building type is conditioned by cultural content. All such distinctions are subsumed, however, by the overriding polarity of spatial *addition* for the first phase and spatial *division* for the second phase.

This first chapter is the longest and the most complex. Frankl is transparently quickened by geometric schemes, and in his Preface he elevates his enthusiasm to a universal dictum by asserting that '*anyone for whom geometric descriptions are tedious and irksome is fundamentally unsuited for the history of architecture*' (p xv). Not only is he very adept at formal analysis of space organisation, an exercise that has not been improved upon appreciably since, but he is also able through this kind of analysis to draw some telling distinctions between ecclesiastical and secular buildings. He stresses the *successive* comprehension of secular spaces as compared to the *simultaneous* comprehension of church interiors, and focuses his analysis of the former on areas of circulation such as galleries, stairs and stairwells, courts, and the like. The princely palace is the only building type to be considered as secular architecture in all phases but the last. This is the natural outcome of an attitude that has changed but little in the study of post-medieval architecture: that the term architecture embraces largely monuments of a ceremonial or elevated nature, and not utilitarian buildings like hospitals, commercial halls, etc, with the possible exception of military works. In fact, the utilitarian viewpoint and the creation of new building types is held in some measure accountable by Frankl for the diffuse and puzzled energies of 19th-century architecture.

Corporeal form, Frankl's second category, is concerned with mass and its articulation. In this chapter the analysis of orders, groupings of supports, rustication, coffering, and frames is orthodox. The all-embracing polarity for the category is described to be that between Renaissance mass as *generator* of forces and Baroque mass as the *transmitter* of forces. The forces are viewed in terms of the human body, in a manner similar to Geoffrey Scott's *The Architecture of Humanism*, published the same year. There was, of course, ample German precedent for this theoretical basis; Robert Vischer and Theodor Lipps had outlined the concept of *Einfühlung* in the last third of the 19th century. In applying it specifically to architecture, Frankl is cautious not to imply any value judgment. He talks of '*the indescribable feeling of torment engendered by the works of the second phase ... caused by the seeming unhappiness of their tectonic corporeal*

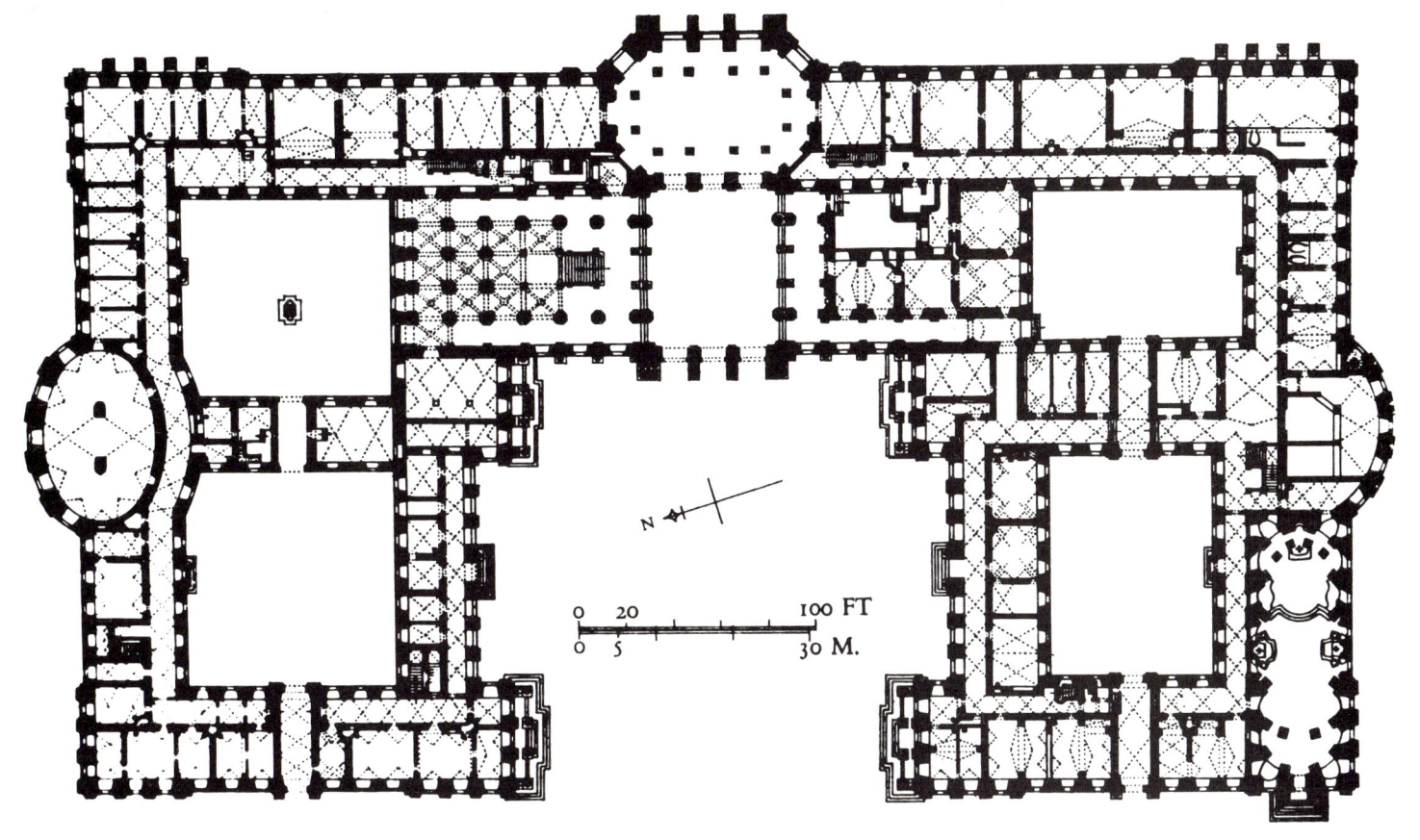

Purposive Intention
Würzburg, Residenz, 1719, plan (*Principles of Architectural History*, fig 91)

forms' (p 130), but goes on to say that *'Happiness and torment are values in human experience, but in art they are forces of expression and are valuable to the extent that they are artistically effective'* (p 131).

The last two categories of Frankl's system are briefly treated but have significant implications. In discussing visible form, he insists on the kinetic experience of architecture. *'To see architecture means to draw together into a single mental image the series of three-dimensionally interpreted images that are presented to us as we walk through interior spaces and round their exterior shell'* (p 142). This concept itself is more important than the arrived at polarity which is that of *one image* for the Renaissance and *many images* for the Baroque.

Similarly, the final category, purposive intention, introduces what should be an elemental concern of architectural history and often is not, even though the results of his particular analysis under this heading are not very rewarding. By purposive intention Frankl understands not only structural and functional propriety, but also a building's *'spriritual import, its content, its meaning'* (p 1). He recognises the obvious truth about architecture, too readily brushed aside by art historians even today in preference for description, formal analysis, and the hunt for sources: that architecture is *'the moulded theatre of human activity'* (p 2), and that *'people are part of architecture'* (p 159). The study of architectural history, with this truth in mind, becomes the study of human institutions and rituals and as such a vital part of cultural history.

But Frankl is caught in some traps of his own making. For one thing, he is confused as to the status of architecture in the cultural history of a period. He rightly points out that the practice of summarising the historical events of a period as a prelude to discussing its architecture is inadequate. Rather than treating a building as mere illustration of its cultural background, *'we must begin with art itself and there seek the threads that bind it to civilisation in general'* (p 160). But at the same time his acceptance of Riegl's *Kunstwollen* and its attendant determinism deflates the standing of individual achievement, and undermines the value of studying past buildings for what they reveal of culture. Art has preconditions. It follows rather than leads. *'An architectural style can begin only when a culture has reached a state of maturity. Philosophy, religion, politics, and science—the whole Renaissance culture—had to be ready before the fine arts could give them expression'* (p 2). Secondly, Frankl believes that *'the meaning of space derives solely from its furnishings'* (p 157); thereby grossly impoverishing architectural iconography. For these reasons among others, the results of this final chapter are both too general and too specific. But the value of this line of research is indisputable, and recent laments[2] on the state of our discipline illustrate the anaemic response to Frankl's call in the 50 years since it was issued. [...]

Notes
1 Cf Introduction by James Ackerman to Paul Frankl's *Principles of Architectural History* (Cambridge, Mass: MIT Press 1968).
2 Cf Bruce Allsopp, *The Study of Architectural History* (New York 1970).

Copyright December 1971 by the Society of Architectural Historians (all rights reserved).

Classicism and Neoclassicism
EMIL KAUFMANN
1891–1953

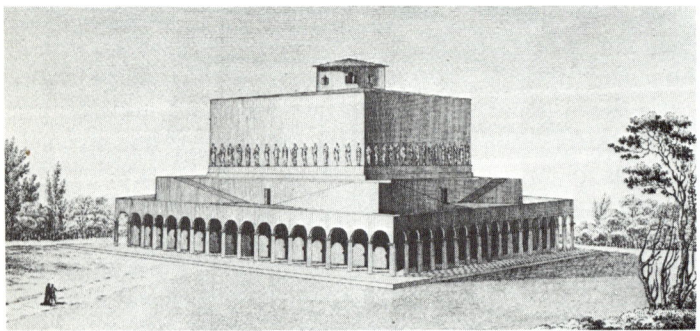

Claude-Nicolas Ledoux, Maison des Gardes Agricoles, *c* 1780; Prison of Aix-en-Provence, 1776; and Panaretheon, 1773–79 (from *Visionary Architects*, University of St Thomas, 1968)

EMIL KAUFMANN was born in Vienna in 1891 and died in Cheyenne in 1953. He studied in Vienna with Max Dvořàk, and wrote his thesis on Claude-Nicholas Ledoux. After emigrating to the United States, he continued his research on eighteenth-century architecture, supporting himself with various research fellowships. He published the first monographs on Ledoux and Boullée in 1933 and 1939, initiating a revival of interest in the significance of their works. Kaufmann's book *Architecture in the Age of Reason* (1955) is heralded as a major contribution to the history of the Baroque and Neo-Classical periods. His other major writings include *Architekturtheorie der französischen Revolution* (1929) and *Von Ledoux bis Le Corbusier* (1934).

The major difference between the two epochs [Classical and Neoclassical] – the one before, the other after the French Revolution – is that Classicism represents not only the claim that everything in architecture should be based on an inner conviction, but also the claim that the building should be harmonious in its whole and in its parts and thus affect the observer through the physical beauty of its appearance. It is in the union of these two postulates that the essence of Classicism lies. Indissolubly linked, they form the architectural aesthetic of France until the middle of the 18th century.

In Neoclassicism, on the other hand, several currents meet and mingle. One of these, resulting from the scientific and literary inclinations of the age, finds expression in a love of antiquity, indeed in a recourse to the forms of the past and especially to medieval forms. Neoclassicism and Romanticism existed side by side [. . .] This becomes clear if we consider the view of a critic who was not French but who was certainly one of the highest authorities. I am thinking of the great German architect, Schinkel [. . .]

Among his ideas and notes on art in general intended for a text-book on architecture, we find the following sentences:
'The visual arts should represent the expression of a spirit or soul, they should represent the state of a beautiful or fine soul. [. . .] *In a sense one can argue that the mind or spirit will give life to corporeal matter through the form which it impresses onto it.* [. . .] *'The work of art should produce – in those who have cultivated a finesse of feeling – depth of emotion, or rather those moods which are the basis of higher moral aspirations.'* There is no insistence, in Schinkel that architectural form should please the eye.

Now there can be no doubt. The contrast between the Classical view and the Neo-Classical view in France goes very deep. In the last third of the 18th century the Revolution separated two spiritual worlds. In the aesthetics of architecture the change became apparent as follows: Classicism demanded of architectural form a meaningful harmony; its apparently cool and intellectual demand that the material should be handled according to its nature and that form should be such as its purpose requires, is nothing more than the demand that the material should be granted its own physical properties and life, and that these should be given expression. This is not the case with Neoclassicism. For Neoclassicism the material is dead. Form has no other function than to be the bearer of ideas, the mediator of moods, to arouse emotions which are distinct from the sensuous material and which the material itself does not contain. The symbol of Neoclassicism is the de-naturalised stone, the stone inhabited by a 'genius'.

Emil Kaufmann, 'Die Architekturtheorie der französischen Klassik und des Klassizismus', in *Repertorium für Kunstwissenschaft*, LXIV, 1924, pp 224–226 (written in 1920).

Mass effect – that is, effect by means of uniform and compact mass and not by means of an ordered, organised collection of individual parts gathered together and sorted – that was the slogan of the architectural movement which developed in the course of the French Revolution. *'Le jeu des masses'*, wrote Ledoux, *'. . . c'est le seul effet que l'on puisse tirer d'un plan qui a pour base la stricte économie'*. (The effect of mass is all one can deduce from a plan based on the strictest economy.) It is only occasionally that we find in his designs antique triumphal arches added to the puritanical walls of his country-houses, or perhaps on the naked walls of his Panaretheon. Sparse plastic decoration, like the dry decor of Neoclassicism, expresses the decline and withering away of the Baroque sense of life.

The hierarchy of rank in the old architecture has disappeared. We no longer find buildings which are worthy of artistic decoration and others which are not. Baroque architecture had limits [defined by] feudal [values]; anti-Baroque architecture is universal [. . .]

Emil Kaufmann, 'Architektonische Entwürfe aus der Zeit der französischen Revolution', in *Zeitschrift für bildende Kunst*, LXIII, 1929–1930, pp 38–39.

Neoclassic and 'Autonomous' Architecture: the Formalism of Emil Kaufmann
GEORGES TEYSSOT
b 1946

Emil Kaufmann (1891–1953) belongs to the disciples of the famous Viennese school of art history. He studied in Vienna under Max Dvořàk, Joseph Strzygowski and Hans Semper. But it was the work of Riegl and Wickhoff which made him an adherent of the so-called 'formalist' school of art history.

Ever since his first article on Claude-Nicolas Ledoux for the Thieme/Becker Dictionary of Art, Kaufmann always claimed to have been the discoverer of the 'revolutionary' architects Ledoux, Boullée and Lequeu. His main thesis on the subject appeared in an article published at the end of the 1920s:

'the projects of the circle around Ledoux and Boullée have an astonishing similarity to the architecture of today (1929). This means that the historical break of 1789 points to the new era which has begun in the realms both of social and artistic life, and that the hiatus of 1800 is as important as that of 1500.'[1]

Among the numerous questions raised by Kaufmann's writings, we have chosen to concentrate on those raised by the concept of *Klassizismus* (usually translated as 'Neoclassicism').[2] As early as 1920, Kaufmann had published an article, 'The Architectural Theory of French Classicism and Neo-Classicism'[3] in which he argued that the 'Classic' (*Klassik*) and the 'Neoclassic' (*Klassizismus*) share a common concern for clarity and truth; but while the first term designates a period which favours a pictorial fusion of elements (sculpture with the wall for example), the second establishes a harmonic coexistence among the parts.[4] On the basis of such formal notations Kaufmann risks an attempt at periodisation: the partial concordance between Classic and Neoclassic sensibilities is of extreme importance for French architecture. It is proof of the absence of a true Baroque period. Thus it has been possible to confer a unity on the period from the middle of the 17th century to the beginning of the 19th by giving it the name of 'classicism' in general. But, continues Kaufmann, once one has understood the true essence of the Neoclassic spirit, one cannot deny the distinct difference between French Classicism and Neoclassicism. The first extends from the middle of the 17th century to approximately 1750; the second continues to the beginning of the 19th century.[5]

How is this distinction established? Kaufmann proposes two levels of interpretation: one 'formalist' (we will examine the sense of this word), the other seeking to link the analysis of form to the 'Spirit of the Age'. The formal explanation is developed thus:

'Classicism demands of architectural form a harmony pleasing to the senses and a clear and easy reading. The material has to

Etienne Louis Boullée, Project for Newton's Cenotaph, 1784, exterior and interior at night (BN, Est, Ha 57, nos 7 & 8)

GEORGES TEYSSOT was born in Paris in 1946 and graduated in architecture from the Instituto Universitario di Architettura di Venezia (IUAV) in 1971. After a year of studies at Princeton University, he returned to Venice as an assistant in the Department of the History of Art, IUAV, under Manfredo Tafuri, and since 1975 has been professor of the history of architecture in the same department. He has carried out several research projects for the Institut d'Etudes de Recherches Architecturales et d'Urbanisme in Paris, of which he is a member. From 1974 to 1976 he was the book editor for *l'Architecture d'Aujoud'hui*. His published work includes articles for *Architecture/Mouvement/Continuité*, *Casabella*, *Lotus International*, *l'Architecture d'Aujoud'hui*, and *Oppositions*. He wrote a book on *George Dance the Younger* (Rome, 1974), the introductions to Emil Kaufman's *Three Revolutionary Architects: Boullée, Ledoux, Lequeu* (Italian, Spanish, and French editions) and to RH Guerrand's *Les Origines du Logement social en France* (Italian edition).

be treated as its essence requires; the form has to find an image reflecting its use, a signification reduced to the intrinsic qualities of the subject and their expression. Neoclassicism is at the opposite pole. For it, matter is dead. Form has no other function than to be the support for thought, to transmit impressions, to provoke sensations which, beyond the plasticity of the material, do not express the qualities of the material itself. The symbol of Neoclassicism is the stone without sensuality, the stone inhabited by a "genius".'[6]

Thus, the Classic exploits the sensuous potential of material while the Neoclassic, art dematerialised, makes the genius 'speak' in the stones. While Kaufmann's method is of 'formalist' origin, one also senses in this brilliant analysis the concept of 'empathy' (*Einfühlung*) developed by the Vischers and by Lipps, which is at the centre of the psychological current in the history of art. 'Empathy' in the definition of R Vischer is the symbolic sympathy which links the sensible to the spiritual by animating the real. Kaufmann seems here to want to relate the concept of 'empathy', that representation which produces the emotive values in things, with that of *architecture parlante* as it was understood at the end of the 18th century. This is only one step from saying that this architecture attracted the attention of Viennese art historians because they could, by means of the bias of 'formalist' (Riegl) and 'empathetic' (Vischer, Worringer) theories, conceive of relationships between it and the art of *Expressionismus*.[7]

Kaufmann's second interpretation, that of seeking to link the analysis of form to the 'Spirit of the Age' (*Zeitgeist*), is expressed in this way: '*For Classicism, clarity is an aesthetic category. For Neoclassicism, it becomes an ethical one.*' Kaufmann finds in Neoclassicism ethical values: the clarity of form corresponds to the purity of moral and political intentions. By means of this analogy, he arrives eventually at the literary world of Romanticism. 'Romantic architecture' is a traditional concept in artistic historiography. Friedrich von Schlegel was the first to make the distinction (in 1809) between 'the theory of the classic and that of the romantic',[8] a distinction which was popularised throughout the 19th century. Kaufmann, in his first article, defined the relations between *Klassizismus* and *Romantik* and opened the way to that ambiguous term 'romantic Neoclassicism' which has invaded the texts of architectural history:

'*In Neoclassicism . . . several currents converge. One of these, deriving from the scientific and literary tendencies of the period, is manifested in the taste for the antique, or, in general, by a return to the forms of the past, in particular those of the medieval period – Neoclassicism and Romanticism go together. Other currents have their source in the new ethic; they are founded on the requirement to produce a spiritual effect (this effect corresponds to the universe of sentiment in Romanticism), but also on the almost opposed demand for verisimilitude of architectural appearance.*'[9]

Numerous German publications insist on the Romantic character of Neoclassicism. This is essentially the thesis developed by Sigfried Giedion in 1922 in his *Spätbarocker und romantischer Klassizismus*.[10] This study is concerned with German architecture from the end of the Baroque to the birth of 'Romanticism'. It attempts to define and locate the point of rupture between Baroque and Romantic sensibilities. Thus, in the historical space which unites these two strong poles – Baroque and Romantic – Giedion recognises a period of transition which 'goes from one to the other [and] can either confuse their boundaries or else describe quite clearly their contours through the different utilisation of antique form.' Giedion calls this later tendency 'Romantic Neoclassicism' (*Romantischer Klassizismus*), and its first concretisation in Germany was the Monument to Frederick the Great designed by the young architect Friedrich Gilly in 1796. This tendency is opposed, continues Giedion, to that of 'late Baroque neoclassicism' (*Spätbarocker Klassizismus*) whose most remarkable spatial realisation is the Church of Sainte Genevieve in Paris by Jacques-Germain Soufflot, begun in 1757.

It is difficult to capture the sense of these periodisations, which at first sight can seem unnecessarily complicated. To judge their usefulness, one must for a moment return to the work of the 'founders' of modern art history: Aloïs Riegl and Heinrich Wölfflin. Riegl had suppressed, or at least displaced, the concept of 'decadence' in his analysis of *Spätromische Kunstindustrie* (*Late Roman Industrial Art*, published in 1901) and of *Die Entstenhung der Barock-Kunst in Rom* (*Roman Baroque Art*).[11] The decadence of the 'late period' is no more than historic divergence between the work of art and the truth of the 'classic' (Greek art, the age of Augustus in Rome, the Florentine Renaissance), but it is the moment of transition where art (all the arts) continues to be 'produced'. Its value is measured in relationship to the techniques and processes applied, to the immanence of the labor contained in it, to the transformation of the spatial models imposed by time. By attaching himself to the idea of the 'autonomy of art', an approach introduced by Konrad Fiedler, the Viennese critic, denies all possible identification of art with the demands of the search for ideal (or 'classic') beauty.

Setting its own limits by the autonomy it has given itself, the new discipline of the history of art denies itself the possibility of constructing an aesthetic *system*: art is an immanent and temporal production, the expression of a *Wollen* (Will) characteristic of a period. The techniques of form-making which are the 'language' of art are conventional and thereby equivocal, subject to transformation.[12] Once the *limits* of a period are set – late Roman art/paleo-Christian, Classic/Neoclassic, Baroque/Romantic, etc – one must determine its structure, that is to say, using Riegl's concept, its *Kunstwollen*, its 'artistic will', the principle which *informs* the work on the formal level in the domain of pure visibility (*Sichtbarkeit*), where only '*contour and colour*, in the plan or in space' enter into play.

It is by such a 'formalist' analysis that Giedion defines *Romantischer Klassizismus*. In this period the overall volume tends to circumscribe itself in order to be materialised in independent and discrete units, playing on the plasticity of cubes. It is the mass, the block, which inspires. One can thus think of Gilly's Monument to Frederick the Great as a crystalline system. Subsequently, with Schinkel: '*Romantic Neoclassicism emerges in its purest form when it expresses itself freely in all its plasticity and gives birth not to space but to volume.*'[13] Finally, in the 'Romantic' plans, there is no longer, according to Giedion, the distinctly marked rhythm of Baroque spaces; one finds instead an intangible slowing down. The

Élévation du Pavillon de Bouchefort

Above Gabriel Germain Boffrand, Pavillon de Bouchefort, (*Livre d'Architecture*, 1745) (p: Bibl Nat, Paris)

Right Charles-Louis Clérisseau, Père Lesueur's room, monastery of Trinità dei Monti, Rome, c 1766

different parts become individual entities that align themselves independently of the whole, and one can invert their order without changing anything of decisive importance.[14] In this analysis one can discern not only the application of the methods of Viennese *Sichtbarkeit*, methods dear to Giedion (who began his studies in Vienna), but also that of the 'formal categories' of Wölfflin, his thesis adviser in Munich.[15]

After 1930, Emil Kaufmann strengthens his contacts with the *Jüngere Wiener Schule*, a school of art history led by Otto Pacht and Hans Sedlmayr. Sedlmayr was also a student of Max Dvořák and Julius von Schlosser, and had later edited the *Kunstwissenschaftliche Forschungen*, a series of critical texts aiming at raising the study of forms into a 'science'. It was in the second volume of this series that Kaufmann presented his views on Ledoux and revolutionary architecture.[16] He further elaborated the same theme in his first book *Von Ledoux bis Le Corbusier*, 1933, where, interestingly enough, Le Corbusier appears only on the title, as if the connection between 18th-century architecture and the Modern Movement was self-evident.

In the texts Kaufmann published in 1933,[17] the Wölfflinian category of *Einheit* (Unity and uninterrupted movement) of the Baroque is opposed to the *Vielheit* (multiplicity and articulation) of the Neoclassic. This opposition reappears in the distinction which Kaufmann establishes between *Barock-Verbandsystem* and *Pavillonsystem*, the former displaying a unitary principle of spatial organisation, the latter the multiple and fragmented, 'autonomous' nature of Neoclassicism. As Meyer Schapiro has noted in his incisive analysis of *The New Viennese School*, 1936, 'whereas Wölfflin and others have treated this formal opposition as an automatic development or reaction, Kaufmann has attempted to explain the artistic changes by specific social changes.'[18] In other words, Kaufmann introduces an idealist dimension as he attempts to link these formalist analyses to the *Zeitgeist* (The Spirit of the Age). By bridging the gap between Gestalt psychology and the German *Geistswissenschaften* (The Sciences of the Spirit), Kaufmann claims that aesthetic categories are intimately tied to moral categories:

'At the time when Kant rejects all the moral philosophies of the past and decrees the "autonomy of the will as the supreme principle of ethics", an analogous transformation takes place in architecture. In the sketches of Ledoux these new objectives appear for the first time in all their clarity. His work marks the birth of autonomous architecture.'[19]

As Meyer Shapiro has pointed out, this correlation between 'autonomous architecture' and the ideology of bourgeois society *'depends more on quotations from Ledoux than on a study of social and economic history.'*[20] Thus, the concept of 'autonomy' is an artificial construction since it presupposes *'an inherent nature of architecture or of building, a pure Platonic nature, apart from the individual concrete historical examples of architecture'.*[21]

The anchoring of aesthetics in ethics, that is, the moralisation of the artistic intentions of Neoclassic architecture, allows Kaufmann, by means of a rapid and hazardous shift, to affirm that 'autonomous' architecture is a 'revolutionary' architecture. The main thesis of his *Three Revolutionary Architects: Boullée, Ledoux, Lequeu*,[22] is a most paradoxical one: it reintroduces, by a purely immanent and automatic determination, notions of *content* within a method (the 'formalist' criticism of art) which attempted on the contrary to eliminate such interferences.[23]

Surely, Meyer Shapiro's attack against formalism was aimed from a materialist point of view; yet it coincided with the liberal, but still very hostile, anti-formalist position of Erwin Panofsky. In an article published in *Logos* in 1932 (later appearing as the Introduction to his famous *Studies in Iconology*), Panofsky stressed the necessity for a theory of *style* and of *types*. Though we cannot expound here on this theoretical dispute, it is worth noting that these events took place under strenuous political circumstances; a possible hint as to why Kaufmann could not settle in any American University after he was exiled from Austria just before the Second World War.[24] The fact that Hans Sedlmayr became in 1941 a full member of the Austrian Academy of Sciences, must have surely interfered with the settling of the formalist school of art in the United States.

In *Architecture in the Age of Reason*[25] Kaufmann takes up anew the term *Spätbarocker Klassizismus* which he calls 'frozen baroque'. Similarly, the idea of 'Romanticism' applied by Giedion to the architecture of Friedrich Gilly, Peter Speeth, Karl Friedrich Schinkel, and Leo Klenze, is extended to all the architecture of the second half of the 18th and the beginning of the 19th century. For Frederick Antal between 1935 and 1943, for Fiske Kimball in 1944, for Vincent Scully in 1961, and more recently for J Mordaunt-Crook or D Lewis, *'the concept of "romantic classicism" in architecture ... henceforth confirmed the essentially romantic character of the movement which previously carried the title of "neo-classic".'*[26] Without dwelling unnecessarily on this tautological affirmation, it seems to us that the main fualt stemming from the application of the idea of Romanticism to the architecture of the second half of the 18th century lies in the lack of an analysis of the very concept of 'Classicism' which one wants to oppose it to. In effect, to take a few examples, if the Richmond capitol built by Thomas Jefferson between 1785 and 1789 is 'Romantic', one must ask whether the work of Clérisseau – who inspired Jefferson – is equally so. Should one not then take into account the *Antiquités of France* (1778), or the false ruin of the room 'of the parrot' which Clérisseau painted before 1766 in the convent of Trinità dei Monti in Rome?[27] And if Clérisseau and his followers (such as Robert Adam) are 'Romantics', then Piranesi, master of all of them, must be as well.... Pevsner's thesis proposes on the other hand to include in the forms of the Rococo not only Piranesi's *Chimneys* of 1769, but also his 'most grandiose visions of Rome',[28] thus posing the *Rokokoproblem* described by Kaufmann,[29] a problem never truly elucidated and which still tends to obscure the historical schema of *Klassik/Klassizismus*

Today, the polemics surrounding the work of Emil Kaufmann might seem outdated. It is necessary, however, to bear in mind our theoretical debt to the tradition of German art history. Surely, our contemporary disputes between Formalists, Iconologists and Empiricists have highlighted new theoretical questions: those of typology, signification, language, ideology, strategy, etc. But they have not managed to erase the question of the 'autonomy' of architecture; indeed, an obsessive theme both with contemporary historiography and architectural practice.

Claude-Nicolas Ledoux, Woodcutter's House and Workshop, 1773–79 (from *Visionary Architects*, University of St Thomas, 1968)

Notes:

1. Emil Kaufmann, 'Architektonische Entwürfe aus der Zeit der französischen Revolution,' in *Zeitschrift für bildende Kunst*, LXIII, 1929–30, p 46.
2. For a discussion on the history of Classicism, see the introduction and notes to Emil Kaufmann, *Trois architectes révolutionnaires: Boullée, Ledoux, Lequeu*, eds Gilbert Erouart and Georges Teyssot, Editions S A D G, Paris, 1978.
3. E Kaufmann, 'Die Architekturtheorie der französischen Klassik und des Klassizismus,' *Repertorium für Kunstwissenschaft*, LXIV, 1924, pp 197–237 (written in 1920).
4. *Ibid*, p 211.
5. *Ibid*, p 224.
6. *Ibid*, p 226.
7. Cf Hermann Bahr, *Expressionismus* (Munich: Delphin Verlag, 1916), esp the chapter 'Wer ist Riegl?', pp 75–82. Nevertheless, the interest aroused by the theory of *architecture parlante* is to be compared, more than to *Expressionismus*, to the 'expressiveness' of the Viennese Secession, an artistic movement of which Bahr was the most brilliant critic.
8. Cf J Guillerme, 'Classicisme et repetition, une approache philologique,' *Recherches Poïetiques*, IV (Paris: Klincksieck, 1979). See also J Rykwert, 'Classic and Neo-Classic,' *Oppositions*, 7, Winter 1976, pp 39–54; P Szondi, *Poésie et Poétique de l'idéalisme allemand* (French translation. Paris: Les Editions de Minuit, 1975).
9. E Kaufmann, 'Die Architekturtheorie . . .' *op cit*, p 224.
10. S Giedion, *Spätbarocker und romantischer Klassizismus* (Munich: F Bruckmann A G, 1922).
11. A Riegl, *Spätromische Kunstindustrie* (1901), Italian translation, *Industria artistica tardoromana* (Florence: Sansoni, 1953), with an introduction by Sergio Bettini and A Riegl, *Die Entstehung der Barock-Kunst in Rom*, ed A Burda and M Dvořàk (Vienna: A Schroll, 1908); cf H Zerner, 'L'Histoire de l'art d'Aloïs Riegl: un formalisme tactique', *Critique*, Nos 339–40, 1975, pp 948–52; on the Viennese *Sichtbarkeit* see R. Salvini, *La Critica d'arte della pura visibilita e del formalismo* (Milan: Garzanti, 1977), anthology of texts. On German aesthetics in general, consult G Morpurgo-Tagliabue, *L'esthetique contemporaine, une enquête* (Milan: Marzorati, 1960); and more specifically E K Mundt, 'Three Aspects of German Aesthetic Theory', *Journal of Aesthetics and Art Criticism*, XVII, March 1959, pp 287–310. On Fiedler, refer to P Junod, *Transparence et Opacité* (Lausanne: L'Age d'Homme, 1976). See also the recent book of H Dilly, *Kunstgeschichte als Institution. Studien zur Geschichte einer Disziplin*, Frankfurt, 1979.
12. Cf M Cacciari, 'Di alcuni motivi in Walter Benjamin', *Nuova Corrente*, 67, 1975, in particular pp 228–35, and by the same author, 'Loos-Wien,' *Oikos, da Loos a Wittgenstein* (Rome: Officina Ed, 1975). pp 13–60.
13. S Giedion, *Spätbarocker und romantischer Klassizismus*. Chap II on 'The Meaning of Space in late Baroque Classicism and in Romantic Classicism.'
14. *Ibid*, Chap III: 'The Sequence of Spaces'.
15. Cf *Hommage à Giedion, Profile seiner Personalichkeit* (Basel and Stuttgart: Birkhauser Verlag, 1971).
16. E Kaufmann, 'Die Stadt des Architekten Ledoux', *Kunstwissenschaftliche Forshungen*, II, 1933, p 131–60.
17. Cf E Kaufmann, 'Klassizismus als Tendenz und als Epoche', in *Kritische Berichte*, 1933, pp 201–14; also, E Kaufmann, 'Die Krise der Baukunst um 1800', summary in *Congrès international d'Histoire de l'Art de Stockholm*, 1933 (XIII), pp 184–186.
18. On the followers of the 'Vienna School' in the Twenties and Thirties, M Schapiro, 'The New Viennese School,' *Art Bulletin*, Vol XVIII, No 2, 1936, pp 258–66.
19. E Kaufmann, 'Die Stadt des Architekten Ledoux', *op cit*, p 153. The reference to Kant will again be quoted in: E Kaufmann, *Von Ledoux bis Le Corbusier, Ursprung und Entwicklung der autonomen Architektur* (Vienna-Liepzig: 1933–34), p 76 of the Italian translation (Milan: Mazotta, 1976).
20. M Schapiro, *op cit*, p 265.
21. *Ibid*, p 266.
22. Cf *Transactions of the American Philosophical Society*, Vol 42, Part 3, 1952, pp 431–564 (reprinted in 1968).
23. Cf E Kaufmann, 'Architektonische Entwürfe . . .', *op cit*, also E Kaufmann, *Three Revolutionary Architects . . .*, *op cit*.
24. A hypothesis expressed by Werner Oechslin in a symposium on E Kaufmann (organised by S A D G, Paris, November 1978; other participants were H Damisch, J. Guillerme, R Middleton).
25. E Kaufmann, *Architecture in the Age of Reason; Baroque and Post-Baroque in England, Italy and France*, Harvard Univ Press, Cambridge, Mass, 1955. Cf J Grote van Derpool, 'E Kaufmann', *Journal of the Society of Architectural Historians*, XII, 3, October 1953.
26. Cf Antal, whose articles published in the *Burlington Magazine* from 1935 to 1941 are collected in F Antal, *Classicism and Romanticism with other Studies in Art History* (London: Routledge and Kegan Paul, 1970). F Kimball, 'Romantic Classicism in Architecture', *Gazette des Beaux Arts*, XXV, Feb 1944, pp 95–111; V Scully, *Modern Architecture* (New York: Braziller, 1961), see p 41; J Mordaunt-Crook, *The Greek Revival: Neoclassical Attitudes in British Architecture, 1760–1870* (London: John Murray, 1972), *passim*. The quote is from D Lewis, 'Il Classicismo romantico in America il tempio nella sua forma completa', *Bolletino CISA. 'A Palladio,'* XIII (Vicenza, 1971).
27. T J McCormick and J Fleming, 'A Ruined Room by Clérisseau', *Connoisseur*, CXLIX, 1962, pp 239–243.
28. N Pevsner, 'The Egyptian Revival', *The Architectural Review*, CXIX, 1956; reprinted in *Studies in Art, Architecture and Design*, Thames and Hudson, London, 1968, Vol I, pp 216 ff.
29. Cf E Kaufmann, 'Die Architekturtheorie der Französischen Klassik und des Klassizismus', *op cit*, pp 236–37.

Perspective as Symbolic Form
ERWIN PANOFSKY
1892–1968

ERWIN PANOFSKY was educated at Berlin, Munich and Freiburg Universities and at the Warburg Library at Hamburg. Between 1926 and 1933 he was professor at Hamburg University, and was visiting professor at New York University from 1931 to 1933. In 1935 he became professor at the Institute for Advanced Study at Princeton University. He was a leading figure in the iconological approach to art history, as exemplified by his work *Hercules at the Crossroads* (1930). Major publications include a study of Dürer's *Melancolia* (jointly with F Saxl), *Early Netherlandish Painting* (1953), and *Renaissance and Renascences in Western Art* (1960). In *Meaning in the Visual Arts*, he brings together a selection of papers examining the themes of art history as manifestations of cultural tradition.

Thus it becomes clear, finally, how the perspectival conception of space (and not only perspectival construction) could be criticised on two completely different grounds: Plato had laready condemned perspectival space because it distorted the 'true measurement' of things by putting individual judgment and subjective appearance in the place of reality and νόμος; while more recent artistic theories reproach perspectival space for being the instrument of a limited and limiting rationalism. The ancient East, classical Antiquity, the Middle Ages, and all archaicising art, for instance that of Botticelli, have rejected it—more or less completely—because it seemed to introduce an individualistic and contingent attitude into the world of the extra—or super—subjective, whereas Expressionism [...] avoids it because it confirms and guarantees that residue of objectivity which even Impressionism had had to remove from the individual figurative will, that is, the three-dimensional space of reality as such. But in fact, this polarity is simply the double aspect of something single and identical, and these negative attitudes aim at a single and identical point. The idea of perspective, whether understood and interpreted in the sense of rationality and objectivism or in the sense of chance and subjectivism, is based, ultimately, on the desire to construct figurative space (though leaving the psycho-physio-logical 'datum' out of consideration) from the elements and according to the schema of empirical visual space: perspective considers this space in purely mathematical terms, but it is precisely this visual space that perspective mathematicises—perspective constitutes an order, but precisely an order of the visual image. In the last analysis, it is merely a question of emphasis whether one accuses perspective of humiliating 'real being' by reducing it into an appearance of things seen, or [whether one accuses perspective] of fixing the free and spiritual representation of form into an appearance of things seen. By means of this peculiar transposition of artistic objectivity into the field of the phenomenal, perspectival representation debars religious art from all access to the region of the magical, [...] but it also opens up a completely new region for art, the region of the visionary. [In perspectival space] the miracle becomes something experienced immediately by the spectator since the supernatural events break into the apparently natural visual space which in turn enables the spectator to 'penetrate' their supernatural essence. Furthermore, perspective offers religious art the region of the psychological—in the highest sense of the word: the miracle now takes place in the soul of the man represented in the work of art. Not only the great phantasmagorias of the Baroque—already announced by Raphael's Stanze, Dürer's Apocalypse, and Grünewald's Isenheim altarpiece, or perhaps even earlier by Giotto's fresco of St John at Patmos in Santa Croce, Florence—but even the late works of Rembrandt would not have been possible without the perspectival conception of space. Perspective, by transforming ο'υδία into φαινόμενον, reduces the divine to the status of a mere content of the human consciousness, while at the same time it broadens human consciousness so as to make it capable of receiving and containing the divine. It is not by accident, therefore, that this perspectival conception of space should have arisen twice during the course of artistic development: first as the mark of an ending, when the ancient theocracy collapsed; second as the mark of a beginning, when modern anthropocracy emerged.

Excerpt from Erwin Panofsky, 'Die Perspektive als "symbolische Form"' first published in *Vortrage der Bibliothek Warburg*, B G Teubner, Leipzig-Berlin, 1927. This extract is taken from the Italian edition of Panofsky's selected essays entitled *La prospettiva come 'forma simbolica' e altri scritti*, (ed) Guido D Neri, Feltrinelli, Milan, 1961, pp 75–77.

Above left Perspective analysis of J van Eyck's *Madonna van der Paele* (St John's Hospital, Bruges, 1436) (*La prospettiva come forma simbolica*, fig 6)

Below left Perspective analysis, Dirk Bouts' *The Last Supper*, (S Pierre, Louvain, 1464–67) (*La prospettiva come forma simbolica*, fig 7)

The Artistic Theory of Erwin Panofsky
GUIDO NERI
b 1935

Erwin Panofsky was born in 1892. Already in 1915, he became known for his distinguished study on *Dürers Kunsttheorie* and soon he began to teach art history at Hamburg University. He studied the writings of Alois Riegl (the most philosophical 19th-century historian of art) having already acquired a deep knowledge of the philosophy of Kant. In fact Riegl and Kant (together with Cassirer, Kant's modern interpreter) were to remain his main references throughout his career. Like Cassirer, Panofsky worked in close collaboration with the researchers of the Warburg Institute in Hamburg, and particularly with the director of the Institute, Fritz Saxl. Following the path opened up by Aby Warburg, Saxl had become the principal advocate of a new type of cultural history; one which stressed the world of images. The Renaissance—which constituted the main area of research—was analysed in depth, revealing an enigmatic world of figures and symbols which could be understood only through a systematic exploration of the texts and mythologies of antiquity. Panofsky, therefore, confronted the task of reconstructing the history of these myths; a task closely related with problems of iconology and interpretation in general. During that period, Cassirer's impact on him—as on other academics of the Warburg Institute—was extremely strong. The Neo-Kantian Cassirer had abandoned the almost exclusively gnoseological orientation of his masters at Warburg and had devoted himself to a complete historical reconstruction of the modern cultural world. He had, in fact, elaborated an anthropological theory concerning the meaning of the 'symbolic' forms (in the areas of myth, religion, language and art) which constitutes human culture.[1]

With the advent of Nazism, these early years of fruitful collaboration came to an abrupt end. The Warburg Institute moved to London. Panofsky, who since 1931 had been teaching at the University of New York, moved to the United States in 1933 and, while keeping his chair at Hamburg,[2] joined the Institite for Advanced Studies of Princeton University. Panofsky's famous text *Die Perspektive als 'symbolische Form'* (*Perspective as 'Symbolic Form'*) has stimulated discussion for more than 50 years; it is, in fact, the best example of his historiographic method. In this text, Panofsky interprets the various historical and artistic forms of spatial representation from the point of view of a particular philosophy of history: one which defends the '*significative*' character of artistic forms (ie against formalist analysis) while calling for the formulation of general interpretive categories of the historical world (ie against empiricist historiography).

The precedents of this formulation have been twofold: first, the historical relativism which all artistic historiography has turned to since the end of the last century; second, the theoretical and historical research of Ernst Cassirer concerning modern spatiality as a mathematical-functional concept.

Concerning the first point, we have mentioned Alois Riegl (1858–1905) whose determining influence on German art historical studies lasted more than half a century. Riegl, a man of complex cultural background, fought against the philologism which then dominated historical studies, thus re-establishing a 'philosophy of art history' of an almost Hegelian flavour. His famous relativisation of artistic intention helped to restore value and autonomy to art forms which were removed from the classical conception of beauty (eg late Roman and Baroque art). This relativisation seems to have been an almost direct consequence of the death and transfiguration of art (particularly of 'Fine Art') of which Hegel had spoken. It was precisely the fall of the classical idea of beauty as an absolute ideal which gave to modern historiography of art its impetus; it tried to remain impartial in its dealings with the individual periods of history and their corresponding artistic styles; it confined itself to revealing the 'artistic will' implicit in the works of each artist and each period.

Concerning the second point, it seems that Panofsky's research converges with Cassirer's as regards the significance of symbolic space.[3] What is common between Panofsky and Cassirer is the latter's attempt to reconstruct the historical world around the notion of space as symbolic form. For Cassirer, the symbolic refers to that typically human activity whereby the exigencies of life—which appear to the conscious subject as 'impressions'—are internalised actively and are given, through a process of mediation, an expressive function. [...]

Panofsky has opened up the possibility of reinterpreting the entire history of art, this time not as a series of psychological-individual expressions nor as a catalogue of formal devices,

GUIDO DAVIDE NERI, born in Milan in 1935, teaches philosophy at the University of Padua. Author of *Prassi e conoscenza*, published in 1976, about the phenomenology of Husserl and his relationship with Marxist thought, he has also published much on the problems of contemporary philosophy. Since 1971, he has travelled extensively in socialist countries, and has published a number of articles on the Czechoslovakian experiences of 1968 in the reviews *Quaderni Piacentini* and *Aut Aut*. His latest book *Aprorie della realizzazione*, published in 1980, is a critical essay on the contemporary philosophy and ideology of the Eastern block.

but as the chronicle of historical encounters (taking place in determined historical situations) between traditions and techniques which together construct and signify the human world. Panofsky's decision to examine artistic life in all the contingency of its real development (corresponding to the continuities and breaks of the historical world in its entirety) makes it clear that his work is in no way to be assimilated—as many have tried—within the general tradition of 'formalism'.[4] On the contrary, his work represents the greatest attempt at penetrating the problems of history and content of the world of forms.

By defending the 'significative' character of artistic forms, Panofsky was, in fact, launching an attack against two traditions of art historical thinking: namely, psychologism and formalism. His early essays of circa 1915–35 are a conscious formulation of this double polemic; a polemic which aimed at salvaging the realm of artistic meaning which both psychologism and formalism were undermining.[5]

The opportunity to attack formalism was given to Panofsky by Wölfflin's distinction between the 'expressive content' of works of art (which depends on the 'individual disposition' of the artist) and the 'forms' as such, conceived as the vehicles of expressive content. For Wölfflin, the forms as such are not dependent on the individual disposition of the artist (since they are common to all the artists of a particular period) but on the 'eye', that is to say on the characteristic way a particular period 'sees and represents'. The artist's spiritual disposition (*Besinnung*) is excluded from the realm of forms which in turn are presumed to be merely 'optical'. Panofsky attacked this Wölfflinian distinction. He maintained that, if we don't want to get involved in absurd discussions about the physiology of vision, we should give to the realm of the 'visual' an extremely elastic meaning. It is not visual perception as such which is different between, say, a Renaissance and a Baroque painter; the difference lies in the spiritual attitude towards sensory data.

Thus, for Panofsky, it is clear that Wölfflin's distinction between form and content has no value whatsoever. In Wölfflin's opinion, forms are empty possibilities, empty 'recipients' into which it would be possible to accommodate the most diverse 'expressive contents'. [...] It should be noted that in Wölfflin's system—who in his turn wanted to rescue the independence of artistic forms from their being linked to the artist's intentions—the formalist assumption cannot but bring into the foreground obscure psycho-physiological considerations; as for example, the argument of the modifications of the 'eye' we have mentioned. To free the life of forms from their immediate links with individual artistic minds meant, of course, that they would have to be referred to a *collective psyche* or to a common physiological nature. [...]

Alois Riegl had, in fact, introduced the concept of *Kunstwollen* (artistic will) as the determining agent of stylistic development beyond all material or technical considerations. The concept of *Kunstwollen* became very popular, for it lent itself to expressing equally well the spiritual attitude of a period and the intentions of the individual artist. The individual personality of an artist could very well emerge from a work while, beyond such personality, one could still feel the weight which the techniques and norms of a school or the general stylistic principles of a period exercised. The balancing, however, between the intentions of an artist and the spiritual attitude of a period was to remain unprescribed; which means that it was to remain open to a free phenomenological analysis. [...]

Thus, the concept of *Kunstwollen* was to be interpreted by art historians and artists alike in a *psychologistic* sense. The psychology of the individual and the psychology of the period were spoken of as determining causes of the reality and evolution of a style. It is precisely this psychologistic interpretation of *Kunstwollen* (from which one can trace another direction, that of the theory of *Einfühlung*) that Panofsky criticised in his 1920 essay on *Der Begriff des Kunstwollens* (*The Concept of 'Artistic Will'*).

Let us try to outline the difficulties which Panofsky saw in such a 'psychologistic' position. They become evident when we consider interpreting a work of art. For if works of art are nothing more than effects of the 'psycho-physical reality' which comprises of the individual or collective psyche, these 'effects' can become intelligible only insofar as it is possible to trace the causal process of their emergence. Often the works themselves, however, are the only clue to the very 'psyche' which ought to be giving the explanation; thus, finding it impossible to trace the causal process, we should give up our interpretation. Nor would the idea of referring to ready-made interpretations (self-analyses construed by the artists themselves) be of any help; the inevitable partiality and occasional conceit would only generate further problems of interpretation. Or still, the theory of *Einfühlung* of Th Lipps and his followers would be rather naive: we have learned by now that there is no common 'empathy' that is based on assumed constants of human nature. [...]

According to Panofsky, when faced with these difficulties all one can do is to affirm the non-psychological character of *Kunstwollen*. [...] '*Artistic will as an object of possible scientific knowledge of art*' wrote Panofsky, '*is not a psychological reality.*' For Panofsky, 'reality' is the total of the physical and psychic phenomena which follow determined laws and which are manifested within objective dimensions of space and time. Furthermore, any phenomenon, to qualify as 'real', must be the 'effect' of a 'cause'. The sense of the work of art, however, (not its material existence as a thing of the physical world) belongs to a world of its own, outside the causal dimensions of physical reality. The work of art is not a 'thing'; instead it points to the sense that resides in phenomena without ever identifying itself with them.

Panofsky, therefore, sees the work of art participating in two worlds: that of physical reality and that of its own sense; a view which is fundamentally indebted to Kant. In as much as a work of art belongs to its own world of sense, it is necessary for the history of art to create *a priori* categories with which to address works of art. [...] Such interpretive categories which aim at a *history of sense*, do not exclude the possibility of an empirical history of art: since works of art belong to the worlds both of reality and of their own sense, there must be two ways of treating them. However, even empirical history itself is based on theoretical-transcendental assumptions.

It is this last point which Panofsky discusses in his essay 'On the Relationship between the History and Theory of Art'.[6] [...] In this essay, Panofsky raises the question: is it *legitimate* to use categories of a theoretical nature in historical research? Faced with the arbitrary evaluations of so many 'theories' of art, Panofsky observes, historians are often sceptical about 'theorising' and instead they consider empirical documentation as the only worthwhile historiographic research. In 1920, the empiricist Max Dorner accused Panofsky of confusing the history with the theory of art.[7] [...] The science of art, maintained Dorner, should simply order the works of art in space and time by classifying them on the basis of their sensory properties, while using concepts which are *currently available*. [...]

Panofsky's reply to Dorner demonstrates how even empirical history requires the utilisation of theoretical categories. Quoting Dorner's article, Panofsky shows how even empirical history is forced to fall back on theoretical concepts like 'pictorial', 'plastic', etc. The fact that such concepts might be *currently available* by no means makes them *less* theoretical. One does not debate here the legitimacy of a theoretical concept as regards its current popularity, but rather the legitimacy of introducing theoretical concepts in art history altogether.

The mere description of sensory properties cannot in itself speak of the artistic work. *'In itself, a description which picks up only the sensory qualities of the work of art,'* wrote Panofsky, *'does not have the slightest right to differentiate between the lines drawn by the artist's hand and the lines which might have been formed by the cracking of the paint.'* [...] But, then, one would have to take the same stance towards artistic phenomena as one takes towards phenomena of nature; that is to say, one would have to compile hundreds and thousands of particular observations only to end up—at best—with a quasi-poetic account of sensory *Erlebnisse* (sensory experiences). [...]

In his book *Studies in Iconology*, Panofsky launched a double polemic: against both the formalism of Wölfflin and the empiricism of Dorner. [...] Faced with the task of describing and interpreting works of art, Panofsky demonstrated that beyond the mere phenomenological sense of representation (that is, beyond the sense which arises without any cultural reference, for example, the 'Resurrection' as 'man hovering in the air') there exists a 'sense of the meaning which goes beyond the concept of a mere observation'. Taking the painting of Maffei in the Museum of Faenza, once we have recognised a woman, a severed head on a plate and a sword held in the woman's hand, it is only through the history of *types* that it is possible to recognise a 'Judith' or a 'Salome'; since the plate (that of John the Baptist) seems to contradict the first hypothesis while the sword (used by Judith) the second. For Panofsky, the *'type is a figurative representation in which the determined phenomenological sense is so closely linked to a determined sense of the meaning that it has become its traditional vehicle.'* Thus, what is *'open'* to be represented by a particular artist conforms to the effective history of figurative types. [...]

In this essay, I have tried to sketch a guiding thread which might make the reading of Panofsky a little easier. Two points seemed to me most important: first, Panofsky's polemic against formalism and second, his polemic against historiographic empiricism. In the first case, it was a matter of defending the *significative* value of artistic 'forms' against an absurd psychologism. In the second case, the defence was against the simplistic claim to a pure history of empirical data.

Panofsky revindicated the rights of a *theory* of art which has as its conscious theme the formalisation of conceptual categories of analysis. If Panofsky's *a priori* categories do not satisfy us and if they seem immersed in the preoccupations of the German *Kunstwissenschaft* (Science of Art) of the first 30 years of this century, we must not conclude that the link he established between theory and history is similarly outdated. For it is necessary—especially today—to give up both the notions of formalist and empiricist art history and to direct research towards the more broken and uneven ground of the historical (that is, significatively concrete) genesis of artistic forms.

Notes
1. On Aby Warburg, see the commemorative article by G Pasquali in *Pegaso*, April, 1930; reprinted in *Vecchie e nuove pagine stravaganti di un filologo*, Florence, 1952. On Fritz Saxl, see the text by G Bing in *Fritz Saxl (1890–1948): A Volume of Memorial Essays from his Friends in England*, London and Edinburgh, 1957. On the activities of the Warburg Institute, see Frances A Yates, 'Le Warburg Institute et les études humanistes', in *Pensée humaniste et tradition chrétienne aux XV et XVI siècles*, Paris, 1950. Cassirer used some of the Warburg Institute's material to elaborate parts of his *Philosophie der symbolischen Formen*, Berlin, 1923–9. The collaboration of Panofsky with Saxl is evident from the study *Dürers Melencolia*; as is his collaboration with Cassirer from the historical-aesthetic work *'Idea', ein Beitrag zur Begriffsgeschichte der älteren Kunsttheorie*, Leipzig, 1924.
2. For Panofsky's activity in America, see his essay 'The history of art' in *The Cultural Migration: The European Scholar in America*, ed W R Crawford, University of Pennsylvania Press, Philadelphia, 1957, pp 321ff. Here are some of Panofsky's most significant works: *Dürers Kunsttheorie, vornehmlich in ihrem Verhältnis zu der Italiener*, Berlin, 1915; *Dürers Stellung zur Antike*, Vienna, 1922; *Dürers Melencolia*, (in collaboration with Saxl) Leipzig-Berlin, 1923; *Die Deutsche Plastik des elften bis dreizehnten Jahrhunderts*, 1924; *'Idea', ein Beitrag zur Begriffsgeschichte der älteren Kunsttheorie*, Leipzig, 1924; *Studies in Iconology: Humanistic Themes in the Art of the Renaissance*, New York, 1939; *Albrecht Dürer*, Princeton, 1943; *Gothic Architecture and Scholasticism*, London, 1951; *Early Netherlandish Painting, Its Origin and Character*, Cambridge, Massachusetts; *Meaning in the Visual Arts*, New York, 1955; *Pandora's Box; the Changing Aspects of a Mythical Symbol*, (in collaboration with Dora Panofsky), 1956; *Renaissance and Renascences in Western Art*, Stockholm, 1956.
3. In his *Philosophie der symbolischen Formen*, Cassirer contrasts 'sensory space' not only with the intellectually conceived space of geometry but also with 'mythical space'; the latter resulting from superimposing sacred values onto the dimensions of empirical reality. Panofsky did not utilise this last point. In the art historical circles, what comes closer to it is the connection established by Pierre Francastel between the mythical conception of the world and 'topological space' (which is based on notions like 'near and far', 'succession and contiguity', etc, all of which are independent of any formal scheme or any fixed scale of measurement). Cf Pierre Francastel *Peinture et Société. Naissance et destruction d'un espace plastique*, Lyon, 1950.
4. Cf Pierre Francastel, *Peinture et Société*, op cit, Appendix III.
5. From Panofsky's early essays, see 'Das Problem des Stils in der bildenden Kunst', in *Zeitschrift für Aesthetik und allgemeine Kunstwissenschaft*, 1915, Vol X, pp 460ff; 'Der Begriff des Kunstwollens', ibid, 1920, Vol XIV, pp 320ff; 'Ein Beitrag zu der Erörterung uber die Möglichkeit "kunstwissenschaftlicher Grundbegriffe"' ibid, 1925, Vol XVIII, pp 129ff; 'Zum Problem der Beschreibung und Inhaltsdeutung von Werken der bildenden Kunst', in *Logos*, 1932, Vol XXI, pp 103ff.
6. On the movement of *Allgemeine Kunstwissenschaft* promoted by Max Dessoir from 1906 onwards, see A Banfi, *La vita dell'arte*, Milan, 1957; also D Formaggio, *Fenomenologia della tecnica artistica*, Milan, 1953; also D Formaggio, 'M Dessoir e il problema della scienza generale dell'arte', in *Rivista di Estetica*, 1958, Vol II. Panofsky was certainly right when he stressed that the fundamental concepts he presented were not empirically derived—as in Wölfflin—but are deduced *a priori* in a Kantian way. But even if one admits that Panofsky's categories do draw the boundaries within which an artistic phenomenon must find its place, it seems to me that art history has little to gain from such a direction. Once the need for categories of analysis is recognised (even for the simplest description), the elaboration of those categories cannot stem from unconditional *a priori* possibilities, but rather from the suggestions which operative history offers us.
7. Cf Alexander Dorner, 'Die Erkenntnis des Kunstwollens durch die Kunstgeschichte, in *Zeitschrift für Aesthetik und allgemeine Kunstwissenschaft*, 1920, Vol XVI, pp 216ff.

In Search of Cultural History
ERNST GOMBRICH
b 1909

Friedrich Overbeck (of the Nazarenes) *Italia and Germania*, 1811–1828

One may be interested in the manifold interactions between the various spheres of a culture and yet reject what I have called the 'exegetic method', the method, that is, that bases its interpretations on the detection of that kind of 'likenesss' that leads the interpreter of the scriptures to link the passage of the Jews through the Red Sea with the Baptism of Christ. Hegel, it will be remembered, saw in the Egyptian sphinx an essential likeness with the position of Egyptian culture in which the spirit began to emerge from animal nature, and carried the same metaphor through in his discussion of Egyptian religion and Egyptian hieroglyphics. The assumption is always that some essential structural similarity must be detected which permits the interpreter to subsume the various aspects of a culture under one formula.

Not only is there no iron law of such isomorphism, I even doubt whether we improve matters by replacing this kind of determinism with a probabilistic approach as has been proposed by W T Jones in his book, *The Romantic Movement*. The sub-title of this interesting book demands attention by promising 'a new method in Cultural Anthropology and History of Ideas'; it consists in drawing up such polarities as that between static and dynamic, or order and disorder, and examining certain periods for their bias towards one or the other end of these scales, a bias which would be expected to show up statistically at the periphery of the Hegelian wheel in art, science and political thought, though some of these spheres might be more recalcitrant to their expression than others. In the contrast between 'soft focus' and 'hard focus' the Romantic, he finds, would be likely to lean towards the first in metaphysics, in poetical imagery and in painting, a bias that must be symptomatic of the Romantic mentality.

Such expectations, no doubt, accord well with commonsense psychology; but in fact no statistics are needed to show in this case that what looks plausible in this new method of salvaging Hegel still comes into conflict with historical fact. It so happens that it was Romanticism which discovered the taste for the so-called 'primitives' in painting, which meant, at that time, the hard-edged, sharp-focused style of van Eyck or of the early Italians. If the first Romantic painters of Germany had one pet aversion it was the soft-focused bravura of their Baroque predecessors. Whatever their bias in metaphysics may have been, they saw in the smudged outline a symptom of artistic dishonesty and moral corruption. Their bias in the syndrome—to retain this useful term—was based on very different alternatives, alternatives peculiar to the problem of painting. Paradoxically, perhaps, they identified the hard and naive with the other-worldly and the chaste. It was soft-focused naturalism that was symptomatic of the fall from grace.

We have met this bias before in the discussion among cultural historians of the symptomatic value of painting styles. It might not have assumed such importance if it had not been such a live issue at the very time and ambience of Hegel and of the young Burckhardt. This was of course the time when the trauma of the French Revolution aroused a new longing among certain circles for the lost paradise of medieval culture. The German painters who became known as the Nazarenes regarded realism and sensuality as two inseparable sins and aimed at a linear style redolent of Fra Angelico and his northern counterparts. They went to Rome where most of them converted to Roman Catholicism, they wore their hair long and walked about in velvet caps considered somehow to be *alt-deutsch*. Now here the style of these artists and their *Weltanschauung* was clearly and closely related, their mode of painting, like their costume, was really a badge, a manifesto of their dissociation from the 19th century. If you met a member of this circle you could almost infer from his attire what he would say and how he would paint, except, of course, whether he would paint well or badly.

It is legitimate for the cultural historian to ask how such a syndrome arose which marks what we call a movement. It is possible to write the history of such a movement, to speculate about its beginnings and about the reasons for its success or failure. It is equally necessary to ask how firmly the style and the allegiance it once expressed remained correlated; how long, for instance, the anti-realistic mode of painting remained a badge of Roman Catholicism. In England the link between Catholicism and a love of Gothic is strong in Pugin, but was severed by Ruskin, while the Pre-Raphaelite Brotherhood even aimed at ascertaining naive and sharp-focused realism.

Even here, though, the style expressed some kind of allegiance to the Age of Faith. Judging from a passage from Bernard Shaw's first novel, this syndrome had dissolved by 1879 ... The syndrome, if Shaw was right, had changed from medievalism to aestheticism and a generalised non-conformism. Burne-Jones was now the badge of allegiance of a progressive creed.

Ernst H Gombrich, *In Search of Cultural History* (Oxford: Clarendon Press, 1969), pp 32–35.

SIR ERNST GOMBRICH CBE was born in Vienna in 1909 and now lives in London. A former Director of the Warburg Institute and Professor of the History of the Classical Tradition in the University of London, he has been Slade Professor of Art at both Oxford and Cambridge, and Professor of the History of Art at University College, London. He has also held a number of visiting professorships in the United States. Professor Gombrich's many publications, including *The Story of Art* (1950), *Art and Illusion* (1959), *Norm and Form* (1966) and *The Sense of Order* (1979) have established his reputation as one of the leading intellectuals of our time.

Gombrich and Cultural History
ALAN COLQUHOUN
b 1921

In his essay *In Search of Cultural History* E H Gombrich discusses the role of the art historian within the context of cultural studies, and in doing so sets out some of the historiographic principles which form the basis of his work. Though he is primarily concerned with the history of painting, these principles apply, *mutatis mutandis*, to architecture, as a cultural phenomenon and a system of aesthetic representation. It will be the intention of these notes to discuss some of these principles and their implications, using the chosen extract as a methodological example—as does Gombrich himself.

The virtue of this passage is that, as a self-contained piece of historical analysis, it can be removed from its context without doing too much violence to Gombrich's thought. Gombrich's writings are unusually resistant to this kind of dismemberment because the ideas they contain unfold gradually, almost in spiral fashion, and it is often only after a rather long passage that his meaning is fully disclosed.

In Search of Cultural History, however, has a complexity all its own. This is due less to the wealth of illustrative material with which the argument is interlaced than to the historiographic problem to which he addresses himself. In elucidating this problem, Gombrich seems constantly to be struggling with and qualifying the premises from which he sets out. As these premises are basically Hegelian, it is with his attitude towards Hegel that his ideas are best approached.

In these notes I do not intend to question Gombrich's interpretation of Hegel's theory of history, or to inquire to what extent ideas imputed to Hegel might not apply in some degree to a whole tendency of German thought in the late 18th century, particularly to Herder. My purpose will be merely to investigate how Gombrich deals with what he sees as the Hegelian problem. The aspect of Hegel with which he is concerned is the theory according to which culture, in all its aspects, is a reflection of the stages through which human history passes in its continuous evolution from lower to higher states. Each stage has its peculiar spirit, which determines the nature of the cultural phenomena associated with it. If one possesses the key to the spirit of the age, one will be able to recognise it even in its smallest manifestation. And, since, at any one stage, history can take one form and no other, every cultural phenomenon can be seen as absolutely necessary. What might appear as 'free' (ie as explicable) would be an anomaly which could, in principle, be resolved by taking more phenomena into account.

According to Gombrich it is this view which has provided

Friedrich Overbeck, *The Artist with his Wife and Son*, 1820

ALAN COLQUHOUN was born in England in 1921. He received his degree in architecture from the Architectural Association, London, in 1949. He has taught at the Architectural Association (1957–64); Cornell University, New York (1968, 1971); University College, Dublin (1972–73); The Polytechnic of Central London (1974–1978); l'Ecole Polytechnique Fédérale de Lausanne (1977); and Princeton University, New Jersey (1966, 1968–70 and 1978 onwards). He has written extensively in architectural and art journals like the *British Journal of Aesthetics*, *Architectural Design*, *Oppositions*, *l'Architecture d'Aujourd'hui*, *Werk-Archithese*, *Architectural Review*, *Arena* and others. His book *Arquitectura moderna y cambio histórico* was published by Gigli, Barcelona, in 1978 and will be published by MIT Press in 1981 under the title *Selected Essays in Architectural Criticism: Modern Architecture and Historical Change*. He is a principal in the firm Colquhoun & Miller, Architects, London.

Jean-Francois Millet, *Men and Women Trussing Hay*, c 1849–50

Art History with its main impetus in the search for an overall pattern of stylistic development.[1] But he also believes that its application has usually led historians to hasty and over-simple explanations which ignore the complexity of artistic and cultural facts. This view is consistent with Gombrich's approach to the interpretation of history, which, in general, follows Karl Popper's principle of falsifiability and is clearly incompatible with a theory of historical teleology. Yet, if the desire to find patterns is itself to be no more than an historical accident, the application of the principle of falsifiability to historical interpretation seems to present a problem. The only way to deal with Hegel's assumptions would be to regard them as 'hypotheses'. But, it would seem doubtful if they can be taken as hypotheses in the sense that Popper uses the word. A valid hypothesis is, according to Popper, one that can in principle be refuted. But, no teleology of history could ever be refuted since it would never be possible to exhaust the facts which would be needed to falsify it. Hegel's theory of history is therefore not a hypothesis in the Popperian sense; it is an apodictic statement. As such it constitutes a belief and like all beliefs it relies on exegesis to make it plausible. Since Gombrich explicitly rejects the exegetical method, it is difficult to see how the Hegelian assumptions behind Art History can be other than an embarrassment.

Reading the earlier part of Gombrich's essay, one finds oneself constantly asking how it is possible for him to accept Hegel as a necessary source of Modern Art History, and at the same time to reject the methodology which the Hegelian doctrine seems to demand. Or, to put the question in a slightly different form, how can one reconcile a point of view that simultaneously holds an assumption to be axiomatic and falsifiable? The application of the principle of falsifiability would seem either to reduce the assumption to a tautology (unity being predicated in the phrase '*the same period*') or make it meaningless.

Gombrich does not attack this problem head-on. But, he does use arguments which suggest ways in which one might retain the essential Hegelian postulates without having to accept his historical teleology. His first argument lies in the distinction between '*periods*' and '*movements*'. It is implicit in Gombrich's view that 'movements' are created by individuals, while periods are constructed after the event. According to Gombrich, Hegel attributed to periods the intentional properties which belong to movements. This criticism seems to be only partially successful, because he accepts that movements are not isolated and random events; they are accompanied by '... *badges, their outward signs, their style of behaviour, style of speech or dress*'[2]—in other words that collective and block-like behaviour which enables one to recognise and isolate historical 'periods'. We see from this that the original distinction between movements and periods is not so clear-cut as it seemed at first sight. If one's only access to movements was through the study of the actions and statements of the individuals who founded them, we would be no wiser than they as to the underlying significance of their actions and history would reveal to us no new information; it would be a kind of biography—the sum total of innumerable psychological events. But history is the study of societies, and individuals within society exhibit collective behaviour which is often at variance with their explicit intentions. If we are not justified in extrapolating from individual psychology, and in attributing to groups the psychological motives found in individuals; and if we cannot postulate a 'world historical spirit' which is somehow endowed with foresight, how are we to establish any coherent relationship between the explicit, individual and atomic events which historical research uncovers? We must have some other principle on which to base a hypothesis which cannot be derived by induction from the events themselves.

Gombrich seems to accept Hegel's underlying assumption of a 'meaning' to history, his insistence that no event in history is isolated, but to reject the method by which Hegel tried to account for such a meaning.[3] He accepts Hegel's general concept of historical development and the need to study the actual events of history *as if* they were all part of a tapestry of meaning, rather than acknowledge or ignore them according to an *a priori* scheme. But, he rejects Hegel's reintroduction of the *a priori* on the higher level at which all events must be shown to be the necessary effects of the 'Will of History'. His historiography of culture thus seems to belong to the general trend of post-Hegelian historiography, whose aim is, as Gombrich himself puts it, to *'salvage the Hegelian assumptions without accepting Hegel's metaphysics'*.[4]

The twin concepts of *'period'* and *'movement'* open up a fissure in this metaphysical fabric, but they do not in themselves solve the problem of how one might reconcile Hegel's broad assumptions with a more 'scientific' and empirical approach. Gombrich's 'solution'—which seems to be central to his whole methodology—lies in another pair of opposed concepts: those of symptom and syndrome.[5]

According to the Oxford Dictionary a *symptom* is a sign or token of the existence of something, while a *syndrome* is the concurrence of, or a set of concurrent, symptoms (of disease). If we attribute to periods the kind of consistency which belongs only to individual intention, we will look for a single cause underlying the events of a period. Visible events will be *'symptoms'* of this hidden cause, and will hold only instrumental interest or meaning in themselves. To this way of interpreting events, Gombrich opposes another. Instead of trying to explain everything in terms of 'hidden' causes, he proposes that we should observe the other events of the same kind which accompany the event being considered. This will provide the tool which is adequate for an explanation, and it has the advantage that it leaves the event which it seeks to explain intact. The event is no longer considered as a symptom, and therefore reducible to another event at a lower level; it is one of a cluster of events which are not arranged hierarchically in a causal sequence, but which nonetheless hang together to form a meaningful pattern—in other words, they constitute a *'syndrome'*.

In thus denying to the behaviour patterns of a period an absolute determination, and in giving them a certain autonomy, Gombrich is implying that they belong to a system of signification, and that the relationship which holds between them is that of signs to other signs. The important thing about historical analysis is not to know how one event is caused by another, but to know one event will elicit a certain set of meanings whose references may be independent of any single determining factor. Thus, in the text which I have chosen to exemplify Gombrich's historical method, we should not assume that, because in a particular case the collection of ideas summed-up in the word 'romantic' may be accompanied by 'soft-focus' forms, it will necessarily be accompanied by these forms in all cases. 'Soft-focus' forms are not a symptom of the romantic attitude; but they and the romantic attitude belong to a syndrome whose elements will regroup themselves in different situations.

It is clear from this that we cannot separate historiographic problems from a theory of signification. The view that all the cultural phenomena of a period are symptoms of the 'spirit of the age' would imply that a work of art 'reflects' an idea and is capable of only one interpretation. Gombrich's notion of the work of art as part of a syndrome implies a different theory of signification according to which the relation of forms to their meanings is, in a certain sense, arbitrary. Meanings cannot be deduced from forms. These can only be deciphered if we know the social and artistic context within which they have been produced.

The fact that forms are capable of multiple interpretations can always give a particular interpretation a *prima facie* plausibility, but this can be shown to be partial by drawing attention to possible alternative interpretations. Thus, in his criticism of Arnold Hauser's *The Social History of Art*, Gombrich paraphrases Hauser's interpretation of French classicism (*'Frigid noblemen will like a rigid style, and agile merchants will be eager for novelty'*) and compares it to an alternative reading (*'Blasé aristocrats love new sensual stimuli, while strict businessmen want their art to be neat and solid'*) to show that both interpretations, though contradictory, are equally plausible (and equally inadequate).[6]

This attitude towards signification, though related explicitly in some of Gombrich's writings to information theory, has a certain resemblance to that of structural linguistics based on de Saussure. According to de Saussure the linguistic sign is comprised of a signifier and a signified, and while these are arbitrarily related, they form an indissoluble unity. The signified cannot be thought of as having an independent existence prior to or outside language itself. The meaning of a linguistic unit relies not on its correspondence with a pre-existent idea, but on its relation to the meanings of other linguistic units within the language. An understanding of how language works does not come from treating it as something which has degenerated from a 'pure' state, or is evolving towards a 'perfect' state, but studying it as a synchronic system. When Gombrich says that cultural historians should *'supplement the analysis of stylistic origins by an analysis of stylistic associations and responses'*,[7] or that *'continuity'* studies should be supplemented by *'contiguity'* studies,[8] he seems to be saying essentially the same thing, though without the implication that the synchronic analysis of cultural events

Left Eugène Delacroix, *Christ on the Sea of Galilee*, c 1853
Right Jean Auguste Dominique Ingres, *Self Portrait*, 1804
Far right Théodore Géricault, *The Carabinier*, c 1814

could ever take the place of the diachronic studies.

It is this tension between the diachronic and synchronic studies of artistic works which creates the dialectical quality of Gombrich's thought—a thought that seeks to accommodate historical continuity and change on the one hand, and a theory of signification independent of historical determination, on the other.

Art history in the modern sense becomes possible and necessary precisely at the moment when history is no longer seen, as it was in the classical period, as a more or less random accumulation of customs obscuring fixed norms. As soon as history is seen as disclosing different artistic periods each possessing it own *raison d'etre*, it becomes necessary to find a logic of historical change and a new theory of artistic meaning. Gombrich's view seems to be that Hegel's attempt to solve both these problems simultaneously by means of a teleological theory of history simply resulted in replacing the classical notion of absolute value before history by an absolute value at the end of history. Far from being a solution, this took away from the absolute all the specificity—in the form of artistic rules, with which the absolute was endowed by classicism—and replaced it by a vacuous notion of the 'Idea', making it impossible to arrive at a theory of artistic meaning except by means of a crude *a priori* scheme. In spite of Hegel's acknowledgement that artistic phenomena have an essential autonomy, this theory is in fact incapable of explaining any artistic phenomenon at all in its richness and specificity.

Yet Hegel's scheme suggests a way in which its own limitations can be overcome. If artistic meaning can no longer be explained by reference to a fixed, external point of reference, partial explanations can at least be expected by taking into account as many as possible of the complex conditioning factors of a work of art. To do this it is necessary to assume at any one moment the existence of a system of values, and to show that these values are a necessary condition of their alteration. Gombrich suggests an elementary model by which to gauge changes in artistic style; it is a Cartesian grid whose coordinates represent a set of images and a set of tasks respectively.[9] The image is always 'necessary' (motivated) but becomes 'sufficient' (meaningful) only when overlaid by the concrete social situation. In this way he implies that any a-historical system of aesthetics (*à la* Arnheim) would be misleading because it would attribute too much importance to the 'natural' and 'empty' sign; he thus calls to mind the theory of 'making and matching' which he elaborated in connection with the theory of representing 'reality' in painting in an earlier book.[10]

In this model Gombrich is also proposing something different from the theory of structural linguistics. Whereas this seeks to disclose the permanent structures which make meaning possible, but leaves the meanings themselves to the unexplored regions of diachronic studies, Gombrich's scheme, in stressing the primacy of the image, makes meaning the core of the study of aesthetic signification. In terms of language, this would imply that it is not the relation between signifier and signified which is important in artistic works, but that between the signified and another signified: in other words, metaphor. This distinction is expressed by Aquinas (as quoted by Gombrich in another context):

'a truth can be manifested in two ways: by things and by words . . . the scriptures contain a twofold truth. One lies in the things meant by the words used—that is the literal sense. The

other is the way things become the figures for other things, and in this consists the spiritual sense.'[11]

For Gombrich the task of the cultural historian is not to 'explain away' the artistic phenomena which he studies. These phenomena contain *'truths'* and values which are perennial, and part of the historian's task is to preserve these truths and values.[12] But, they can no longer be taken for granted and their preservation depends on a constant work of interpretation. Interpretation requires analysis and the deconstruction of myth; the removal from the image of its original aura, and the 'explanation' of artistic works in terms of the infinitely complex web of meanings of which they are a part.

It may not be altogether outlandish to suggest that, in the delicate balance which Gombrich maintains between history as the accumulation of value, and history as a continuous process of demythification, we can see an echo of the Hegelian project of reconciling idealistic dualism with a holistic metaphysics, even though the Hegelian closure is constantly denied.

The problem which Gombrich tries to solve, and which faces all modern historiography, can also be seen, in more modern terms, as the conflict between the heritage of 19th-century philology, with its positivistic bias, and the 'aesthetic revival' of the early 20th century, which saw the individual work of art as the only valid object of art-historical study. Gombrich wants to preserve the freedom of the artist, as the creator of unique works of art, against the tendency to 'explain' these works deterministically. To do this he leaves the door of analysis ajar by saying that the typological fixity of art is merely that which the artist finds at his disposal and which constitutes his ground of meaning. The artist and the art historian must start from this system of values and must believe in them. But they are able to alter these values and this constitutes their condition of freedom. In this way art as social communication (relative, arbitrary and conventional) and art as the expression of transcendental value no longer present themselves as logically irreconcilable.

Notes

1 *'No type of historian has a greater stake in this [Hegelian] approach than the historian of art. Indeed it might be claimed that a history, as opposed to a critical evaluation, of the art of the past only became possible in the light of this interpretation.'* E H Gombrich, *In Search of Cultural History* (Oxford: Clarendon Press, 1969), p 13.
2 *Ibid*, p 37.
3 On the dilemma caused by the breakdown of the Hegelian tradition, Gombrich writes: *'no culture can be mapped out in its entirety, but no element of this culture can be understood in isolation.' Ibid*, p 41.
4 *Ibid*, p 25. In fact, the rivalry between empirical historiography and certain tendencies in the philosophy of history goes back to the beginning of the 19th century. It was already implicit in Wilhelm von Humbolt's essay 'On the historian's task' of 1821, in which he warned against the philosophical temptation to explain history in terms of final causes, and to see it as a teleological process. Although this was, presumably, an attack on the rationalism of the Enlightenment, it prefigured the anti-Hegelian position of 19th century historians such as Leopold von Ranke, and instituted a tradition within historicism itself, of which, in many ways, Gombrich is a latter day exponent.
5 *Ibid*, p 30.
6 E H Gombrich, *Meditations on a Hobby Horse, The Social History of Art* (London: Phaidon Press, 1963).
7 Gombrich, *In Search of Cultural History*, p 38.
8 *Ibid*, p 43.
9 E H Grombrich, *Symbolic Images, Studies in the Art of the Renaissance* (London: Phaidon Press, 1972), p 8.
10 *Art and Illusion* (London: Phaidon Press, 1960).
11 Gombrich, *Symbolic Images*, p 13.
12 *'If we want to keep open our lines of communication which permit us to understand the greatest creations of mankind we must study and teach the history of culture more deeply and more intensely than was necessary a generation ago.'* Gombrich, *In Search of Cultural History*, p 45.

The City's Adventures
LEONARDO BENEVOLO
b 1923

Dutert, Galerie des Machines, Paris Exhibition, 1889

Strictly speaking, artistic research has made a decisive contribution to the establishment of Modern Architecture. After the crisis of 1848, the agreement between bureaucracy and property—that is, between landed capital and the rest of capital—for the management of the city resulted in the isolation of technicians and artists into their respective sectors. In the artistic sector this established the circulation of experiences, giving rise to the need for a common ideological (eclecticism) and organisation platform (the circuit of exhibitions, specialised commerce, magazine and newspaper criticism, etc). Artists of the avant-garde reacted by overturning the conditions imposed on them by the power structure; conditions which had frustrated internal debate and the revision of directions to a point that it had become impossible to bear. Thus, in the first decade of the 20th century, they liquidated the entire patrimony of visual usage inherited from tradition, and with it art's role as the regulating activity of such patrimony. In the void of figuration obtained, they were able to begin a systematic investigation of the newly constructed scenario in order to liberate, not to limit, the day-to-day life of everyone. In this investigation the division of roles was no longer the ideological one imposed by tradition—artists and technicians—but one of function; a division of roles that was more complicated and continually variable, necessitated by the empirical progress of their research, just as in every other field of modern scientific research.

Artists educated for traditional roles arrived at the crossroads of the two methods during the second decade of the 20th century as, for example, in the case of Mondrian. The few who were willing to do their work in the laboratory of architecture (like Le Corbusier and Van Eesteren) gave up the isolation and immunity of their initial condition, and became planners like all the others, satisfied or dissatisfied with the particular results they achieved. The majority continued to be artists. Over and over again they repeated by themselves operations which had already been performed collectively in the first post-war period. In other words, they discovered the precarious character

LEONARDO BENEVOLO studied architecture in Rome where he graduated in 1946. He was Professor of the History of Architecture in Rome from 1955 to 1960, and in Florence until 1963, when he became Professor at the faculty of Architecture in Venice. In 1973 he became Professor of the History of Architecture at the University of Palermo. Professor Benevolo is also a practising architect. He has written several books on architecture, including a *History of Modern Architecture* in two volumes, *The Origins of Modern Town Planning*, and the two volume set *The Architecture of the Renaissance*.

of their professional position and oscillated between total satisfaction in practising it with no further external responsibility (Picasso) or total dissatisfaction since they were no longer able to perform a task useful to others (the contesting artists of whom Argan speaks at the end of his book).

Meanwhile, society's attitude towards artists had changed. When their work began to threaten the still undisputed cultural traditions, avant-garde artists were ostracised and reduced to conditions of misery. Now that this tradition is widely disputed, and now that an alternative body of research is available (the research of modern architecture), the work of avant-garde artists helps prolong the existence of a specialised artistic circle which shifts the proposals of modern architecture from the field of everyday life to that of casual escapism, of free time, and of fiction. Society is prepared to progressively raise the rewards for those working in that circle. The decisive point, even for such goals, however, is the institutionalised arrangement, and not the value of experience. [...]

Let us translate these indications into the language of theory: all products of 'pure work' and 'models of doing things according to free choice' are to be segregated into museums and administered to the public as a category clearly distinct from that of useful objects. Outside, in the city, there are only impure products; work constrained by profit.

It is exactly the opposite of the programme of modern architecture as defined by the very artists and architects who participated in the change 50 years ago. In the twenties, what Mondrian had criticised was that very separation of art from everyday life:

'*The environment, like life, seems to have deteriorated to a state of imperfection and arid necessity. In this sense, art becomes a refuge. One looks to it for beauty, for harmony, qualities which do not arise from, or which one seeks in vain, in life and in the environment. Thus beauty and harmony have become unrealisable ideals: inasmuch as they are* art, *they have been placed outside life and outside the immediate environment. [But] will art always be necessary? Isn't it perhaps a poor artifice, useful only as long as beauty is lacking in life? Beauty is achieved in life: this must be more or less possible in the future. Then it will be natural that life itself discards art ...; once discarded, its true content will remain: art will transform itself. It will first become palpable in our environment, then in society, in all aspects of life which will at that time become truly human.*'

The programme is precisely '*the end of art as something separate from everything surrounding it; for entire centuries, art was the surrogate that reconciled man with his exterior life; [today] painters and sculptors are necessary because the skills obtained in painting or in sculpting can lead to accomplishments in the technical part of construction. [But] for those who will live in these buildings, paintings and statues will cease to exist. Art can be seen as a substitute that compensates for the lack of beauty in life.*'

In the following 50 years, the obstacles of this transformation have been assessed and the simple optimism of Mondrian ('*with a little good will, it will not be impossible to create a kind of Eden*', 1927) has come to an end. In recompense, the structure of the city that tolerates art as a temporary reward has been analysed, and alternatives (which are possible with present technological means) have been determined and, in part, experimented with. The forces are, in fact, divided between those who accept this type of city as the only one possible and those who are working on a project for the development of a different type of city. A project which is to be completed only after a general transformation of society takes place; yet a project which can start now, precisely in order to weaken the oppressive physical order which helps to maintain existing social relationships.

The important objective is not, in fact, the safeguarding of art, but the safeguarding of everyone's life: pure air should not only be in museums as masterpieces, but outside, for everyone ...

Leonardo Benevolo, *Le avventure della citta*, Laterza, Bari, 1973, pp 130–32, 134–35.

Benevolo's *Storia*
CESARE DE SETA
b 1941

The point from which to follow the historiographic activity of Leonardo Benevolo is, no doubt, the publication of his *Storia dell'architettura moderna* of 1960. Not because it was his first work—he had already completed the seminal studies on Sant'Ivo della Sapienza (1953) and on Bomarzo (1955)—but rather because it launched him as an historian of international calibre.

The most celebrated histories of Modern architecture, of course, had been Sigfried Giedion's *Space, Time and Architecture* of 1941 and Nikolaus Pevsner's *Pioneers of the Modern Movement*, 1936. In Italy, there had been a *Storia* already: Bruno Zevi's *Storia dell'architettura moderna* of 1950; a work which, on account of its breadth of information, its insistence on updated historiographic material, and its decisive polemic against the lingering establishment of positivist art history, had surely surpassed all previous literature on the subject. Benevolo's point of reference was Zevi's *Storia* which, however, already after ten years of life, was showing signs of wear. Scanning through the contents of the two works, one notices a clear difference in their positions: F L Wright, for instance, the 'Sacred Spring' from and into which the diverse streams of Zevi's Modern Movement flow, is radically demystified by Benevolo. The American maestro continues to appear amidst the protagonists of the new architecture, now, however, stripped of the messianic and sacred halo which Zevi's *Storia* had conferred upon him.

In direct contrast to his predecessors, Benevolo's history is not a sequence of the biographies of the masters of the Modern Movement: his history is one which consciously 'burns the bridges' to all modes of neo-idealism. This is the philosophical foundation of his historiography: a complete impermeability to Croce's idealist concepts of *creation* and *artistic personalities*. Instead, Benevolo singles out three levels as constitutive of the historicity of events: the mechanisms of production, the evolution of technique, and the socio-economic dynamics of a historically determined society. When compared with the philosophical premises of his predecessors, the shift is total: what in idealist histories was but the blurred background against which the 'maestros' performed, has now become the propelling force of history.

Benevolo's historiography shows strong Weberian influences; Weber's principle of *causality*, for example, has been lucidly applied by Benevolo, in a manner that avoids the pitfalls of doctrinaire artificiality. Benevolo is, thus, both indebted to and critical of the typical risks of European culture: he has shed away all idealism and with it the belief in

William Morris, Chintz, 1896

CESARE DE'SETA is professor of Architectural History at the University of Naples. His major publications include *La cultura architettonica in Italia tra le due guerre*, Laterza, Bari, 1972; *Storia della città di Napoli dalle origini al Settecento*, Bari, 1973; *Citta, territorio e mezzogiorno in Italia*, Turin, 1977; *Architettura e citta barocca* (with Anthony Blunt), Bari, 1978.

the self-sufficiency of art; at the same time he has distrusted all positivist thought (for example, Choisy's or Viollet-le-Duc's) and with it the deadening effects of determinism. And yet, the name of Max Weber never appears in his writings unlike those of William Morris, Marx, or Engels. In the Preface to his *Storia*, he adopts William Morris' definition of architecture: '*Architecture embraces the consideration of the whole external surroundings of man . . .*'[1] Is this definition a theoretically generic one? Perhaps; but without entering into a theoretical debate, Benevolo claims that only such an understanding of architecture can prove comprehensive enough to embrace the diversity of phenomena set in motion by what is usually referred to as the industrial revolution.

It is the period around 1750 which, for Benevolo, constitutes the outer limits of what was to become the Modern Movement: '*Just as industry has made it possible to produce tools and amenities in sufficient quantities to allow everyone to benefit from the same material opportunities, so the task of modern architecture is to transmit equally, to all men, certain cultural opportunities which were originally differentiated according to the social hierarchy; and it can, therefore, be described as a "programme for the redistribution of artistic goods" acording to the needs of modern society.*'[2] In Benevolo's interpretation, the Modern Movement is linked to the evolution of the architectural language as well: such links are, however, treated with caution and with a reductionist ethos. Consider the way he treats Art Nouveau: as a relationship between architectural language and a number of political and social processes otherwise (that is, to an idealist mind) peripheral or external to the history of art.

With an unprecedented insight, Benevolo weaves tightly together the transformation of the processes of production with the growth and political evolution of the working class; with the history of ideas on social thinking; with the emergence of Socialism and the foundations of Marxism. Political and social events are brought in; the functional organisation of the 19th-century city is revealed through its most telling enterprise: the bourgeois and post-liberal practice of town planning of the Second Empire. Benevolo's treatment of Hausmann's Paris is, certainly, among his most original historical formulations and has pressed heavily on anyone who has since dealt with urban history. For Benevolo, the 19th century acted as a melting pot for the transformation of production, cities, and architecture. The logical chain of consequences that these events have had—the Weberian concept of causality is markedly present—give rise, eventually, to '*a coherent line of thought and action*' called Modern Movement.

For Benevolo, the Modern Movement shared the same vision with Morris: that of integrating production with everyday objects and the built environment. To turn this vision into reality, wrote Benevolo, '*we must find a method suited to making it come true: a method general enough to bring together various individual efforts and capable of rendering the results obtained communicable.*'[3] In Benevolo's view, this step was first taken by the Bauhaus: '*Strictly speaking, this is the point at which one can begin to talk of the Modern Movement.*'[4] The second volume of the *Storia* is devoted to the period spanning the foundation of the Bauhaus and the end of the Second World War. In this volume, Benevolo adopts two classificatory themes: Le Corbusier and the Bauhaus. Throughout the book, these *topoi* serve as frames of reference against which to measure the various national schools which branch off. And though Benevolo devotes an entire chapter to American developments, the New World is deprived of the significance it has had in previous histories. All along, however, I have been referring to the first edition of Benevolo's *Storia*; a choice which, given the numerous editions of this book, might be misleading.

Benevolo, in fact, has been one of those rare authors who have had the courage to rewrite their books. Examining the various Italian and foreign editions of the *Storia*, one realises that self-reflection and the suggestions of his critics have had an enormous effect on the re-writing of the book. An obvious case—which Benevolo himself recalls—has been the 1973 edition; it shows how seriously Benevolo took Banham's review as well as the latter's *Theory and Design in the First Machine Age*. To this fifth edition, the author has added an explicit clarification: '*The starting point can be chosen at will, but the finishing point* is *the present moment which is important because it is the context we must operate in.*' These words reveal an essential characteristic of Benevolo's historiography: it is in continuous and close relationship to what is happening today—especially in matters concerning territorial planning—that history finds its *raison d'être*.

This insistence on rendering history intelligible by confronting the past with the present makes Benevolo's historiography a militant one. For Benevolo, there is no such thing as a disinterested history. It is clear, therefore, why Le Corbusier has been given such an important role in Benevolo's *Storia*: his commitment as an architect and planner went beyond aesthetics aiming at an integration of everyday life. Similarly, the most important contribution of Benevolo's *Storia dell'architettura del Rinascimento* has been the climate of re-appraisal it initiated in connection to the use and function of the old town in contemporary urban development. To be sure, it is by no chance that the first plans for the restoration of historic Bologna were Benevolo's. However, his *Storia dell'architettura del Rinascimento* (the title of which is rather misleading) is not a history of the Renaissance but a history of the development of classical language and of the role the city has played in the modern world. If we want to study Palladio, Benevolo's *Storia* is of little use; if, instead, we want to understand why Pienza is made in a certain way, then the *Storia* is an indispensable source. If we want to learn something about Michelangelo, Ackerman's monograph is certainly more useful; but if we want to understand the contributions made by the Italian planning tradition to Modern European and American planning, then, Benevolo's *Storia* is an essential text.

Benevolo's works, despite their popular success, have often been regarded with condescension—especially by Italian critics and by the 'Venetian School'. We will not concern ourselves here with pedantic misprint hunters. The critics of the Venetian School, however, have exposed a 'weakness' in Benevolo's historiography: his tendency towards simplistic schematisations and the manifesto-like quality of his writings. There is a parenthesis to be opened on this subject. In Italian culture, torn as it is between old and new idealism (albeit in the guise of Marxist criticism applied to architecture), word

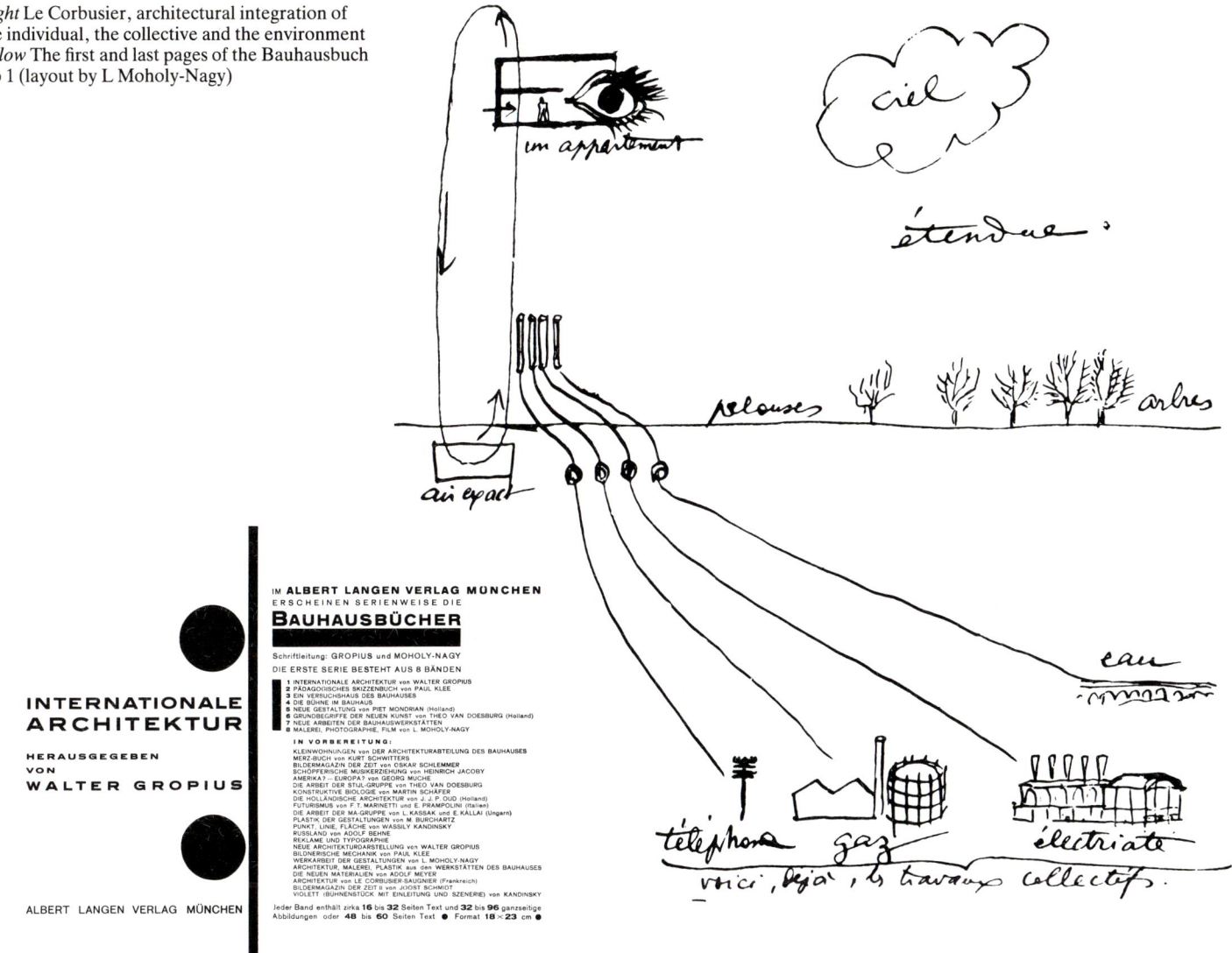

Right Le Corbusier, architectural integration of the individual, the collective and the environment
Below The first and last pages of the Bauhausbuch No 1 (layout by L Moholy-Nagy)

has it that Benevolo is a *rara avis*; that is, he reacts with an uninhibited empiricism which is too close to factual reality. It should remain an open question, however, whether his empirical method of analysis is less (or more) useful than the meta-linguistic commentaries of recent theoreticians. [...]

In view of the current crisis in architecture, an objective limit of Benevolo's historiography is his obstinate faith in a Modern Movement of which at the moment we see but meaningless scraps. His faith in the Modern Movement, however, should be traced back to a faith in the fortune of the western middle classes; a faith which perhaps seems to us disparagingly optimistic. [...] To be sure, the Modern Movement had already exploded in the 1930s, at a time when it stood assured of the excellence and infallibility of both the theory and practice of its International Style. But the crisis of the Modern Movement is more than just a crisis of language. It is a crisis of the programmatic undertaking that was so dear to Gropius, Le Corbusier or the CIAM: it is a crisis of the Enlightenment faith in the objectivity of reason. [...]

And yet, one cannot but be impressed by the popularity his texts have enjoyed in the course of the last 20 years. His *Storia dell'architettura Moderna* and the *Origini dell'Urbanistica Moderna* have had, between them, 35 editions in eight languages. There is no doubt that they have become *the* architectural bestsellers. That is because Benevolo writes for a huge audience. In that sense, his influence on Italian historiography and practice is ultimately irrelevant. What still remains to be studied is the particularities of his international appeal and the extent to which such an appeal formulated the consciousness of the profession. In 1961, the most authoritative and intelligent Italian critic of the third generation had written about the *Storia*: '*There are more than a few reasons which have made Benevolo's work useful if not indispensable: from now on, [the* Storia*] can be recognised as a fundamental step in the study of the history of architecture and town planning of the last two centuries.*'[5] Some 20 years later, Manfredo Tafuri's opinion should perhaps be revised: Benevolo's work remains a decisive contribution to the international historiography of the last 50 years.

Notes

1 Leonardo Benevolo, *Storia dell'architettura moderna*, (1960), English translation taken from the 1971 edition, Routledge and Kegan Paul, London, Vol 1, p *x*.
2 *Ibid*, Vol 1, p *xi*.
3 *Ibid*, Vol 1, p *xi*.
4 *Ibid*, Vol 1, p *xi*.
5 Manfredo Tafuri, in *Argomenti di architettura*, No 2, April 1961.

Mechanization Takes Command
SIGFRIED GIEDION
1888–1968

Above Edgerton, Speed photograph of a tennis player, 1939 (*Space, Time and Architecture*, pl 265)
Below Picasso, *Guernica*, 1937, detail (*Space, Time and Architecture*, pl 266)

SIGFRIED GIEDION was born in Switzerland and educated there, in Germany, and Italy. His doctoral thesis for Heinrich Wölfflin on *Spätbarocker und romantischer Klassizismus* came out in 1922. Giedion assumed professionally the roles of critic, journalist, architectural and cultural historian, and social anthropologist. He was instrumental in disseminating the principles of the Modern Movement and acted as secretary of CIAM. He taught in the United States at the Federal Institute of Technology, and was also Mellon Lecturer at the Washington National Gallery and Charles Eliot Norton Lecturer at Harvard University. His books in English include *Space, Time and Architecture* (1941); *Mechanization Takes Command* (1948); *The Eternal Present: The Beginnings of Art* (1962); *The Eternal Present: The Beginnings of Architecture* (1964); and *Architecture and the Phenomena of Transition* (1970).

Our aim throughout has been to trace the two basic types of bathing: the bath as an ablution and the bath as total regeneration. Both types are often found together, one usually dominating the other. Closely connected with the type of bath is its social significance. The ablution bath, by its very type, easily leads to the position that bathing is a private matter. Of this view, the tub bath, especially in its present-day mechanised form, is the chief exponent.

The regeneration bath, by its very type, favours social intercourse and almost automatically becomes a focus of communal life.

Periods have developed various types of regeneration just as they developed various types of comfort. The Greeks, in their regenerative type, were able to interweave invigoration of the body and invigoration of the mind to a degree unequalled by any other culture. Operating within a universal framework, their bath type did not have to be a complicated one. The Greeks of the fifth century BC were little inclined to technical refinement.

Not until post-Alexandrian times did the scientific thought of the Greeks move closer to practical ends. The basis which Alexandria had laid in the third and second centuries BC, Roman engineering fully elaborated in the first. The thermae of the Roman masses have their centre in the now-dominant hot-air bath and its accessories, the universal Greek framework, however, not being altogether discarded.

But in the Islamic type of regeneration, the games and athletics—self-invigoration—fall away. Instead, the organism is penetratingly worked upon by various massages, especially cracking of the joints, perhaps brought from India.

The Roman bath and the Islamic bath must rely upon numerous attendants. Both drew upon a plentiful labour supply. The Russian bath is the simplest of regeneration types, and perhaps the most natural. It calls for no massive buildings, no technified apparatus, and no slaves. The whole pattern suggests an origin in remote times, now lost in historical darkness. The austerity of the Russian bath corresponds to a humble standard of living. It is at the same time the most democratic and the most long-lived type of regeneration.

After late Gothic times, the bath ceased to be a social institution. We tried to show the chaos and helplessness in which the 19th century lingered before making a small part of its technical genius available to human requirements. Finally, this century, in the time of full mechanisation, created the bath-cell, which, with its complex plumbing, enamelled tub, and chromium taps, it appended to the bedroom. Yet the fact cannot be lost from sight that this convenience is no substitute for a social type of regeneration. It is tied to the plane of simple ablution.

A culture that rejects life in stunted form voices a natural demand for the restoring of the bodily equilibrium of its members through institutions open to all. Whether as Roman marble halls or as Siberian log-cabin is unimportant. Neither, as so often claimed, is finance the decisive factor. Financial considerations are often no more than pretexts.

A period like ours, which has allowed itself to become dominated by production, finds no time in its rhythms for institutions of this kind. That is why the 19th century failed in its efforts to revive the regeneration of former ages or to devise new types shaped to our specific needs. Such institutions stood in contradiction to the period.

Regeneration is something that cannot arise in isolation. It is part of a broader concept: leisure. Jacob Burckhardt found in the word ἀρετή the key to Greek conduct. Leisure, in this sense, means a concern with things beyond the merely useful. Leisure means to have time. Time to live. Life can be tasted to the full only when activity and contemplation, doing and not doing, form complementary poles, like those of a magnet. None of the great cultures has failed to support this concept.

Sigfried Giedion, *Mechanization Takes Command*, W W Norton & Co, New York, 1975, pp 711–12.

Giedion in America: Reflections in a Mirror
KENNETH FRAMPTON
b 1930

'It is no felicitous metaphor to call art the mirror of life, and a survey which takes the history of art essentially as the history of expression runs the risk of disastrous one-sidedness ... The content of the world does not crystallise for the beholder into an unchanging form. Or, to return to the first metaphor, beholding is just not a mirror which always remains the same, but a living power of apprehension which has its own inward history and has passed through many stages.'

Heinrich Wölfflin, *The Principles of Art History*, 1915.

'History is a magical mirror. Who peers into it sees his own image in the shape of the events and developments. It is never stilled. It is ever in movement like the generation observing it. Its totality cannot be embraced: history bares itself only in facets, which fluctuate with the vantage point of the observer.'

Sigfried Giedion, *Mechanization Takes Command*, 1948.

It is one of the paradoxes of history that the Swiss architectural historian Sigfried Giedion should come to make his debut as a writer of world stature in America when, in 1941, at the age of 54 he published his first major work *Space, Time and Architecture*; an achievement which was followed seven years later by an even more seminal study, *Mechanisation Takes Command*, with which his reputation became immediately secure. It is curious given the author's nationality that both of these texts should be published first in English and equally strange that the reality of America should have been a primary influence in the maturation of his historical vision; all the more so since Giedion was to stay in the United States for but two short periods; the academic year 1938/39 when he was at Harvard – no doubt at Walter Gropius's invitation – and the longer research visit, which kept him in the country from 1941 to 1945.

Running into four editions and translated into eight languages, *Space, Time and Architecture* has been continuously read by almost every architecture student for the past 40 years and, reviled or revered, it has exercised an important influence on every account of the Modern movement which has appeared since. The reasons for the longevity and the wide-ranging influence of this text are surely not hard to find, for written in a brilliantly persuasive and forceful style, the book is as much a polemic for modernity and for a particular modern mode of beholding as it is any kind of factual account; although its standing in this last respect is by no means to be dismissed. Variations in methodology notwithstanding, that

Above Griffon and Vincent, *Graphic representation of a horse's gait*, 1779
Below Marcel Duchamp, *Nude Descending the Staircase*, 1912

KENNETH FRAMPTON was born in England in 1930. He is a Fellow of the Institute for Architecture and Urban Studies, New York, and a member of the faculty at the GSAP, Columbia University, New York. From 1959 to 1965 he was an associate of Douglas Stephen and Partners, London. From 1962 until 1965 he was technical editor of *Architectural Design*, and from 1966 until 1972 he was a member of the faculty of Princeton University. The low-rise housing prototype on which he worked with UDC architects was completed in 1976 as the Marcus Garvey Park Village, Brownsville, Brooklyn, and is now fully occupied. He has written extensively in architectural and art journals, and he is the author of the book *Modern Architecture: A Critical History*, Thames and Hudson, London, 1980.

part of the text entitled 'The Evolution of New Potentialities' expounds at length on the development of ferro-vitreous construction throughout the late 18th and 19th centuries, culminating in the grandeur of the World Exhibitions, Henri Labrouste and the Chicago School – a range of subject matter and an emphasis on the anonymous, which for the time was certainly virgin territory. (See also his *Bauen in Frankreich: Eisen, Eisenbeton*, 1928.)

Space, Time and Architecture thus oscillates uneasily between the dictates of a complex and often contradictory modernist polemic and the documentation of Giedion's initial research into the anonymous history of 19th-century America. It was in fact the public record of his Charles Eliot Norton lectures given at Harvard in 1938/39, and as such it contained the fruits of the first research seminars which he was to conduct with American students. While all of this is fairly understandable, given the context, one is surprised by Giedion's extremely distant attitude to the advent of the Second World War, particularly as one of the essential theses advanced in the book is that the 20th century is a spiritually fractured era; shattered to pieces as the result of the modern split between thought and emotion. This demonstration of academic 'coldness' could be construed as historical objectivity were there no mention of war at all. However, the author does allude to the phenomena of war but he does so only in a generic sense, as though it were a remote possibility, happening somewhere, but certainly not in any part of the globe that he or the reader might occupy. Thus we find him writing, after the highly idiosyncratic argument advanced by Le Corbusier in *La Ville Radieuse*, that

'even to day the threat of attack from the air demands urban changes ... it is becoming clear that the best means (of defence) ... is by the construction, on the one hand, of great vertical concentrations, which offer minimum surface to the bomber and on the other hand, by the layout of extensive free, open spaces. How serious the dangers of war will prove to be in the future there is, of course, no way of knowing ...'[1]

The strange tone of this passage becomes all the more curious when one discovers that while Picasso's *Guernica* is prominently featured in the text, the author fails to mention that it was painted as a passionate protest against the German dive-bombing of a Basque village in 1937. He refers to the Spanish Civil War but the specifics of the conflict are discretely omitted. Thus, after comparing Picasso's cubist composition to an Edgerton stroboscopic photograph of a tennis player made in 1939, he merely remarks: *'Out of the unknown, an artist like Picasso can produce intuitively symbols for a reality which, as in this instance, is afterwards confirmed by scientific technique.'*[2]

We may safely assume that the black humour of this passage was fortuitous and that Giedion was merely anxious to demonstrate the second major thesis of his text, namely that in this instance, there was an unconscious 'space-time' parallelism between an *artistic* conception of a violent spatial transposition – not to say literal disembodiment – and a *scientific* tracking of the co-ordinated gestures of a tennis player as recorded by high-speed photography. From such labored comparisons the case can be made that the dichotomous *parti pris* running through *Space, Time and Architecture* reflects an unacknowledged division in the author himself; one which it is worth examining in detail since it affords an insight into Giedion's ideological position and into the contradictory discourse which was to arise as a result.

The first intent of *Space, Time and Architecture* was to reveal after John Dewey's *Art as Experience* (1934) how the whole of modern economic and cultural development was permeated by a ubiquitous split between thought and feeling, a rift whose ultimate origins lay in the division of labour. The second intent – stemming in part from Wölfflin's theory of periodicity and in part from Apollinaire's assertion that a parallelism existed between Analytical Cubism and the 1908 'space-time' model[3] advanced by theoretical physicists – was to evoke the re-integration of man through the unifying force of the *Zeitgeist*. Giedion conceived of this integration as being realisable through the practice of architecture and design. The first of these intentions was to correspond to a materialist method of analysis which, latent in *Space, Time and Architecture*, emerged with full force only in *Mechanization Takes Command* – so much so that Le Corbusier seems to have been shocked by the consequences. The second intention derived from Wölfflin's hypothesis that all cultural development necessarily passes through a cyclical waxing and waning; a mutation which was characterised in the fine arts in terms of polarities.

Thus in passing from the Classic to the Baroque, conceived according to Wölfflin as generic conditions, linearity gives way to painterliness, planar frontality to recession, closed form to open, multiplicity to unity and finally in terms of clarity, the absolute is replaced by the relative. In this spectrum the Baroque is seen as compounded out of receding, open and yet unified forms. Its primary sign is the atectonic, undulating wall as opposed to the tectonic and elemental purity of the classic.

Giedion's materialism, which he absorbed in part through Dewey and to a much larger extent through the Neue Sachlichkeit wing of CIAM, was patently in conflict with the formalist training that he had received in Munich at the hands of Wölfflin. It is clear from the rather inconsistent taxonomy employed in his definition of what he called *constituent facts* that such a contradiction had no possibility for resolution outside dialectical materialism – a theory which he was to stubbornly resist throughout his life. The text in this instance speaks for itself:

'Constituent facts are those tendencies which, when they are suppressed, inevitably reappear. Their recurrence makes us aware that these are elements which, all together, are producing a new tradition. Constituent facts in architecture, for example, are the undulating of the wall, the juxtaposition of nature and the human dwelling, the open ground plan. Constituent facts in the 19th century are the new potentialities in construction, the use of mass production in industry, the changed organisation of society.'[4]

It is not the axiomatic assertion which is questionable in this instance, but rather the categoric inconsistencies that are evident within the passage; the fact that the constituent facts of the 19th century are of an exclusively material nature, whereas those applying to the 20th century are formal and strangely suspended in time by Giedion as though they were in some way generic, and yet on reflection it is easy to see that the *open ground* plan, like the *open* form, is not generic to architecture *in se*. This sleight of hand suggests that the constituent facts of the 20th century are going to be read in Neo-Baroque terms, and in what follows the undulating wall is indeed regarded as the common link connecting Borromini to Le Corbusier; whereas the close juxtaposition between nature and dwelling is seen by the author as obtaining to an equal degree in both Versailles and Falling Water.

And while these analogies may be sustained at the level of resemblance and the existence of certain common conditions, the way in which such imminent forms are supposed to relate to the constituent facts of the 19th century is left embarassingly unclear, particularly as the text makes evident that the new technical potentialities of the previous epoch cannot be considered defunct simply because that century has drawn to a close. Such was the hypnotic hold of 'form-follows-function', and such was Giedion's paradoxically formalistic anti-formalism – that is, his curious aversion to the very idea of style – that he seems to have been unable to countenance the possibility that technical facts and expressive forms may be mutually mediated. On the other hand, the appearance of certain fundamental forms such as the undulating wall are seen as evidence of the mysterious workings of the *Zeitgeist*.

This contradictory approach is evident from Giedion's rather prejudiced treatment of Louis Sullivan, in particular his distaste for Sullivan's manipulation of the steel frame in his Wainwright and Guaranty Buildings of 1891 and 1896. I am referring to Sullivan's projection of giant vertical 'flutes', in brick or terracotta facing, at double the interval of the steel frame, which unified the middle section of the standard highrise, tripartite format – bottom, middle and top. These tall office buildings, 'artistically considered', are conspicuously left unillustrated by Giedion (as is Sullivan's Auditorium Building), and the author unabashedly declares his reason for the omission:

'*But the skeleton – whether iron or steel or reinforced concrete – is essentially a neutral spatial network. Its "cage construction" bounds a certain volume of space with complete impartiality and no one intrinsic direction. In his typical buildings Sullivan picks out and emphasises the vertical lines of force in this network. In the Carson Pirie and Scott Store, however, it is the neutral and impartial equilibrium in the skeleton construction which Sullivan chooses to project upon the facade of the building.*'[5]

Naturally Giedion *does* illustrate Sullivan's store in order to substantiate his point – in fact it is even shown twice – and moreover its detailed facade is seen by him as directly anticipating Gropius's Chicago Tribune entry of 1922. In fact the *Zeitgeist* thesis attains scandalous dimensions at this juncture, for the Neo-plastic manipulation of the frame, indulged in by Gropius and Meyer in their Chicago Tribune tower, is passed over by Giedion in silence. Unlike Leonardo Benevolo who dealt with virtually the same period in his *Storia della architettura moderna* of 1960, Giedion seems to be either unwilling or unable to recognise that, as Benevolo writes, '*The relation between classical rules and technical rules was the central problem of neo-classical culture and Jefferson's conception belonged broadly speaking within this setting.*'[6]

As with Jefferson, so with Sullivan – as the latter's essay of 1892 'The Tall Office Building Artistically Considered' makes abundantly clear – Giedion would have been as loathe to recognise Sullivan as a Neo-classicist as he was unwilling to regard his esoteric decoration as being related to the Art Nouveau. A comparable blindness is evident in Giedion's characterisation of Burnham's refusal to follow the Sullivan principle of gradation in his addition to the Carson, Pirie and Scott store, as nothing but '*a few unimportant changes*'. One wonders how Giedion must have treated Schinkel in his doctorate thesis completed under Wölfflin's direction in Munich in 1922 (*Spätbarocker und romantischer Klassizismus* Bruckman, Munich 1922).

Giedion's inconsistent approach to anonymous history is evidenced further in his assessment of American urbanism, in which, along with the ubiquitous parkway, he applauds the *verticality* of Raymond Hood's Rockefeller Center, not only on the grounds that it constitutes a new urban entity but also because the vertiginous clustering of its towers is to be seen as a realisation of the 'space-time' continuum. To this end, he once again draws analogies with Edgerton's stroboscopic photography, only this time it is not *Guernica* but a collage of fore-shortened views of Rockefeller skyscrapers that forms the subject for comparison.

Post-war urban development has superficially conformed to Giedion's 'parkway' vision of the future inasmuch as the ubiquitous autoroute and the open-ended block have, in various forms, emerged as the universal elements of today's Megalopolis, although the poetic and baroque image of the glittering Cartesian tower, set amid parkscape and fed by a sensuously undulating freeway, has become a banality; the lost Corbusian dream which in the Thirties was heroically projected onto the pampas or the corniche of Algiers. Even then this image already had the status of an ideological mirage which prevented Giedion from perceiving the anonymous history of the American city as a fabric. While his materialist analysis enabled him to identify the predisposing causes, the inventions, the tools and the available resources, he was strangely unwilling to allow the same methods to reveal the historical reality of the colonial grid, to which these productive forces were applied. He could recognise the criticality of the sawmill, the importance of Jesse Reed's nail machine (invented in 1790 and capable of turning out 60 000 nails a day), as he could identify G W Snow as the inventor of the balloon frame (in 1833); but he could not bring himself to confront the empty, gridded chequerboard upon which these devices operated – that abacus so beautifully characterised by Benevolo when he wrote 20 years later:

'*American towns had the same regularity (as the Baroque European town) but not the sense of perspective unity; the street system was undifferentiated, the few distinct elements – a wider street, a square or an important building – simply interrupted the uniform texture, without producing any related intensification in the adjacent buildings; the organism was temporarily bounded by natural limits or geometrical lines, but was open in all directions, the streets running in a way that suggested that they might vanish gradually into the surrounding country side . . .*'[7]

And it was a comparable blindness – his refusal of the dialectic mode – which prevented him from understanding why the brilliant inventions of the Chicago avant garde – Sullivan, Wright, etc – were soon to give way to the normative principles of classicism, not only because classical elements and their deployment were the only principles which could be rationally transmitted (at both a professional and societal level), but also because classicism represented the republican virtues of freedom and order; the one within the other, on which the entire constitution of the United States had been predicated.

Benevolo's filling in of these ideological 'voids' made his work the retroactive critique of Giedion's failure to acknowledge in *Space, Time and Architecture* that technique is invariably mediated by cultural value, and that technique finally has to have an ideological field within which to operate. Thus that which Giedion paradoxically regarded, after the Chicago avant garde, as the cultural 'betrayal' of Burnham (that is, his adoption of the Beaux Arts style for the Columbian Exposition of 1893) is seen by Benevolo in rather different terms:

'Jefferson's type of realism, which led Americans to attribute cultural values with a sort of material and independent existence, enabled Chicago architects to interpret certain of the needs of a modern centre in an extremely open-minded way, and therefore to make advances in the direction of the "pure-forms" mentioned by Giedion, anticipating the work of European architects by several decades; at the same time however, it prevented them from systematizing these results, because that involved a consideration of the connections between the various values, which American thought was not inclined to assess . . . the results attained [by Jenney, Root, Holabird, Roche and even Sullivan] *could be neither standardized nor diffused, and the only consistent way of abstracting a general norm from them, when changed economic and functional needs made this necessary, was to go back from the single experiments to common cultural premises, though it was precisely the original element of these experiments that was lost during this operation; what was left was, of course, the basic eclecticism, and the necessary lowest common denominator could be none other than classicism . . .*

Burnham's behaviour was therefore quite logical; he interpreted in the only way possible the organizational demands that arise when a city reaches a certain density, whereas Sullivan remained entrenched in his individualist position which was soon to be by-passed by events.'[8]

The relevance of *Mechanization Takes Command*, set down in its final form during Giedion's stay in the States between 1941 and 1945, stems not only from the complexity and urgency of its argument, but also from the fact that in this work Giedion has the temerity to broach the issue of ideology directly. He does so through his notion of *ruling taste*: a concept on which he had been working since his first researches into this theme, carried out in the Bibliothèque Nationale in the summer of 1936. That ruling taste and ideology were more or less one and the same in Giedion's usage is borne out by a passage in which the term is first introduced (without any prior definition), in Part II of the book:

'Herbert Spencer, most influential spokesman for the creed of progress as the second half of the century came to understand it, surely did not intend his evolutionary teachings in the sociological sphere (before Darwin) as license for commercial irresponsibility in the name of laissez faire. *Evolution is now used interchangeably with progress, and natural selection with the results of free competition. In this roundabout way Herbert Spencer was turned into the philosopher of the ruling taste. He provided the theoretical bulwark. A sociologist has recently observed that over 300 000 copies of Spencer's works were sold in America in the space of four decades.'*

Giedion then goes on to show how the *ruling taste* of biological evolution and scientific progress was to be subsumed in the 19th century, by the ideology of production as an end in itself:

'Belief in progress is replaced by faith in production. Production for production's sake had existed ever since the Lancashire cotton spinners first showed the world what mechanization on the grand scale was capable of doing. With the waning of faith in progress, floating as a metaphysical banner over the factories, there entered that faith in production as an end in itself. Fanaticism for production as such was heretofore confined to the manufacturing groups. In the time of full mechanization, faith in production penetrated every class and ramification of life, thrusting all other considerations into the background.'[9]

Mechanization Takes Command oscillates between two modes of analysis: one which addresses itself to ideological and practical transformations in respect of criteria governing our notions of comfort, beauty, hygiene and vegetation – one may think of it as *the pole of desire in relation to nature*; and another which documents the determined response of the machine and mechanisation to the demands of necessity – *the pole of need and economy*. The overlapping of these two, particularly at the level of furniture and furnishings is one of the convincingly didactic demonstrations of the text.

In many respects *Mechanization Takes Command* extends the Loosian thesis of the primacy of the anonymous object as it had been developed by Le Corbusier in his anti-decorative art polemic of 1925, *L'Art decoratif D'Aujourd'hui*. However, unwilling to restrict himself like Le Corbusier to demonstrating the process of typification as the natural selection of industry, Giedion showed instead how mechanisation had entered into every walk of life. The parallel Giedion drew, between the taylorized slaughtering of hogs in Chicago (*The Mechanization of Death – Meat*) and the automated production of automobiles in Detroit, was as distressing as it was deliberate. This much Le Corbusier seems to have sensed when he wrote to Giedion in May 1948, after receiving a copy of the text:

'My dear Giedion, Many thanks for your great book, with its disturbing and menacing American title. It is the mirror of that terrible century: the 19th. A hundred years of emerging machinism – blind and idiotic. Your title? Well, if you wish: Prolegomena, Volume 1, 1948, mechanization has taken command; second book, Volume II, 1950, the overcoming of machinism – man has recovered command. I have leafed through your book, page by page. It is very well written, finely interpreted. But the American atmosphere only gives it a surrealist perfume and a sense of clandestine eroticism. My

Above Louis Sullivan, Carson Pirie Scott and Co department store, Chicago, 1899–1904
Right William Le Baron Jenney, The Fair Building, Chicago, 1891, skeleton

God, these Americans know so little about living! This much I agree with; they are the place, the field for experiment, the abundant market and the laboratory. By the side of the old nations of Europe they are conceited. By the side of France, old and intelligent as a monkey or a chinaman, the Americans are poor guys deluded by their apparent abundance, who manifest a true unconsciousness ...

One can take a more optimistic attitude to the subject of your book Mechanization Takes Command *if one admits that the works of the first machinist era must be swept away like so much shit: the* villes tentaculaires *and all the other things ... Then let us look at Giedion and his book. It is very gratifying to have traced the road of discovery from* le tohu-bohu *to the bazaar. There is a fresh eye and a lively mind. I hope to find the time to read it for certainly there is a point of view ... a spiritual aesthetic mixed with an ethic ... which equals a point of view. Very soon atomic energy will be at everyone's disposal. That will be the end of the dilemma of USSR and USA which are the shadows echoing events that have already passed from the stage. Thus the river will flow between its banks. The work will consist in distinguishing between* sterile and fertile consumer objects. *There we shall have the true* esprit. *Congratulations Giedion on your great and beautiful work. Corbu.*'[10]

Mechanization Takes Command was to cause Giedion to confront the issue of culture in a mass society as he never had before, while references to class and cultural identity are constantly cropping up throughout the text. The author traces the evolution of ruling taste from Napoleon as the prototypical self-made man to the middle class triumph of the nineteenth century upholsterer of whom Giedion wrote:

'*Thus in the last decades, the authority of the upholsterer was ever increasing. He was the man to gather superficially loose ends. He provided oil paintings and their gold frames for a middle class unable to afford originals. He arranged still lives from the bric-a-brac of a mechanised past.* Décorations mobiles, *the French of 1880 called these strange compositions that were set up with an air of casualness on tables or chairs. Cushions and heavy draperies completed the effect.*'[11]

In paralleling Walter Benjamin, for he surely knew nothing of Benjamin directly – Giedion went on to show how patent furniture shifted the centre of reality from the home to the office and *en route* sought to achieve the normative (that is, the most efficient) ergonomic posture, so as to influence medical equipment and nomadic furniture in general. In travel, of course, the criterion of comfort and spatial economy, of dual use and transformability, etc, were to determine the objects in a precise way, and Giedion has nothing but admiration for the way in which function, production and use were to limit the shape of military equipment and were to bring about the universal Pullman-style furnishing of steamships and railroad cars.

In his final chapter however, dedicated to 'the Mechanization of the Bath', Giedion returns to consider the more complex interaction of culture, identity, class and production. After treating at length the history of bathing as regenerative culture, he concludes by evaluating modern plumbing in terms which, while appreciative of hygiene, remain nonetheless sceptical as to the cultural deprivations of the normative domestic bathroom. He was to write:

'*A culture that rejects life in stunted form voices a natural demand for the restoring of the bodily equilibrium of its members through institutions open to all. Whether as Roman marble halls or as Siberian log-cabins is unimportant ... A period like ours, which has allowed itself to become dominated by production, finds no time in its rhythms for institutions of this kind.*'[12]

It is interesting to note how this was to distinguish his position from that of Reyner Banham who a decade later, in 1960, in his *Theory and Design in the First Machine Age*, was to acclaim Buckminster Fuller as the promise of an objective

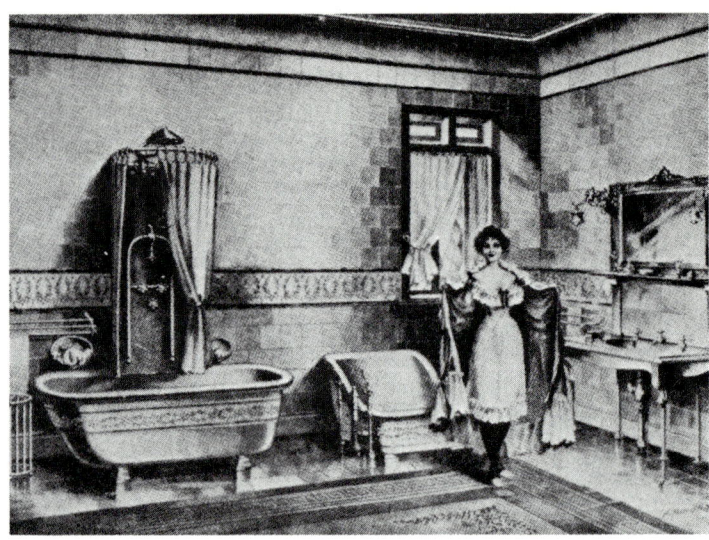

Left Albrecht Dürer, 'The Women's Bath', Nuremberg, 1496
Above English Bathroom, 1901

and scientific architectural future. Of this Neo-Futurist prospect Giedion was to write in 1948:

'Buckminster Fuller was among the first to recognise that the bath is no isolated unit, but demands combination with the various other mechanisms of the house. In his first mast-house (1927) he gave shape to this idea ... Here too is seen how new materials and constructions ... easily lead to grotesque throwbacks ... The idea of resting a house on a central prop dates back well into the 19th century ... But as a standard form, multiplied by millions, these self-enclosed huts become a city planner's nightmare ... The mechanical core must share in the general direction to be followed by the coming development as a whole: co-ordination and freedom of treatment ... the task of mechanization is not to deliver ready-made, stamped-out houses or mechanical cores, but flexible standardised elements, admitting of various combinations, so as to create better and more comfortable dwellings.'[13]

The distinction that Giedion was to draw in this penultimate chapter, between the bath as a form of *private* ablution and the bath as a *public* act of regeneration, almost certainly reflects something of the specific context in which the final sections of *Mechanization Takes Command* were written: in general, the peculiarly optimistic cultural climate of the late New Deal – in particular, the summers of 1944 and 1945, which Giedion spent with Fernard Leger and his wife at Rouses Point, Lake Champlain, on the US/Canadian border, working on the final stages of the book. For, as Giedion makes clear in *Architecture You and Me* (1958), this was a period in which both men started to re-think, however hesitantly, the terms under which a modern culture worthy of the name could come into being; with Giedion taking his distance from Neue Sachlichkeit dogmatism and Leger looking at the promise and pitiful achievement of the Popular Front.

For both men, the partially lost but traditional celebration of collective institutions and forms (such as the public bath) was to become a critical issue. They were among the first, along with Jose Luis Sert, to call for a new monumentality, issuing jointly their *Nine Points on Monumentality* in 1943. In anticipating the theme of CIAM XIII Congress, 'The Heart of the City', held in Hoddesdon in 1952, they expressed their mutual concern for the tendency to privatise every aspect of modern life. Following the early Soviet preoccupation with the problem as to what should be the form and content of the new social condenser in a progressive society, and after the subsequent false monumentality of both Stalinist Social Realism and the Neo-Classicism of the Third Reich, they asserted in the first point of their manifesto that:

'Monuments are human landmarks which men have created as symbols for their ideals, for their aims, and for their actions. They are intended to outlive the period which originated them, and constitute a heritage for future generations. As such they form a link between the past and the future.'[14]

In calling for the re-integration of the arts in the service of the collective monument, it would seem that both men still had the enduring image of Rockefeller Center in mind, although they recognised the difficulty of representing with modern programmes and modern artistic means the symbolic form and memory of the people. With this manifesto on monumentality, written five years before the publication of *Mechanization Takes Command*, Giedion's role as a polemical historian had come full circle, for he was compelled to recognise that the space-time syndrome which he had posited in 1941 as the prime syntax for the re-integration of man was in fact incapable of doing so, since hardly any connections existed between the abstract forms of modern art and the traditional representative forms of collective memory. The countermanding reflection was virtually instantaneous and for Giedion, from now on, it was nothing but a long haul back through the ancient past to re-discover the eternal language of the eternal present.

Rain Bath for Medical Purposes, France, c 1860
The doctor, watching from his observation platform, controls the treatment. 'It is no rare thing to see a subject who at this first shower betrays actual terror, shouts, struggles, runs away, experiences frightening suffocation and palpitation; and it is not rare to hear him say after a few moments "So that's all it is"' (L Fleury, Traité thérapeutique)
(*Mechanization Takes Command*, fig 470)

Garments for the Atmospheric Cure, Dr Rikli, c 1870
In the sixties, the Swiss Arnold Rikli (1823–1906) attempted to exploit systematically the beneficial effects of radiation. Sun bathing and open-air exercise were the basic elements of his cure. Rikli made his patients wear shorts, sandals, and open-necked and short-sleeved shirts. In the time of parasols these garments were worn by a few eccentrics walking behind the high fences that surrounded his sanatorium. (Dr Arnold Rikli, Let There Be Light, or The Atmospheric Cure, 5th ed., 1895)
(*Mechanization Takes Command*, fig 466)

Notes:

1. Sigfried Giedion, *Space, Time and Architecture*, Harvard University Press, Cambridge, Mass, 4th ed, 1963, p 721.
2. *Ibid*, p 446.
3. Giedion took his 'space-time' concept from Cubist aesthetic theory which, aside from parallels in theoretical physics, had both a metaphysical and a mystical origin – the one in Henri Bergson's idea of a 'becoming' reality as set forth in his *Creative Evolution* of 1907; the other in Uspensky's vision of an ultimate reality as determined by time, first advanced in his *Tertium Organum* of 1911. Apollinaire could have been influenced by both sources when he wrote in his book, *The Cubist Painters* of 1914, *'Regarded from the plastic point of view, the fourth dimension appears to spring from the three known dimensions: it represents the immensity of space eternalising itself.'*

    This avant-garde, anti-perspective space gained much of its authority from Einstein's theory of relativity of 1905 and still further confirmation from Riemann's theory of *'four-dimensional hyper-space conceived as an isotropic curved continuum.'* (See *Cubist Aesthetic Theories* by Christopher Gray, Baltimore, 1953.)
4. Sigfried Giedion, *op cit*, p 18.
5. Sigfried Giedion, *op cit*, p 388.
6. Leonardo Benevolo, *History of Modern Architecture*, MIT Press, Cambridge, Mass, 1971, Vol I, p 201. First published in Italian in 1960.
7. *Ibid*, pp 194, 195.
8. *Ibid*, pp 229, 230.
9. Sigfried Giedion, *Mechanization Takes Command*, Oxford University Press, New York, 1948, p 31.
10. Paul Hofer and Ulrich Stucky, eds, *Hommage à Giedion*, Birkhäuser Verlag, Basel, 1971, pp 50, 51.
11. Sigfried Giedion *Mechanization Takes Command*, p 387.
12. *Ibid*, p 712. Giedion's work on the culture of bathing had been first carried out for an exhibition staged in the *Kunstgewerbe Museum*, Zurich, in 1935, under the title *Dar Bad im Kulturganzen*.
13. *Ibid*, pp 709–711.
14. Sigfried Giedion, *Architecture, You and Me*, Oxford University Press, Cambridge, Mass, 1958, pp 48, 49. It is important to note that this book was originally published in 1956 as *Architektur und Gemeinschaft – Tagebuch einer Entwicklung*. This title evoked the German critical concern, dating from the mid-19th century for distinguishing between a society based on rootedness and fraternity (*Gemeinschaft*) and a society based on the Enlightenment concept of the social contract, on mere abstract association (*Gesellschaft*).

Pevsner's Progress
REYNER BANHAM
b 1922

Antonio Sant'Elia, *Stazione Aeroplani*, 1912

REYNER BANHAM was born in Norwich in 1922. He received his early education locally and spent the war years with the Bristol Aeroplane Company. After the war he went to study at the Courtauld Institute in London where he received his BA Degree in 1952 and his PhD in 1958. He was on the editorial staff of *Architectural Review* from 1952 to 1964; and in 1960, the year of the publication of his first book *Theory and Design in the First Machine Age*, he took up a teaching post in Architectural History at University College, London, where he taught until 1978. The years from 1964 until 1966 were spent in Chicago on a Graham Foundation research scholarship; and in 1978 he decided to set up home in the USA, first in Buffalo and then, in 1980, on the West Coast. As well as contributing regularly over the years to periodicals like *New Statesman*, *New Society* and *The Listener*, he also published several books including *Guide to Modern Architecture* (1962), *The New Brutalism* (1966), *Architecture of the Well-Tempered Environment* (1969) and *Los Angeles* (1971).

Pevsner's success as a stylistic talent-spotter could be due to a number of things; luck, undue influence on later events, or a true perception of how things happen in history. All three are indeed there; he was clearly fortunate to be set on course by Gropius almost before he knew that such a thing as a 'Modern Movement' might exist; he certainly was influential in shaping the ideas of two if not three generations of architects, historians and critics, so that all were inclined to make his prophecies come true. And at least one of the reasons he was so influential was that his historical generalisations looked true at the time, and in many cases still look good.

Anyone who believes he can find direction and purpose in history must be capable of producing comprehensible pictures of the historical process and they will be comprehensible only in so far as they can cut through the glitter and confusions of 'the Brownian movement of random events' to reveal patterns (true or false) that lie within. The discovery and delivery of such generalising patterns is one of the services that historians render to the lay members of society. Indeed, the ability to generalise convincingly and usefully is one of the tests of a great historian, and is also one of the reasons historians' reputations are so perishable since changing circumstances will undermine the conviction and utility of any generalization. But it also explains Pevsner's impact in the 1930s, 1940s and even 1950s, when architects and lay-folk alike needed help in understanding what was going on.

Given such generalisations it is, admittedly, very easy to endow them with personalities, parts and passions, and it is—alas—not a very long step from such glib observations as 'The Roman Baroque prefers elliptical floor-plans', to more sinister historicist rhetoric about 'the architectonic mission of the German *volk*'. Yet their utility persists, and, Watkin avails himself of them as much as any historian: 'the historicist and *Zeitgeist*-inspired historian will tend to regard modern collectivist ideas as right; he will be ever anxious to deal wholesale with humanity, to label individuals as types, to identify them in classes...'—a sentence in which he himself labels individuals as types and identifies them in classes.

The relative blackness of pots and kettles is not the point at issue here: Pevsner's performance is. He got it right. He got it more right than Giedion or Henry-Russell Hitchcock. It behooves any of us who disapprove of his methodology, or dislike his particular favourites and are concerned at his omission of *our* particular favourites, to recognise that he produced a picture of the architecture of his own time which was useful, applicable, and has had demonstrable predictive power. If it was Whiggish historicism, or the kind of moralising that comes naturally to a self-made Lutheran, that made it possible to do that, then so much the worse for Butterfield and Popper.

Indeed, a good Popperian, I feel, should salute rather than abuse Pevsner for having offered a falsifiable hypothesis about the main style of 20th-century architecture in the Western industrialised world, and having seen that hypothesis resist falsification for 40 years. It is, of course, only one of the many historical services he has rendered us, but its success should command respect, and give pause to those who would deprecate any of his methods.

Reyner Banham, 'Pevsner's Progress', *Times Literary Supplement*; 17 February, 1978.

Reyner Banham: the Plenitude of Presence
ROBERT MAXWELL
b 1922

The excerpt cited is from the review Reyner Banham made of David Watkin's book *Morality and Architecture*.¹ It is a short text, and it may seem invidious to reproduce just part of it. However, what I have omitted, is largely taken up with the polemics of reviewing, whereas the passage quoted, being mainly a defence of Nikolaus Pevsner, is one of the few passages where Banham addresses himself to the job of the historian. It has the advantage of being recent, and of dealing with the Modern Movement as a single event of history. This essay is not an attempt to summarise Banham's achievement, but to clarify his method: I will, thus, amplify the excerpt chosen by references to his more important books.

The polemical passages are in crisp *TLS* manner, not so much avoiding beating around the bush as simply eradicating it. Banham identifies Watkin's book as a piece of Butterfieldian-Peterhousey anti-Whiggery; an attempt perhaps at an *'academic take-over of the current fashion for knocking Modern Architecture'*. Apart from affording us a glimpse of a Banham who is basically 'for' Modern Architecture, this also shows us a Banham who, in spite of being an academic, does not wish to be in any way associated with academicism. Confined, as most historians are, to the rear-wards view, Banham has a quick eye to grasp the actuality of events as they swirl into the field of vision. His interest in the virtually unchanging profile of the distant mountains is as low as his trust in the redeeming power of the *Phileban* solids.² Whereas most historians work to dislodge past events from the dust which has already immobilised them and which might efface them, Banham seems to prefer events which are still in motion, on which the dust has not settled. His view of culture emphasises its inertia, its accumulation, and suggests that, like all accumulations, it constitutes clutter. His telling phrase— *'the history of the immediate future'*—reveals much of his motivation; and his writing, has the intrinsic interest of revealing a picture *for the first time*.

This combination of virtues has certain journalistic consequences like the danger of being 'wrong', or simply of mistaking the momentary for the momentous; but I would be the last to reproach him for his tone of light banter, or take exception to the occasionally portentous result of bending his mind to minutiae like clip-boards or alternative neckties. What is refreshing in him is especially his refusal to reject apparently light-weight evidence, since this increases our awareness of the historical dimension in our own lives 'as lived'. If his achievement as an academic has been no more than to employ more frequently the normal lens of the

From top Walter Gropius, Body for Adler Cabriolet, 1930; Sir Charles Burney, Streamlined cars, 1930; Buckminster Fuller, Dymaxion ground-taxiing unit, 1933 (from R Banham, *Theory and Design* p 304)

ROBERT MAXWELL was born in Northern Ireland and educated at Liverpool University. After graduating in 1949 he worked in London as an assistant architect in various offices before joining the Architectural Association in 1958. In 1962 he moved to the Bartlett School at University College and at the same time commenced an association with the firm of Douglas Stephen and Partners. He is now Professor of Architecture at the Bartlett and a partner in the same practice. He is the author of *New British Architecture* (Thames & Hudson, 1972) and of many critical articles, including 'Teaching and Learning' (*RIBA Journal*, October 1970), 'Sweet Disorder and the Carefully Careless' (*Architectural Design*, April 1971), 'Architecture, Language and Process' (*Architectural Design*, Vol 47, No 3, 1977) and 'The Venturi Effect' (*Architectural Monographs*, Vol 1, No 1, January 1978).

amateur in preference to the wide-angle or telescopic lenses of the expert, we are already in his debt.

And yet there are still some doubts to raise about his method. Banham is, after all, a *writer*. The eye for fast-moving objects, which we have attributed to him, is only a metaphor. What is the controlling framework which allows his roving camera-work? My guess is that we should seek this control in the form of his work, rather than in its content. Yet his reputation has been so strongly linked to his concept of a history 'of the immediate future' that we must first try to unravel his method from his purpose—which appears to be prediction. His confidence in handling fast-moving objects seems closely related to his confidence in the Zeitgeist-ian motion of the train, his anticipation of a future increasingly focused on the possibilities of technological development. We, the architects, have been constantly chastised by him for our backwardness; to the point where *we* appear to be more concerned with the past than *he*, whose job it is to analyse the past.

'The architect who proposes to run with technology knows now that he will be in fast company, and that, in order to keep up, he may have to emulate the futurists and discard his whole cultural load . . .'[3]

In the pain of receiving this admonition we have perhaps failed to question its assumptions. Did the Futurists discard their whole cultural load? They reacted against it, certainly, but did they *shed* it? Like Abbé Laugier's prescription for a fundamental architecture, their designs now seem quaint, locked into their moment in history, and Futurism was to remain an 'ism' and not become the model for architectural advance. But then we, the architects, have perhaps been too pained in general with Banham's admonitory tone to notice that his own preferences suggest the idiosyncrasy of a sensibility rather than the regularity of a dogma. He has on the whole been soft on the Futurists, hard on the Purists, soft on Fuller and hard on Corb, soft on Parkhill and hard on the Unité, soft on Archigram and hard on Beaubourg, soft on Philip Johnson and hard on Venturi, hard on the profession of architecture, soft on his friends engaged in the practice of it.

The question then is how this kind of variability can be related to the constancy required in a historical method. Here we must be careful to detach Banham's preferences, as a critic of architecture, from his assertions as a historian. If we do this, we will find that he makes no wild claims, but remains anchored very close to established fact. The motion he imparts to facts affects them very little, but affects our view of them considerably.

Notice how, in the last quotation, he does not demand that all architects should shed their cultural load, but only those who propose to run with technology: a strong assertion which has the unassailability of a tautology. Yet it insinuates the idea that not to be in the select group who want to run with technology is not to be in the running at all. This passage well represents the Banham style: at once rigorous, self-evident and seductive.

The matter of prediction *is* dealt with in our quoted excerpt. Here Banham is concerned to show that Pevsner correctly predicted the success of the Modern Movement by defining it not simply in visual terms, but in terms of its basic attributes: functionality, honesty to materials and structure, and social responsibility. Broadly speaking, an architecture with such characteristics did take shape and is still with us. The revolutionary theoretical ideas which emerged from the Great War did indeed result—not in a short-lived 'ism'—but in a normative practical sequel, as *'the main style of 20th-century architecture in the western industrialised world'*.

'Now, Pevsner's success as a stylistic talent-spotter could be due to a number of things; luck, undue influence on later events, or a true perception of how things happen in history. All these are indeed there . . .'

Pevsner, says Banham, was indeed lucky in being set on course early by Gropius, but most important was his *performance* as an interpreter of history. His interpretation amounted to a selective definition of modernity, as much by its hypothetical characteristics as by the chosen exemplars. It involved an action of generalisation, in order to make the pattern perceptible and comprehensible; and this involved a risk of leaving something essential out, of getting it wrong.

This judgement raises some interesting points. First, the acknowledgement that the telling of history involves making an interpretation. The individual historian must then be subject to bias; but he can be proved right, or at least not entirely wrong, by the subsequent march of events. His subjectivity must however be illuminated by a *'true perception of how things happen in history'*; a revelation, presumably, of the real forces determining the immediate future. Hence the capacity of predicting this future with the possibility of having the predictions falsified by the outcome. [. . .]

One wonders indeed if Banham takes seriously the proposition of refutability encapsulated here. Are we to take it that he means that Pevsner showed conclusively that, given the premises of functionality, *only thus* could architecture evolve? Or was it rather that Pevsner perceived that the new kind of architecture free from traditional constraints was more responsive to actual conditions and therefore more acceptable and more likely to endure? These points are not dwelt upon, and indeed there is a suggestion that it was not so much the operational hypotheses, but the stylistic characteristics, which Pevsner got right: that he anticipated merely the broad outlines of a kind of architecture largely emanating from the Bauhaus and approximating to the International Style.

In any case one may doubt if Pevsner's work, however important in other ways, was effective as prediction. The discovery that Modern Architecture was from the start less functional, less honest to material, less responsive to people, than its protagonists claimed, has been going on for almost as long as the Modern Movement itself. Reyner Banham has played an important part in that discovery, just as he has been right in insisting that style alone does not bestow functionality. Modern is now a compendious style embracing many practical and stylistic transformations which suggest a process of adaptation to economic and social pressures. This process of change in real time has little relation either to the intellectual process by which a set of hypotheses may be refuted by argument, or to the empirical process by which they may be disproved by experiment. To suggest that Pevsner, as historian, has established the fundamental premises of the new style in refutable terms is a large claim, and one which skirts

PAESTUM, 600–550 B.C.

THE PARTHENON, 447–434 B.C.

When once a standard is established, competition comes at once and violently into play. It is a fight; in order to win you must do better than your rival *in every minute point*, in the run of the whole thing and in all the details. Thus we get the study of minute points pushed to its limits. Progress.

A standard is necessary for order in human effort.

HUMBER, 1907

DELAGE, "GRAND-SPORT," 1921

Le Corbusier, *Towards a New Architecture*, pp 124–25

the extreme complexity of identifying and defining the role of causality in history. Admittedly, we should not expect to find these questions laid to rest in a review article, but we might expect to find them raised, if only in the role of *caveat*. It would have been more convincing to present Pevsner as a percipient critic, won over to a set of ideas already embodied and communicated in a style by architects.[4] The view of him as a propagandist (presumably of an ideology) was, according to Banham, not unacceptable to Pevsner himself—conversationally at least.[5] And in spite of the talk about prediction, it is the picture of Pevsner which we are effectively given.

It will be seen that Banham's defence of Pevsner, while communicating sympathy with the latter's achievement, does not amount to an endorsement of his method. Still less does it commit himself to a deterministic view of history. The historian stands well back from the risks cheerfully accepted by the critic. His description of an historian's job, which in the context we may take as applying to Pevsner, we must not take as applying to Banham. All that we can assume is that the discovery and delivery of generalised patterns within the random motion of events—just one of the services that historians render to the lay members of society—is an essential part of the job of the historian. It is one which happens to describe very aptly most of what Banham himself does. His generalisations have indeed been effective in their aim of sweeping the here-and-now into a comprehensible story, a story often admonitory, often controversial even, but issuing from his sensibility as a critic rather than from the rectitude of a historical methodology. If his comprehensible generalisations arouse doubts, it is not in relation to the historiographical questions which they offend, but to the critical view of architecture which they enclose. This has always been bent in one direction, towards an 'other' architecture, one which would be light, adaptable and responsive, technologically progressive and therefore of the immediate future, stronger in space and function than in form and structure. While, according to Jencks,[6] Banham believes in the possibility of an '*entirely radical*' architecture which would once and for all put paid to the architects' persistent tendency to monumentalise, he has not projected this architecture as historically inevitable, but as morally desirable. '*It is Banham's strength [said Rowe] to be the possessor of a crucial and simple idea ... [he] has believed, and continues to believe, that modern architecture should be, and can be, exactly what it was claimed to be, ie an objective approach to building deriving from the unprejudiced scrutiny of facts.'*[7]

This position appears to stem from belief rather than from conviction, and to be in that sense beyond attack. It has enabled him to criticise *all* contemporary architecture as in various crucial ways failing the test of being entirely radical. His hope that architecture would consistently evolve closer to engineering technology and away from formal games, is not invalidated by the fact that it seems to be reverting to formal games and anti-technological attitudes. History, since the energy crisis, has provided Banham—and all of us—with a few surprises.

And yet, in spite of Banham's enthusiasms, and they are many, it is his disappointments which come through. In *Theory and Design* there is no concealing his disenchantment with the failure of Modern Architecture to match the early promise of the Futurists. In *The New Brutalists* he is confronted with a sad decline from ethic to aesthetic, a promise laid to rest before he even takes up his pen. In *Megastructures* he again records the story of an idea which had already degenerated beyond hope. Since these writings all involve the story of a promise unfulfilled in the performance, one marvels that expectation can stay high. He is too perceptive and too sympathetic a critic to ascribe these failures merely to the pigheadedness of the architectural profession, even though architects do collect a fair share of the blame. This built-in capacity to be disappointed could be explained as endemic optimism; a temperamental bias to be grateful for in good times and bad times alike. But it could also be explained as an ontological blindness to the fact of culture: to the processes by which culture accumulates its clutter and to the way in which the individual delves in this clutter in order to identify the points of criticism and hence of renewal.

By characterising culture as primarily *'a load which must be shed'*, Banham seems to disregard the dialectical nature of history. Does he really think that culture only clutters? It surely has both negative and positive effects. It keeps enmities alive, and the home fires burning. But is it not also the source of divine discontent? The only entirely radical idea is the one which has not yet been assimilated, which has not even been communicated. Obviously there is a meaning to be attached to radical, but the *truly radical* one may suspect is a myth.

But while we may feel that Banham's critical view of architecture is unjustifiably optimistic and his experience of it unnecessarily disappointing, it would be wrong to see this as invalidating his approach *as an historian*. On the evidence more of his books than of our excerpt alone, Banham appears no fantasist, but straightforwardly a pragmatist. An exponent, one might say, of the British Brutalist view of history which prefers the brute fact to the smooth story, the evidence to the interpretation. There is a distinct air of Dr Johnson in his view of ideality and his refutations are likely to take the form of kicking out at something solid. This preference for solid evidence can intrude at levels concerned purely with imagination. In his discussion of Archigram's Walking City (in *Megastructures*) he praises its wealth of *graphic* detail as if this detail were evidence of its essential practicality. Earlier megastructuralists had been excessively vague about detail:

'*... It is noticeable—alarming even—how few of them actually offer any nut-and-bolt proposals as to how the transient elements should be secured to the megaform, or what precise devices and services are required for the physical activities of homo ludens.*'[8]

Archigram, on the other hand, produced reassuring images which not only had a certain verisimilitude, but indeed provided a wealth of technical detail verging on the production of working drawings. But is 'Walking City' concerned with the idea of technicity as part of an essential practicality? Surely its purpose is to project us into a fantasy where walking cities are already commonplace. We are brought to accept the fantastic as if it had already been actualised. The diminishing telescopic legs are not involved with technical questions but with rhetorical questions.

Such a rhetorical use of graphic detail has nothing to do with making megastructures real, but with making fantasy realistic. It does, however, have the effect of effacing the ideological basis of 'Walking City', by focusing on its actuality. One can but agree with Banham when he comments:

'*The reasons why the British alone seemed prone to finnick over detailing are diverse, and often personal, but do seem somewhat connected to a national tendency to take refuge from ideology in pragmatics.*'[9]

Though conversational in tone, as always, this passage suggests that Banham indeed believes that pragmatics are, or can be, independent of ideology. The pragmatic is his base for the criticism of architectural ideologies, and the fact that it is always identified by a concrete instance obscures the critical role it plays as a category. Thus in *Theory and Design* Bucky's Dymaxion Ground-Taxi-ing Unit was pragmatically superior to Gropius' Adler cabriolet; and the Dymaxion House to 'Les Heures Claires'. As Colquhoun has pointed out,[10] Banham has ignored or preferred not to see, the ideality present in both Fuller products; just as he has passed over in silence the Beaux-Arts content in Sant'Elia's Futurist city-scapes. His blindness to formal and rhetorical content in his own preferred examples suggest that, like the Smithsons, he believes rhetoric to be both reprehensible and avoidable.

Yet is Banham himself not a master of rhetoric? Is it not as much his presentational skill as his insights in selecting the hard evidence, which constitutes his strength as a historian? In saying this, I do not mean to call in question his good faith nor his use of the facts. But the conviction of his narrative stems not from the facts as pragmatic evidence alone, but from the impact these facts create within the empire of his text. In shying away from epistemological questions, in limiting the use of generalising frameworks to the duty of communicating true perceptions of history to a lay audience, Banham is asserting the primacy and immediacy of the fact, thereby diverting our attention from the text to the event outside of it:

'*As far as can be ascertained, the phrase "Fun Palace" was coined, and applied to the project Cedric Price was designing for Joan Littlewood, on the sidewalk in 42nd Street during a visit they paid to New York (in 1962).*'[11]

In such passages it is we who become eyewitnesses to the making of history; and we are astonished to find that history is real, not bunk.

In 'Memoirs of a Survivor', the concluding section of *The New Brutalism*, Banham states his involvement with the

Above Ron Herron of Archigram, *Walking City*, 1963

events described, more categorically than could have been possible with *Theory and Design*:

'The reader will have deduced, if he did not already know, that this book is the work of someone fairly deeply involved with the events it describes. I have in fact been personally acquainted with most of the British Brutalists and Quasi-Brutalists mentioned ... The book, therefore, has a built-in bias towards the British contribution to Brutalism: it is not a dispassionate and Olympian survey, conducted from the cool heights of an academic ivory tower.'[12]

In projecting the immediacy of the events, what is being stressed is the role of the historian as eye-witness. History in these terms becomes a question of access. The further away we are from the event, the less we know about it. The event itself is unequivocal. It has an intrinsic reality which validates the account by the degree that the account is close to it. It is the *plenitude of presence* which authenticates.[13]

But the historian cannot be close to every event he describes. In *Theory and Design* the majority of the events took place far away and long ago. It is a problem not unknown to historians, and there is a well-known answer. Quotations from documents are themselves pragmatic facts; when inserted into a text, they become real events. Some historians emphasise and enjoy the dust-stained aspect of these documentary relics, like the Clerk-of-Works records which figure so largely in 19th-century historical works. Banham has a different method. In him these quotations speak with the vibrancy of key people interviewed on television. Quotations form a hefty chunk of the text in *Theory and Design*. Far from deadening the narrative, they sustain it and give it life.

Banham's power of narrative is based on the skill with which he uses these quotations to create a rhetoric of actuality. A framework of relations is set up, by which the writing animates, and is animated by, the events which it takes as its ostensible content. Thus, what real events are to the author's project (the book), real quotations are to the author's narrative (the text). We see the event—the quotations—but we don't see the text. Events and quotations are evidence of life; they indubitably exist as facts; and being outside of the author's purposes, they impart to the text an authenticity which is that of life. Viewed as parts of writing, however, they are events which are breathed into new life by the way in which they are sewn into the congruity of the text.

This amounts to little more than saying that Banham is a damned good writer; true, but in the context of an historiographical debate it enables us to locate him in an array of other talents and other methods. As a pragmatist he will tend to ignore the framework by which he works; yet this framework does constitute a method and a way of valuing the subject matter of history. Banham remains suspicious of comprehensive classifications and ideological frameworks, and prefers reality as found. That this reality is not tainted by the very act of grasping it, Banham does not appear to doubt. But, despite his seductiveness, his *'rhetoric of the real'* often fails to convince us that he has achieved a true perception of how things happen in history. It is his performance, not his promise, that has us in thrall.

Notes

1. Cf *Times Literary Supplement*, Feb 17, 1978.
2. The Plileban solids may be included in Le Corbusier's list of *les constants humains*—regular human preferences which link us to our distant ancestors and provide archetypes for the immediate future.
3. From the concluding admonition in Reyner Banham, *Theory and Design in the First Machine Age*.
4. *Pioneers of the Modern Movement* was published in England in 1936, by which time the main lines of the new architecture had already crystallised. Johnson and Hitchcock's book had been out for some four years, the key masterpieces built, Weissenhof dispensing its influence, and layouts of white-walled housing by Gropius, Scharoun and others, already lived in.
5. The suggestion that Pevsner himself was a pioneer is but a suggestion. Banham's text reads: *'... conversationally at least he [Pevsner] has acknowledged himself a propagandist for that kind of architecture which was pioneered from William Morris to Walter Gropius.'*
6. Charles Jencks, 'History as Myth', in *Meaning in Architecture*, ed Jencks and Baird, 1969.
7. Colin Rowe, 'Waiting for Utopia'—a review of Banham's *New Brutalism* and Venturi's *Complexity and Contradiction* which appeared in the *New York Times*, 1967.
8. Reyner Banham, *Megastructures*, p 84.
9. *Ibid*, p 85.
10. Alan Colquhoun, 'The Modern Movement in Architecture', *The British Journal of Aesthetics*, Vol 12, No 1, Jan 1962.
11. Reyner Banham, *Megastructures*, *op cit*, p 84.
12. From *The New Brutalists*, p 134.
13. The position from which I have approached the work of Reyner Banham is somewhat near to that expounded by Jacques Derrida in *De la Grammatologie*. Derrida discusses *'writing'* in relation to *'speech'*. Truth can never be grasped in a text, but only glimpsed in the relations conveyed. In this view, rhetoric is not an avoidable weakness, but rather the main vehicle by which the incommunicable is communicated. Rhetoric is capable of recreating the illusion of presence; and the plenitude of presence is the experience which all *'writing'* tries to shadow.

Art et Technique
PIERRE FRANCASTEL
1900–1970

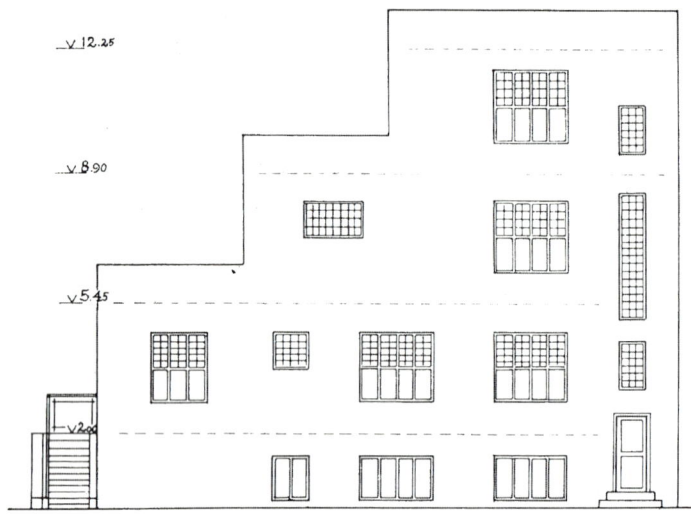

Adolf Loos, Haus Scheu, 1912, elevation

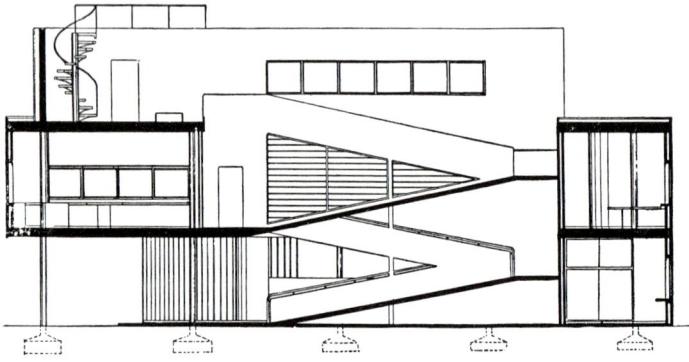

Le Corbusier and P Jeanneret, Villa Savoie, 1928–30, cross-section

PIERRE FRANCASTEL was born in 1900. Before turning to the study of the history of art, he studied classical literature. Between 1925 and 1930, while working as an architectural advisor at the Versailles Palace, he published the books *Girardon* (1929) and *La sculpture de Versailles* (1930). For the next six years, as professor at the Institut Francais de Varsovie, he travelled extensively in Poland and in 1936 he became professor at Strasbourg University. After the publication of his book *L'impressionisme* (1937), Francastel devoted himself to the critical study of the work of art historians. The first of these studies, *L'histoire de l'art, instrument de propagande germanique*, was a critique of the nationalist overtones of German art history and though completed by 1940, it was not published until after the war in 1945. In 1948 Francastel received the chair of the sociology of art at the Ecole Pratique des Hautes Etudes, a position which he held until his death in 1970. His books include: *Peinture et Société. Naissance et destruction d'un espace plastique de la Renaissance au Cubisme* (1951); *Art et technique* (1956); *Les architectes célèbres* (1959); *La réalité figurative* (1964); *La figure et le lieu: l'ordre visuel du Quattrocento* (1967).

The truly original content [of the architecture of Loos] is best seen in two stylistic formulae: the first consists of substituting traditional [composition] with a method of multiplying plans and volumes through addition, juxtaposition, and through the packing of interior volumes; the second [...] on the other hand, concerns the exterior style of buildings. Buildings devoid of cornices, reduced to bald, uninterrupted surfaces, had never been seen before, except in Arabic domestic architecture [...]

Moreover, the houses of Loos—distinct from preoccupations such as Berlage's which consisted of impoverishing the surface of a wall without the slightest sensibility towards volumetric [composition], and which remained within the context of Western historical styles—are not the only buildings of the early 20th century to be based on a sensibility of related volumes [there follows a list of buildings primarily similar to the examples cited by Giedion or Zevi]. These are the principal realisations which, in the course of 30 years, have defined a new style. All the major architects of the century have, at one or another time, contributed to it. It would be untrue to consider it [the new style] as the application of a strictly formulated doctrinal system consisting of a certain symmetrical opposition between the free treatment of interior space and the intentional austerity of the exterior [...] The fusion between the sensibility of related volumes and the use of a smooth wall is rarely achieved in one and the same building [...]

An altogether separate position should be reserved for Le Corbusier's *Maison Savoye*. Undoubtedly, this is the most fresh and perfect work in the whole series [...] The *Maison Savoye* introduces effectively a primordial element: movement. Here, volumes are truly interlocking, even penetrating each other. In the interior of the villa [...] an 'architectural promenade' develops autonomously within the volume of the whole. The work is treated as a sculpture. For 50 years now, nobody else has achieved anything so daring and so complete [...] In the *Villa Savoye*, one can discern at least three buildings inscribed in it [...]

Concerning the links which existed between the 1890s and 1930s, between technique and architecture, [...] a few guiding principles might be in order.

It was not concrete [construction] which inspired the crusade of Loos against ornament. Concrete, as was previously the case with steel, had been known for a long time; and yet it had not provided—by means of a dialectical relationship with necessity—any [theoretical] foundations for a doctrine. Loos and his contemporaries utilised concrete only because it allowed them to satisfy demands of a figurative nature.

Nor was it solely the calvinistic logic of Loos which, hostile to all decorative fancy, had inspired the sensibility of his early work. To express his rejection of the 'useless', he recalled things he had already seen. It is perhaps necessary to research the links which exist between his initial solutions and certain reminiscences of Oriental architecture—be it Arabic or Archaic. But above all, we should keep in mind the influence of contemporary developments in the figurative arts.

Pierre Francastel, *Art et technique*, Editions de Minuit, Paris, 1956, pp 175–78.

Francastel's Interdisciplinary History of Art
YVES ALAIN BOIS
b 1952

It would be difficult to maintain that Pierre Francastel followed a particular 'method' of historical analysis. Instead, the strength of his writings—almost 20 books—seems to derive from his extraordinary intellectual curiosity, as well as from his revolt against the sclerosis of a philological history of art. Of course, he recognised the latter's relative importance; yet, he never ceased to expose its limitations. Francastel criticised the disciplinary esotericism of art historical studies and, instead, he attempted to widen art history's scope by means of an interdisciplinary cross-fertilisation. Genetics, child psychology, mathematics, sociology, economics, philosophy, are but some of the disciplines Francastel drew from while analysing a work of art. It is exactly such an 'opening' which accounts for the richness of his work; but also for the ostracism he suffered by his colleagues and contemporary historians.

Apart from a few articles, Francastel's work on architecture consists of two books: *Art et technique aux 19e et 20e siècles*, 1956; and *Les architectes célèbres*, 1959. In *Art et technique*, Francastel studies the way in which the technical developments of the last two centuries modified the symbolic systems of the Western World. This book—the outcome of a seminar held at the *Ecole Pratique des Hautes Etudes*—is presented as a series of lecture notes in which the author challenges the interpretive schemas of the historians of Modern architecture. The main thesis of the book is that the 'Industrial Revolution' occasioned a fundamental rupture in the systems of production and culture of the Western World. Francastel, therefore, rejects Mumford's '*mystique of progress*' according to which the machine civilisation is the ultimate revelation towards which the whole history of mankind had been steadily advancing.

He also rejects the Rousseauesque '*catastophism*' of Giedion and criticises the latter's idealism and trans-historicism, for its '*vision is a sort of an eternal Man-type, a kind of standard Man who could possibly serve as the ideal of a certain America, but who could never be considered the king of creation.*'[1] To those, like Pevsner, who overemphasised the Arts and Crafts movement, Francastel replies that the latter was but a version of 19th-century '*eclecticism simply enlarged by the discovery of primitive art.*'[2] Francastel questions the significance which, according to the historians of Modernism, the Crystal Palace, the Baloon Frame or the American tradition had in the formation of the Modernist sensibility. Instead, he underlines the instrumental role played by 19th-century structural moralists like Viollet-le-Duc. Elsewhere, Francastel underplays the contribution of Wright and he accuses Le Corbusier of

Le Corbusier, Villa Savoie, bird's eye view

Adolf Loos, Haus Steiner, 1910

promoting a vision of the world similar to a '*concentration camp*'.[3]

These examples of Francastel's critique may suffice for the moment. For, having rejected the classificatory categories

YVES-ALAIN BOIS was born in 1952. He studied at the Ecole des Hautes Etudes under Roland Barthes and received his doctorate in 1977. Since 1974 he has been publishing extensively on twentieth-century painting in *Critique*, and in 1975 he published a book on Picabia. Yves-Alain Bois and Jean Clay founded *Macula* in 1976, a periodical addressing historical and theoretical issues in painting and the arts. Since 1977, Bois has been working towards his Doctorat d'Etat on Mondrian and De Stijl. He is currently preparing a book on the history of axonometric projection.

which the historians of Modern architecture had used, Francastel proposes *a new mode of historicity*: all possible historical ruptures—he maintains—can only be of a global and synchronic nature. In his *Les architectes célèbres*, therefore, Francastel maintains that the Modernist rupture occurred when the new technique of concrete construction was combined with the pictorial preoccupations of Cubism. However, such rupture was originally of a theoretical nature: Loos must have probably been the first 'Modernist' with a sense of exterior surface and a liking for volumetric displacement.[4] For Francastel, the Cubist sensibility becomes the primary category with which to periodise Modernism: the first phase of Modern architecture (from the end of the 19th century to circa 1930) was directly indebted to Cubism; the second phase (that of Aalto and the second Wright) coincides with the decline of Cubism and the emergence of a new fascination with the sensuousness of materials. In any event, *'the majority of the masters of contemporary architecture,'* writes Francastel, *'have done no more than combine, in diverse proportions, the tendencies which were defined at the beginning of the 20th century by the creators of a new plastic sensibility adapted to the machine.'*[5]

One of the richest areas of Francastel's work, however, is the anthropological dimension he imparts to his discussion. In spite of his wrong reading of Marcel Mauss,[6] Francastel's inquiries, based on the idea of *'figurative object'*, led him to the study of the history of perception. For Francastel, *'there exists a common background of sensation and activities which serves as the basis for all specific modes of human activity in the course of a given historical period.'*[7] Such a common sensibility might be, for example, the feel of a polished surface in the Stone Age (which Brancusi attempted to revive), the use of iron in the Middle Ages, or the importance of numbers in the Renaissance.[8] In modern times, *'positive ideas such as "fatigue" or "precision" have changed both their meaning and form.'*[9] Functions such as *'caring'* are no longer practised; and the reality of *'rhythm'* has invaded the experience of contemporary man.[10]

Speaking of the constructive innovations of Modern architecture—eg the process of serialisation or montage[11]—Francastel makes observations similar to those of Manfredo Tafuri; yet, he does not reach the same conclusions. What for Tafuri constitutes the *'crisis of the object'*, for Francastel becomes the future possibility of new links with technique. Francastel's work, however, is marked by omissions similar to those of Tafuri and of all the historians of Modern architecture: one rarely comes across any description proper or formal analysis of a building.

In *Les architectes célèbres*, Francastel returns to a number of issues he had raised in *Art et technique*: the tertiary nature of technique; the failure of Modern architecture to adopt the aesthetics of Viollet-le-Duc, the Arts and Crafts, and Art Nouveau; the appeal to Cubism to compensate for this 'aesthetic vacuum'; or the rejection of the periodisation of Modern architecture into Rationalist (Le Corbusier and Gropius), Organic (Wright), and Neo-Functionalist (Mies van der Rohe). The two most interesting features of this book, however, are the way in which Francastel envisages the 19th-century 'break' (*coupure*) and his choice of illustrations or individual remarks which accompany his general introductions.

Francastel describes the 'birth' of 19th-century modernity in much the same way as Tafuri might analyse historic ruptures such as those of the Renaissance or the Enlightenment: the exhaustion of forms borrowed from tradition the re-appraisal of the Gothic style, historicist eclecticism, or the technical innovations; they all introduce a *consciousness of history* which leads to a critical upheaval of architectural norms. In fact, Francastel maintains that while for centuries the architect had been the servant of a precisely defined ideology—that of the Church and the Crown—the ideological uncertainties of the 19th century created a situation in which architects were asked to *define the architectural programme* themselves.

The illustrations of this book play a twofold role. Firstly, there are illustrations which accompany particular articles written by specialists—some of whom Francastel had severely criticised in *Art et technique*. Giedion and Mumford, for example, are featured here. Labrouste, Viollet-le-Duc, Eiffel, Sullivan, and Van de Velde are discussed in the chapter on *technique*. Gaudí, Loos, Maillart, Mendelsohn, and Perret appear in the chapter on *style*; Wright, Freyssinet, Gropius, Mies van der Rohe, Le Corbusier, Aalto, and Nervi comprise the main body of the chapter entitled *Masters of our Time*. Secondly, there is a collection of illustrations of buildings which, instead of enhancing the conceptual unity of their respective architect/author, they rather point to an anonymous diffusion of Modernist 'traits'. Thus, lesser known works, such as Lafaille and Peirani's *Engine Shed*, Avignon, 1946, are illustrated side-by-side with Saarinen's or Kenzo Tange's buildings.

Francastel's contribution to the theory and history of Modern architecture is, thus, closer to the 'archaeological' studies of Michel Foucault.[12] The diversity of his knowledge and his anthropological interests, as well as his passion for discovering underlying categories of aesthetic thinking should provoke architectural historians to be a little more adventurous with their discipline. Francastel's ability to establish comparative categories of analysis enabled him to propose new historical periodisations, to place new emphasis on works which had been generally ignored, and to use as primary material theoretical problems which had, heretofore, been totally neglected by the majority of architectural historians. His insistence on the influence which painting and aesthetic theories had on architecture, as well as his theory of 'the tertiary nature of technique', constitute a serious repudiation—in spite of the idealism in which they are expressed—of the technical determinism which had been the prominent historiographic tool for the analysis and explanation of architecture ever since Gottfried Semper.

Notes
1 Pierre Francastel, *Art et technique*, Editions de Minuit, Paris, 1956, p 59.
2 *Ibid*, p 30. 3 *Ibid*, pp 78, 95–96, 62, 70, 41–42. 4 *Ibid*, pp 174–8. 5 *Ibid*, p 202. 6 *Ibid*, p 125. 7 *Ibid*, p 138. 8 *Ibid*, p 138. 9 *Ibid*, p 135. 10 *Ibid*, p 136.
11 'The most original contribution made in this field [construction] during our times,' writes Francastel in *Art et technique*, p 191, 'is a particular conception of "montage" which is dependent less on the possibility of transport or rapid manufacture of raw materials, than on the general comprehension of the mechanical processes involved in the production of the object.'
12 Cf Michel Foucault, *L'archéologie du savoir*, Gallimard, Paris, 1969, specifically pp 23–24.

Marxist Historicism and the Philosophy of Art
STEFAN MORAWSKI
b 1921

FUNDAMENTALS OF MARXIST AESTHETICS

Historicism,[1] in establishing the relevant facts and patterns among all the events and processes that are discovered, and then in classifying these data, in analysing their place in the given context, and so on—historicism, thus set apart, must be understood as philosophy, the philosophy of history.

Historicism is, accordingly, one of the fundamental resorts utilised by humanity to get to the core of its status, its civilisation, its beginnings, its evolution and future. Three systems of orientation seem to be available when one reflects on the meaningful existence of humanity: God, History and Nature. These can be drawn on exclusively or in combination. Historicism bases itself on the social history of humanity as its system of reference. In its extreme version, nothing but social history is considered relevant; in its moderate version, social history is not the exclusive but the decisive system of reference.

Historicism in this broader sense, then, is an apt correlative for the philosophy of art. Yet we first have to clarify the historicism we have in mind, for there are many differing approaches. There is a version of historicism which stresses primarily the ontological status of social phenomena; a good example is Jaspers' or Sartre's pre-1945 writings, or R Poulin's 1944 work, *La création des valeurs*. Or consider the late 19th-century historicism which sees historical process as linear evolution, and likewise as a permanent and relentless progress of the species. Clearly this version treats cultural history as being parallel with the evolution of nature, and from this positive assumption, provides an optimistic estimate of the fate of humanity.

Another version of historicism, also modelled on nature, offers a cyclical theory of wax and wane. Launched in the 18th century by Giambattista Vico, in more recent times this philosophy has turned pessimistic as in Brooks Adams, Spengler, or P Sorokin. The methodological premises of this version of historicism were elaborated by the schools of Windelband, Rickert and Dilthey, as well as by the studies on *Historismus* by Meinecke and Troeltsch. We find still another approach in the epic heritage of the historicism of Hegel, rooted in Winckelmann and Herder, later modified by Marx in one way and then by Croce in another.

My purpose in this essay is to focus on the correlations between Marxist historicism and the philosophy of art. Marxism, genuinely understood, has never been a monolithic world view; the exception is in the two socialist empires and their

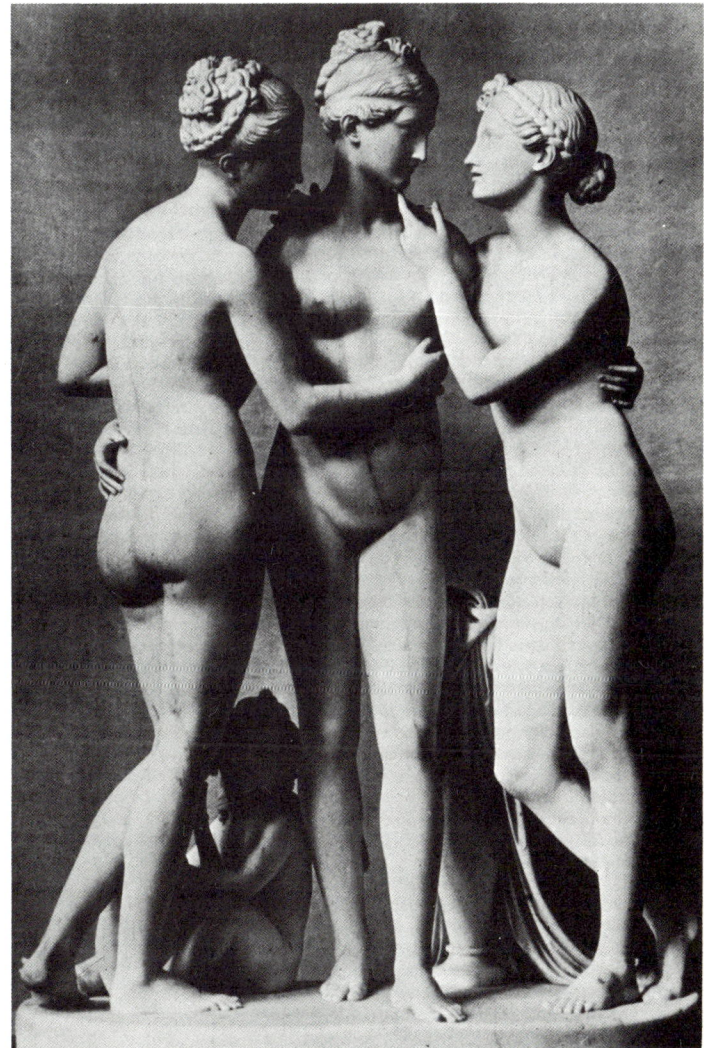

Bertel Thorvaldsen, *The Three Graces*, 1819

STEFAN MORAWSKI held the Chair in Aesthetics at Warsaw University during the 1960s and was editor of *Studia Estetyczne*. His numerous writings in Polish include a three-volume work on aesthetics in 18th- and 19th-century England, France, Germany and Poland, as well as a study of recent Soviet aesthetics entitled *Between Tradition and a Vision of the Future*. In addition to his essays and film criticism, he has written the following books: *L'Absolu et la Forme* on the aesthetics of Malraux and existentialism; *Il Marxismo e l'Estetica*; and a collection of essays entitled *Inquiries into the Fundamentals of Aesthetics*. Since 1970 he has been a research professor at the Polish Academy of Sciences, and a visiting professor at the universities of Amsterdam, Princeton, Boston, Washington (Seattle) and California (Berkeley). His forthcoming book *Marxist Thought After Marx and Engels* will be the second volume in the DOMA series (Documents of Marxist Aesthetics) edited by Lee Baxandall and published by International General, New York.

most faithful satellites where, strikingly, official doctrines are competing with one another. In this sense, it is understandable that historicism, too, is variously regarded by different versions of Marxism. Some scholars treat historicism as but one tenet, if a very important one, of the body of Marxist philosophy. Another approach, led by Althusser, is suspicious of historicism, describing it as the taint of 'utopian humanism'.

Still another interpretation is provided by the young Lukács and by Gramsci, locating in historicism the very foundation of Marxism. This position provides my starting point; it requires that we ask of each and every social phenomenon exactly when and where and in what circumstances it emerged and developed and waned. The stages of the complex relations between the given 'x' and its concrete context cannot, however, be studied as synchronic occurrences only. We must further see the on-going diachronic processes from which the patterns surrounding the occurrences emerge in turn. Moreover, historicism requires that we grasp the totality of the setting, with its important traits brought out. The approach of genuine historicism is to seek the invariants which can be discerned over an extended period of time, if one separates the variables. It seeks also the antinomies which develop in the form of consciousness; antinomies which are relatively independent, but at the same time rooted in the social structure.

Before proceeding any further, I feel I should make it clear that among these concepts, I shall select those which most usefully concern the history of culture. Moreover, I shall regard the Marxist theory of historical process and social development in a specific way. I accept, of course, the main Marxist concept that *being* determines *consciousness*, but I hold reservations concerning the thesis that the productive forces, or the socio-economic relationships, or even both together, are the sole forces of human history. Neither technologism (absolutising the means of production) nor economism (absolutising the property relations) does justice, as is well recognised, to the original ideas of Marx. And even taking the two factors together, there remains the often repeated warning of the classic Marxist texts that the basic social phenomena are moulded in turn by the superstructure and, let me add, by the social consciousness, which includes the cultural heritage, the utopian line of thought, and so forth. Understandably, then, I am keen on interpreting this main concept—'being in relating to consciousness'—with the awareness that the *entire human praxis* confronted with the extra-human world (nature) produces the fundamental opposition between *the objective and subjective conditions*. This opposition provides for the conscious effort to shape reality and transcend the *status quo*.

Now, this sketch of an interpretation does not doubt the fact that Marxist theory made its contribution to historicism precisely because it stressed the relevance of the productive forces and of class antagonisms as motive powers of social change. Not even non-Marxist thinkers can deny that. What my interpretation implies, instead, is simply the *primacy* of the described opposition. Let me specify more closely this description of historicism.

(a) Anything occurring in the context of social life is regarded as conditioned by both human nature and human culture. Human nature, which includes unconscious and irrational components, is a relatively constant factor. However, it is necessarily and continually modified by the culture which surrounds it. The point of mediation between nature and culture can only be the human individual, who variably contributes to social events and products in the framework of cultural norms, the job role, the social era, location and so forth. The way to understand Marx's *das merischliche Gattungswesen* is not entirely clear. It seems, however, that Marx had in mind that there was both an *a priori* given to the human constitution and an *a posteriori* variant moulded by culture. It is exactly this mediation between nature and culture, therefore, that reveals the very ambiguity and aporetic character of man's existence.

(b) The forms of consciousness—science, philosophy, religion, morality, politics, everyday practices, etc—once socially moulded and observed to be distinctive from one another, further evolve through an interaction and interdependence of their autonomous discourses. Their status is affected by shifts of roles and hierarchies within the ever-evolving socio-historical structure. Here rules the *Uberdeterminierheit* principle (the principle of 'overdetermination') whereby, in the ever-recurring interplay of mutual dependencies, certain discourses or aspects of them, prove stronger and determinant.

(c) Class conflicts have shaped the global structure of the societies which developed civilisation to the present. Conflicts of classes have been articulated into latently or explicitly conflicting ideological positions. Such ideological positions have been influential within all the aspects of the social consciousness and especially in such primary institutions as the State. Even so, some aspects neutral to class will occur in consciousness—due to the influence of culture, with its social 'dreaming', its utopian projections, and due also to accretions to civilisation such as some moral tenets, eg fidelity, loyalty, heroism, etc. Through class-neutral aspects, we continually find confirmation of *Allgemein-Menschliches*, that is, of eternal human values. The entanglements of class and strong ideological commitments lead time and again to mystifications: inflected by the biases of class, utopian visions often reappear as mythologies. Lucidity amid this tension derives from developing a sharply critical stance towards the prevailing social norms, the shibboleths and conventions, and from self-awareness in regarding one's position. On this kind of basis can emerge the *potentielles Bewusstsein*, that is, the potential consciousness of understanding the evolving historical forces. But this lucid consciousness cannot be wholly preserved from alienation; look, for example, at Marx himself, or at Lukács in the 1920s.

(d) Linear social development is a delusion. Nor does history change by hazard and leaps. History demonstrates some laws, but no ironclad regularities. One can only find discernible long-term 'tendencies', which, as Marx noted in *Capital*, prove that the same cause and effect relationships do repeat themselves in given social circumstances. Thus, although the socio-economic basis permeates any society, the chief decisive forces and forms of consciousness will be the consequence of the complete social *praxis* in a specific historical setting (here one must refer to Marx's notion of 'unequal development' or to the 'overdetermination' of modern Marxist vocabulary). And again, the moving force of any society will prove to be as much the teleology of the collective subject as the material and technical capability, which is inert. The future of a society is at once determined and open. At its basis lies the advance of the productive forces and of the relations in economy and society. These include the responsiveness of the people who are oppressed. And in the end, a future-oriented vision and a strategy for *praxis* after revolution, can alone shape a forthcoming society which will have more than affluence, which will have pervasive justice and freedom.

(**e**) It is the goal of humanity to have a harmonious and voluntary cooperation among individuals. The realisation of human potentiality safeguards against alienation and loss of freedom. But humanity will not realise its goal unless it continually transgresses its given status, unless it endures a dramatic tension between means and ends, unless it understands the historical reality as always developing to a point beyond control, beyond planning, eluding prediction. Thus, too, the projection of a disalienated human community must be taken more as what is at the limit of our present horizons than as a precisely defined paradise.

(**f**) Marxist historicism offers definite answers to some basic axiological questions. For example, does value have an empirical character or is it irreducible to an empirically given syndrome of qualities? The Marxist view is that the bio-psychological conception of human appetites, interests and satisfactions will not explain value. Nor will the existentialist approach (the individual project of overcoming the naked *condition humaine*), nor will a socio-cultural theory (eg that of Durkheim and his disciples). Values have to be socio-historically determined, in the historicist view. Their ontological status cannot be other than culturally delimited. They do have a privileged status in ideology, but not even the sciences—the model of a sterile detachment—are value-free. Values emerge from the subject/object relationship in a given context. Whenever they are said to be of a transcendent (or transcendental) character, this is a kind of mystification, which in turn can be explained.

This outline does not exhaust the major points of a Marxist historicism. It exhibits, however, the main dialectical tools with which to address the chief antinomies of our thought: nature and culture, the historically relative and universal, the particular and the general, determinism and teleology, scientific prediction and utopianism, the notion of an ideal of perfectibility and a continually open-ended tension. These dialectical issues demonstrate that Marxism is of aporetic character. The studies of the Frankfurt School here seem very relevant.

Having outlined the general philosophical points of Marxist historicism, we shall now turn to a discussion of the historicist philosophy of art.

(**1**) No work of art will fail to engage the whole mind, the unconscious as well as the conscious. Yet the more one understands that what is analysable concerns the rationalised experiences of art and its objectified results, the more one is aware that no creative process can be apprehended to the very end. Every great work of art will, thus, have something of the mysterious in it, irreducible to a logically organised *explanans*. The historian's concern is obviously on the side of the rational mind. It ferrets out what is communicated and shared with others by means of a given code and system of norms.

Certainly the creative individual is conditioned as much as the rest of us by social setting (which includes the cultural tradition). However, what distinguishes the artist can be described as his memorable and at times even eccentric moulding and transmutation of these outside influences. In short, regarding the artist from the standpoint of the conscious mind and its objectified products, we have a subject matter both socio-historically determined and in some way beyond this determination. For the artist is *additus culturae* to the extent that he maintains control over his own creative dispositions.

This uniqueness which stems alike from the unconscious and conscious composition, resulting in effects which are irrational, mysterious, unexpected and original, is near to the wellspring of any genuine creativity. The *natural* endowment of the artist is brought into play. Thus we have a classic instance of the nature-vs-culture antinomy. Culture implies an historical conditioning that necessarily mediates all natural expression; as a result, the artistic process seems to be an archetypal case of the struggle to maintain and reveal an unsullied spontaneity against all convention, fixed rule and stereotype. This struggle is doomed both to failure and to a constant resurgence. The artist tries to inject nature into culture by virtue of his pristine selfhood, and more than others he is an example of *homo additus naturae* as he serves to channel the fundamental cultural resource to the surface of rapidly changing social life.

The nature-vs-culture antinomy also has another level. The artist seeks to bring forth the essence of nature itself. Thus, the chronicles of art and aesthetics are filled with notions of *natura naturata* and *natura naturans* and the recurrent practices founded on these ideas; the varying conceptions of Democritus, Plato and Aristotle on the question of mimesis are with us today, although the formulations have changed. The nature-vs-culture antinomy comes especially to the fore when artificiality seizes the upper hand: Boileau's prettified courtly 'nature', the neoclassical ideal, Baudelaire's dandyism, pop art's intensifications of the detritus of civilisation—all are examples of this. When nature is thus emphasised, one finds either the longing for a more perfect harmony between culture and nature, or a confused if spirited protest against the culture which shuts humanity off from nature. This dramatic tension between the natural and cultural can only be acted out on the stage of social history. Art, too, lives only on that stage.

(**2**) Art, in the process of birth, becomes gradually distinct from the other forms of social consciousness. Its genesis must be hypothesised, but the indications are that it emerged from two chief extrinsic sources which later, under changed circumstances and in altered frameworks, remained permanently as coordinates: these are *production* and *magic*. From the latter emerged religion, science and philosophy. Production has always involved technology and everyday practices. Then, as social life advanced and became more differentiated, one could add morality and politics to the motivating sources of art. Each of these social forms had influence on the artistic domain, and in turn borrowed from it. The distinctiveness of art always was somewhat in doubt due to this interchange. The autonomy of art was both real and unreal. The other forms of consciousness that threatened to infringe upon the artistic domain changed through time: from ancient to medieval times, one finds mythology, religion and craft considerations; in the Renaissance, technology and science; in the 17th and 18th centuries, politics and morality; from the 19th century onward, politics, economics and ethics. The alterations depended on the evolving economic and social structure, the phase of cultural evolution, whether one or another heritage was in decline or ascent, and, of course, the entire historical setting which conditioned the social structure.

Yet art held to its own conditions, it defended its prerogatives, it brought in the outside world only to recompose it. The result was a semi-independence which was fundamental not only to art's place in the larger setting, but also to the 'virtual' character of art. Virtuality, the German *Schein*, or appearance, employs the specific formal order and expressive qualities of the work of art which it combines with fictitiousness in many domains, leading to a simultaneous strength and weakness. Strength, because the incorporation of a virtual or 'rival' world allowed for transcendence of the world itself, a challenge to its intractable and unacceptable characteristics. Strength also because art was like religion, although more *in* the world—because it could offer some compensations, could nourish the dreams of a more acceptable reality, and could produce a human beauty against all-pervasive and choking ugliness.

And yet there was weakness because art could easily become a kind of narcotic (the Nietzschean *Rausch*): it pacified the spirit of revolt, it demobilised the practical energies that looked to reshaping the unendurable world. There was weakness even when the art was truly revolutionary: for the consequences of even this art were (alas) minimal. After the poets have strummed their angry song, the world remains as it was.

(3) From the start of civilisation, works of art have been ideologically biased and necessarily partial owing to their class complexion. Only occasionally, however, is there blatant connection between a class ideology (whether prevalent within the work, or resisted) and the ideological character of a given work of art. Usually that occurs only in times of overt class conflict, or of ostentatious class dominance. Most commonly it occurs in artistic fiction. Especially it is found in propaganda-laden works, where the aesthetic semi-autonomy is neglected so as to favour the moral, philosophical or political message.

Many are tempted to find a universal principle of class bias in art. This must be resisted on several grounds. First, there is the acknowledged difficulty of defining a class ideology for each distinct set of beliefs, attitudes and strivings, which, in effect, excludes the possibility of finding enough class equivalents to match the ideological syndromes. Second, in many works of art—even outstanding ones—ideology is all mixed up; the messages are confused. Moreover, in many works of music or painting, the ideological substratum is hardly decipherable. Third, since ruling-class patronage began to dissolve with the end of the 18th century, the creative intelligentsia has increasingly adopted an inter-class position sometimes identified as 'Bohemian'.

It is manifest that the ways in which the recent avant-garde has responded to the changes in civilisation cannot be reduced to a given class ideology. Thus, while Marxist historicism considers class involvement to be one of the key aspects of the socio-cultural context of any work of art, it is incorrect to proceed as though a key aspect were an all-deciding one. That is a methodological abuse, for although all works of art are historically conditioned, they are not necessarily to be described in terms of an equivalence in overt class conflict. Some works of art, and probably the greatest among them, are not adjusted to their context: they demand or imply what is not possible at the time. Nourishing this tendency is a store of archetypes collected in art by many generations who have experienced painful and often cruel social history. This antinomy between class-boundedness and the *Allgemein-Menschliches* (eternal human values) runs through all art and is made especially manifest by its best specimens. In fact—as already Marx observed in 1859—the values which endure through time are not the class-entangled values, but those springing from man's revolt against his alienation.

(4) The artists (and their works of art) involved to greater or lesser degree in the ideological controversies are by the same act drawn into mystifications which no one can elude. Any kind of utopian projection on the future or the past as an attempt at panacea is a mode of self-deception. The mystifications are the outcome of the alienation which has dogged human hopes since the beginning of history. One task the historicist philosopher of art faces is to analyse and explain the different modes assumed by the alienational situation and to establish the artist's attitude toward them.

Works of art can present evidence of alienation in various ways. They may fully correspond to the prevailing dominant class consciousness with its narrow horizons. They may be products of a shallow protest which ends in patent aestheticism. They may raise a challenge to alienation which is trenchant if they offer a ruthless critique of the dominant catch-phrases. The highest potential of a work of art for counter-alienational commitment is double. It may lucidly and thoroughly survey both the period's and the artist's own limitations. Or it may project a utopian vision of a disalienated world, anchoring such vision in the real potentials of history.

(5) As I said earlier, to speak about art means to discuss artistic values. Artistic values, once generated in early human history and developed to greater distinctiveness, are re-established in constant interdependence with other values. The aesthetic function of any work of art is enmeshed with its non-aesthetic functions, since other values (moral, political, philosophical, technological, etc) are inherent to artistic structures.

Another important assumption of methodology concerns the discrepancy between the variable canons of art at any given moment and the enduring aesthetic paradigms which enable one to regard the status of art as relatively stable through its long history. The antinomy between invariants and variants can be thought of as deriving from some 'laws of artistic valuation'. From such laws, however, no strict determinism follows.

A Historical Outline

I shall now survey the theories claiming to belong to the Marxist tradition. Chronologically, the first Marxist aesthetic theory was the 'scientistic' approach. It was presented by Plekhanov who had come under the influence not only of Taine, but also of the contemporary naturalistic tendencies in aesthetics. In the footnotes to *The Letters Without an Address*

Fernand Léger, *The Constructors*, final version 1950

André Fougeron, *National Defence*, 1950

we read: '*Scientific aesthetics does not provide art with any rules, of which so many were provided by Hegel.*' An aesthetics that provides no rules was understood by Plekhanov (according to his writings of the years 1897, 1905 and 1911 on Bielinski and Czernyszewski, and the polemics with Wolynski and Lanson) as a descriptive science, modelled on biology and physics. He explained the origins of a particular phenomenon by resorting to the sociological method and thus the answers he obtained were to be—in his view—assertions of ballistics.

According to Plekhanov, 'philosophical' or 'critical' aesthetics were equivalent to a position of maximum objectivity, founded on laws discovered by sociology. Furthermore, Plekhanov did not see any fundamental difference between aesthetics and art history, since both, while formulating the most general interdependencies between facts, had eventually to explain them in terms of the same unavoidable social laws. A similar theory was proposed by Mehring in his *Aesthetic Explorations*. In the 1920s this trend was continued by Bucharin, Szmit and scholars of the Fricze and Pieriewierzew research centres. These groups were connected with the Marxist philosophers who advocated the mechanistic approach.

The conception promoting the use of the 'philosophical' approach in aesthetic investigation (the roots of which can be traced back to Marx) was clearly formulated in the writings of Lukács and Gramsci. According to this conception, genuine Marxist investigation lies in the dialectical analysis of artistic knowledge, artistic alienation, and aesthetic ideal. In fact, none of these issues—so the theory went—can be properly scrutinised without the philosophical method. The inquiry is now directed towards artistic values and their hierarchy; the processes of valuation and ranking are analysed against the background of a more general anthropological set of problems. The analysis of cognitive, moral and socio-political values takes priority over the analysis of mere formal-compositional values.

A philosophical method of analysis concentrates on artistic production as formulated within a particular socio-cultural process and on its ever-changing cause-effect relations with outside factors. This method is particularly effective as a means to penetrate into the internal contradictions of an artistic phenomenon. A model for such a philosophical analysis was proposed by Lucien Goldmann. According to Goldmann, in all research—aesthetics included—we cannot but start with a certain total vision which has to be eventually particularised.

Thus, we proceed from external empirically verifiable factors back towards our general assumptions. Explanation and hermeneutic procedures cannot eliminate the axiological engagement: while studying, we are invariably evaluating. This occurs immediately when we accept the implicit or explicit categories of selection. Secondly, we are forced—especially in the case of the humanities—to take into consideration our own selves (the cognitive subjects), as we are involved in the historical process that constitutes the object of investigation.

Following Lukács, Goldmann labels such valuating attitudes brought by the subject as 'ideology'. He certainly, however, does not abandon—as does Lukács—the defence of its objective or scientific character. For, we (as the cognitive subjects) are an empirical fact in the framework of a specific social structure. This means that certain value judgements make it possible to understand our position and the position of others, our own ideas as well as those of others and, by referring to social reality, to point to their internal conflicts.[2]

One cannot eradicate the limitations of the cognitive subject, but it is possible—through a critical attitude toward one's own presuppositions, through methodological doubts with respect to the ideas acquired and established around us—to determine what points of departure are acceptable. For Goldmann, socio-metric and psycho-sociological studies are insufficient. The reality of a phenomenon is unmasked only through the dialectical method of establishing objective-subjective values.

This is why, in his *Recherches dialectiques* of 1959, speaking of the methods of investigation of a historian of literature, he stresses the importance of the philosophical attitude and not the scientistic attitude *sensu stricto*. Every artist—writes Goldmann—communicates a specific way of feeling, thinking and evaluating. A scholar is expected, therefore, to clarify by referring to the socio-historical infrastructure and the philosophical premises contained in the work of art—the specific value perspective of the artist, the internal logic of his work, its immanent contradictions and its relation to existing or potential consciousness.

The method practised and recommended by Lukács and Goldmann has certain points in common with Deborin's school in the USSR, where philosophic analysis replaced scientistic analysis. But one must not confuse Lukács' orientation with the attempts which, since the 1930s, may be encountered in certain Soviet textbooks and monographs. In such textbooks, Hegelianism—devoid of any living methodological content—was mostly a verbal game. Similarly, in more recent works—by Kagan, Stolovicz, and others—nothing is said about the peculiarities of the method, while it is tacitly assumed that there must be unmitigated agreement with the premises of the Marxist philosophy.

J Boriev[3] speaks of the 'historical' method. By historical method he understands a process of investigation whereby artistic phenomena are studied in their emergence and evolution. Though promising, such a methodological outline has been neither sufficiently developed nor made relevant to the inquiry into aesthetic investigation. There are still other basic theories that lead to the same theme in Marxism; as, for example, the aesthetic conceptions of the Englightenment, of the young Germany and of the French artistic disputes of the mid-19th century.

Sometimes, as still in the Soviet Union, the idea of the dialectical method is identified with the idea of the scientistic method. It is impossible to say, then, whether philosophical and scientistic procedures mean the same or perhaps something different. In other words, do they have in mind an autonomous philosophical method that can be scientifically verified, or do they treat dialectics as a general, highest possible science?

Returning to Lukács and Goldmann, yet another reservation must be made. Goldmann—as his arguments indicate—does not reject the applicability of strictly scientistic methods; he simply considers them insufficient. But this opinion is formulated so vaguely that one cannot be certain whether, for example, psycho-sociological methods in the investigation of art are recommended by him or whether they should be abandoned, or, to put it differently, whether they are helpful, neutral or harmful. On the basis of Goldmann's initial assumptions, it would appear that psycho-sociological methods of analysis should be encouraged since external facts under investigation as well as the investigating subject involved are empirical data themselves.

Goldmann, by refraining from stating an opinion on the subject, leaves the question of sociologism open. And yet, the research procedures of both Lukács and Goldmann exhibit a tendency towards subordinating sociological analyses to a most general, philosophical point of view. Their position, however, is less radical than that of Gramsci or Block, who do not admit that the philosophy of art can be verifiable. Such a viewpoint, while not undermining the relative relevance of scientism, maintains that the fundamental truth about art is mainly arrived at through philosophical insight and not through scientific verification.

Another methodological interpretation was offered by Lunaczarski and M Raphael. The former never abandoned the scientist interests of his youth, when, influenced by Avenarius and Spencer, he wrote the *Fundamentals of Positive Aesthetics*. However, already during 1905–1917, he accepted the anthropological-historical interpretation which he based on Marx's legacy. Later, in his *The Fundamentals of the Sociology of Music*, 1927, attempting to assimilate the results of scientific inquiry, philosophical investigation and psycho-sociological analysis he writes:

'... *every complete theory of art should contain: a) a physical analysis that would examine the elements of a particular art in an experimental and mathematical fashion, b) a physical analysis containing primarily reflexiology and also, of course, the study of the development of certain organs and the function of the nervous system, c) a sociological or psycho-sociological analysis, namely the theory of a particular art as a social phenomenon ...*'[4]

Lunaczarski examined particular artists, their work and their developing style, by taking into consideration the physio-psychological components as well, stressing the importance of genetic and functional analysis. In his 1909 studies on Russian Symbolism, Gorki and Mayakovski, entitled *Philosophical Poems in Colour and Marble*, as well as in his interpretation of Modern Art, Lunaczarski adopted a philosophical method of investigation, very similar to Goldmann's.

In his essay *Lenin and Literary Criticism* of 1932, a vagueness even more striking than that seen in Goldmann's methodological credo is evident. His theoretical declarations leave enough room for two interpretations: the interchangeability of the philosophical and special methods, or the integration of the special methods within the framework of the philosophical method. His research practice supports rather the first version.

A similar case may be found in the work of Max Raphael. In his essay *Empirische Kunstwissenschaft* of 1941, there is evidence of the author's inner struggle. He wanted to reconcile the empirical with the mathematical approaches to art, and, in addition, to subordinate these specific methods to the philosophical method (the dialectical theory). Raphael's doubts may be seen clearly in the fact that Marxist dialectics were to appropriate also the phenomenological method characterised, in fact, in such a way that it would be difficult to ascribe it to Husserl and his followers.

In his studies, Raphael[5] wavered between a descriptive analysis, a genetico-functional one, and an axiological interpretation aiming at supra-historical values. The inconsistencies and weaknesses of Max Raphael's arguments demonstrate that he was unable to cope positively with the methodological issues formulated here. What is important, however, is the presupposition which, as in the case of Lunaczarski, seems to result from the correct understanding of the Marxist legacy and may lead toward a promising path of inquiry.

Roughly speaking, the same aesthetic strategies are operative in present day Marxist orientated aesthetics. Pierre Macherey's *Pour une théorie de la production littéraire* of 1966, extends Althusserian premises and conclusions into the study of artistic phenomena. *Mimesis* is questioned as the basic category, while the production of an autotelic world by means of peculiar media and discourse is emphasised. The meaning of any given work of art is uncovered through a *lecture symptomale*, that is, through a reading that reflects not so much upon the content and form of the artistic message as on its ideological limitations, omissions and concealments. Anthropological approaches of analysis are rejected as totally arbitrary (since they are based on the ideas of creative impulse, expression, transcendence, etc), leaving the scholar unable to explain the implications and complexities of artistic communication.

Anthropology rests on ideological presuppositions which cannot explain ideology. The work of art is always misunderstood and mystified when one takes it literally (textually); or in direct relation to reality; or as permanently ambiguous, open to any kind of reading (because of the mysteries of the human spirit); or as conforming to a canon which must be fulfilled (normative aesthetics). Once the sense of artistic production (with the aesthetic operative procedures pertaining to it) is apprehended as establishing an indefinite object for study, there arises the demand for a critical, beyond-ideology production. This is to say that criticism, similar to proper philosophy, *produces* the subject-matter of its study, never identical with the artistic message because the appropriate meta-artistic discourse employed by the art theorist or critic is and must be distinctive, ie, scientific.

One reconstructs ideology by displacing oneself from it totally; one analyses the artist's parodistic use of the ideological references; that is, one explicates the artist's meaning-free decisions, which nevertheless let the work speak more than he wanted. Why? Because art is bound to ideology and is always at odds with it. Thus, the labyrinth to be described and classified is the ideological nexus of the given time and space, not the ineffable work of art. The work's pitfalls—its 'deep truth'—are indeed ideological absences and presences; they reveal the clashes of the surrounding world. The techniques of analysis need to pinpoint them.

This scientific approach in aesthetics is seconded by the Poznari school. In the book entitled *Value, Work of Art, Meaning* of 1975, edited by Jercy Kmila, the latter and his disciples assume that any artistic process is rational and meaningful; its results constitute particular values which are to be interpreted within the codes and norms dominating the given cultural setting. Thus, the way in which any work of art is analysed, judged, and referred to its socio-historical context, bears on the rules sanctioned by that system of culture. These basic rules are called the principles of interpretation. This rational psycho-sociology, rooted in the foundations of historical materialism, needs no special complementing, philosophical method. It is incompatible with the historiosophic approach (art as the utopian project, the challenge to reality, steered by the disalienational ideal) which lies at the core of the aesthetics of Bloch, Fischer, or Garaudy.

For, in the latter context, the philosophico-aesthetic discourse grasps the essential features of human condition exactly through artistic objectified expression. Both the artist and the philosopher are conscious that there remains always something residual, *not* explicated, to the very end. Art and aesthetics, philosophically comprehended, are seen here as the most revealing ways of enhancing man's antinomic dialectics of existence, his *ought* against *is*, his dependencies on the given socio-historical mediations and his constant attempt to transcend the necessities of the here and now. Philosophy of defeat and hope, adjustment and revolt, cognition and envisioning, replaces here scientific comprehension, the sheer explaining and verification of the feedback relations between artist and audience, against the background of the given socio-cultural tradition.

This essay has been able to offer only the most condensed sketch of the difficult and intricate questions it raises.[6] To offer more, I fear, would require treatment at book length; this stands, therefore, only as a set of preliminary notes.

Notes

1. By 'historicism', Stefan Morawski refers to a *philosophy of history* which, however, is not merely empirical or relativist, nor captive to an abstract idea, but which observes and constitutes the patternings in historical occurrences. Morawski, in fact, works with the *logisch-historische Methode*, well known to be that of Marx and Engels. In other words, he bases his inquiry on the strategem outlined by Marx in the *Grundrisse*, according to which humanity is found '*in der absoluten Bewegung des Werdens.*'
2. Cf Lucien Goldmann, *Materialisme dialectique et histoire de la littérature*, Paris 1959, pp 55–56. In an essay of 1947 entitled *Materialisme dialectique et histoire de la philosophie*, Lucien Goldmann maintains that a scholar should deal with (a) a total world view, (b) the inconsistencies within it resulting from conflicts caused by philosophical survivals, (c) its internal quarrels resulting from the elimination of conflict themes with respect to reality, and (d) its limitations arising from a personal version of the world; cf pp 39–40.
3. Cf J Boriev, *Wiediednije w estietiku*, Moscow 1965, pp 16–21, 25–28.
4. Cf Lunaczarski, *W mirie muziki*, Moscow 1958, pp 149–50.
5. Cf Max Raphael, *The Demands of Art*, Princeton 1958.
6. Many of the aspects have been treated in my collection of essays dating from 1961–67 and revised in 1972, *Inquiries into the Fundamentals of Aesthetics* (MIT Press, Cambridge, Mass 1974).

Fourier, or the Arcades
WALTER BENJAMIN
1892–1940

Interior of a Parisian arcade, c 1810 (from J F Geist, *Passagen*, Munich, Prestel, 1969)

Most of the Paris arcades came into being during the decade and a half which followed 1822. The first condition of their emergence was the boom in the textile trade. The *magasins de nouveauté*, the first establishments that kept large stocks of goods on the premises, began to appear. They were the forerunners of the department stores. It was the time of which Balzac wrote: '*The great poem of display chants its stanzas of colour from the Madeleine to

> **WALTER BENJAMIN** was born in 1892. He studied philosophy and literature, and as a student he was an active member of the radical literary movements of pre-war Germany. After the First World War he worked as a freelance critic and translator. Following the Nazi take-over, Benjamin left Germany and moved to Paris. He committed suicide in 1940 while attempting to escape from occupied France to Spain. In 1955, the two-volume German edition of Benjamin's writings was edited and introduced by his first and only disciple Theodor W Adorno. This publication, under the title *Schriften* (Suhrkamp Verlag, Frankfurt AM), brought Benjamin an immediate posthumous fame. Among the English translations of his writings, we note: *Illuminations*; *Charles Baudelaire: A Lyric Poet in the Era of High Capitalism*; *The Origin of German Tragic Drama*; *Understanding Brecht*.

the gate of Saint-Denis'. The arcades were centres of the luxury-goods trade. The manner in which they were fitted out displayed Art in the service of the salesman. Contemporaries never tired of admiring them. For long afterwards they remained a point of attraction for foreigners. An illustrated Paris guide said: '*These arcades, a new contrivance of industrial luxury, are glass-covered, marble-floored passages through entire blocks of houses, whose proprietors have joined forces in the venture. On both sides of these passages, which obtain their light from above, there are arrayed the most elegant shops, so that such an arcade is a city, indeed a world, in miniature.*' The arcades were the setting for the first gas-lighting.

The beginnings of construction in iron constituted the second condition for the appearance of the arcades. The Empire had seen in this technique a contribution to the renewal of architecture in the sense of ancient Greece. The architectural theorist Bötticher expressed the general conviction when he said that '*with regard to the art-forms of the new system, the formal principle of the Hellenic mode*' must come into force. Empire was the style of revolutionary terrorism, for which the State was an end in itself. Just as Napoleon little realised the functional nature of the State as instrument of the rule of the bourgeois class, so the master-builders of his time equally little realised the functional nature of iron, with which the constructional principle entered upon its rule in architecture. These master-builders fashioned supports in the style of the Pompeian column, factories in the style of dwelling-houses, just as later the first railway stations were modelled on *chalets*. '*Construction occupies the role of the subconscious.*' Nevertheless, the concept of the engineer, which came originally from the Revolutionary Wars, began to gain ground, and the struggles between builder and decorator, Ecole Polytechnique and Ecole des Beaux Arts, began.

With iron, an artificial building material appeared for the first time in the history of architecture. It went through a development whose tempo accelerated during the course of the century. This received its decisive impulse when it turned out that the locomotive with which experiments had been made since the end of the twenties could only be utilised on iron rails. The rail was the first iron unit of construction, the forerunner of the girder. Iron was avoided for dwelling-houses, and made use of for arcades, exhibition halls, railway stations – buildings which served transitory purposes. Simultaneously, the architectonic areas in which glass was employed were extended. But the social conditions for its increased utilisation as a building material only came into being a hundred years later. In Scheerbart's *Glass Architecture* (1914) it still appeared in the context of the Utopia.

Chaque époque rêve la suivante.

Michelet, *Avenir! Avenir!*

To the form of the new means of production, which to begin with is still dominated by the old (Marx), there correspond images in the collective consciousness in which the new and the old are intermingled. These images are ideals, and in them the collective seeks not only to transfigure, but also to transcend, the immaturity of the social product and the deficiencies of the social order of production. In these ideals there also emerges a vigorous aspiration to break with what is out-dated – which means, however, with the most recent past. These tendencies turn the fantasy, which gains its initial stimulus from the new, back upon the primal past. In the dream in which every epoch sees in images the epoch which is to succeed it, the latter appears coupled with elements of prehistory – that is to say of a classless society. The experiences of this society, which have their store-place in the collective unconscious, interact with the new to give birth to the utopias which leave their traces in a thousand configurations of life, from permanent buildings to ephemeral fashions.

Walter Benjamin, 'Paris – the Capital of the Nineteenth Century', (translator Quintin Hoare) in *Charles Baudelaire: a Lyric Poet in the Era of High Capitalism*, NLB, London, 1973, pp 157–159.

Residues of a Dream World
KURT FORSTER
b 1935

Walter Benjamin (1892–1940) began as a historian of literature and ended up a radical critic of the very culture that had made him and his subject a specialty. One of the finest minds in a century-long tradition of literary culture in Germany, Benjamin came to penetrate the isolation to which both institutional culture and his scholarship had committed him with his growing recognition of its historical conditions. His studies of 19th-century literature opened a shielded past to the questions of later generations. Instead of immobilising works of art in their own epoch, he investigated them like a detective from a later time, inspecting the abandoned sites of life, turning up clues to events one could know only from hindsight. Keeping track of what happened to works of art after their time led him to recognise both their contingency and their potentially lasting validity.

But their validity could not be static, quintessentially representing their time; rather, as Benjamin wrote in 1938 with critical reference to Plekhanov, the validity of a work of art changes with the *'different epochs that turn their glance back on it. To define its significance with respect to the social structure at the time of its origin amounts to a definition of the work's capacity to give access to the time of its creation through the history of its impact, even to the most remote and alien later epochs.'*[1] Not only does the work of art change its nature when approached through the history of its impact, art itself ceases to be a province with secure boundaries.

When Benjamin attempted to map the topography of Baudelaire's imagination by extending his reading of the poet into a panoramic view of 19th-century Parisian culture, the city herself rather than the poet emerged as the protagonist of historical change. *'What is unique in Baudelaire's poetry is that the image of women and death are permeated by a third, that of Paris,'* observed Benjamin. He found both the remote vanishing point and the contemporary frame for his image in the city:

'The Paris of Baudelaire's poems is a submerged city, more submarine than subterranean. The chthonic elements of the city—its topographical formation, the old deserted bed of the Seine—doubtless left their impression on his work. Yet what is decisive in Baudelaire's 'deathly idyll' of the city is a social, modern substratum. Modernity is a main accent in his poetry ... It is precisely modernity that is always quoting primeval history. This happens here through the ambiguity attending the social relationships and products of this epoch. Ambiguity is the pictorial image of dialectics, the law of dialectics seen at a standstill.'[2]

This state of ambiguity could not last. As the century

Entrance to the Passage des Panoramas from rue Vivienne (from J F Geist, *Passagen*, Munich, Prestel, 1969)

KURT FORSTER was born in Zurich in 1935. He studied in Germany, England, and Italy, and received his PhD in the History of Art and Architecture from Zurich University in 1961. He has taught at Yale University, the University of California at Berkeley, and Stanford University where he is a full professor specialising in the history of Renaissance art and architecture. He has also served as director of the Swiss Institute in Rome and he is a frequent lecturer at schools of architecture. His articles have appeared in *L'Arte*, the *Journal of the Society of Architectural Historians, Architectura, Archithese, New Literary History, Daedalus, Oppositions*, and elsewhere; he is now completing a book on the urban architecture of Mantua during the Renaissance, and further articles on Giulio Romano, the traditions of vernacular building, and on Palladio.

progressed, the historical realities breached the sphere of the individual work of art and began to shift the boundaries of art itself. Benjamin's study of Baudelaire raised the historically and imaginatively submerged city of Paris from her bed and isolated six sites in a kind of Surrealist dream of her 19th-century history: the Arcades, the Panoramas, World Exhibitions, Interiors, the Streets of Paris, and the Barricades.[3]

Hovering on the periphery of aesthetic and utilitarian categories, all are as much images, even fetishes, of themselves as they are enterprises of purpose. Yet they are undeniably also the latter. In ascending order, they project the massive physical transformation of the city into highly particular operations, such as the shopping arcades and the creation of commodity festivals in settings of advanced engineering for the world exhibitions, and they culminate in the dialectically linked private interior and the public phantasmagoria of panoramas. The near perfect imitation of nature in the panoramas suspends the category of painting just as the connections between the place of work and the private sphere are abolished by the antithetical terms of the interior as 'the retreat of art'[4] against the anonymous marketpace of the streets. Here the crowd reigns, but only its hum penetrates into the preciously insulated interior:

'The crowd is the veil through which the city lures the flâneur *... In it the city is now a landscape, now a room. Both, then, constitute the department store that even puts* flânerie *to use for commodity circulation.'*[5]

It is difficult to say whether Benjamin's shorthand of historical analysis or his clinical diagnosis of 19th-century ills is more compelling, but nobody before him had singled out the *sites* of profound historical change with such somnambulist certainly. In the commonplaces of the century he recognised what was common to them as places of historical fate. These *topoi* of the industrial age—the commercial arcade, the cult of commodities and progress, the anonymity of the streets, and the fetish of an artificial reality in the panoramas and in photography—constitute the landscape of a new age in which the language of man-made things replaced the dialogue with nature.

Benjamin began as a student of texts and, as early as 1916, his thoughts on language can only be compared with later tendencies toward a universal theory of semiotics.[6] He had a remarkable sense for the spatial range of texts, an ability to map out the structure of narrative. In his writings on Berlin, and especially in the vast project of *Paris, Capital of the Nineteenth Century*, he deciphered the topography of the city. But this book has no author and no definite date, it needs the student of palimpsests and the philologist. Benjamin was well prepared for both: able to decipher the displacements and distorted fragments, and to recognise the transformations, inserts, and falsifications. The unspoken escaped him no less than the spoken lie, and, above all, the language of *products* betrayed the processes of their making.

Benjamin understood the fundamental change in the very essence of architecture to be its removal from nature and craft to industry and planning. As an industrial product architecture can be analytically divided into the parts from which it is assembled. The discontinuous process of fabrication and assembly and the separation of design into increasingly unrelated branches effect the assimilation of building into industry.

Benjamin collapsed the historical distance between the architecture of his own and that of Baudelaire's times into the recognition of buildings as commodities, objects of speculation, and instruments of ideology. He exposed the truth in a novel history of the city in which Surrealist devices of shock, estrangement, and involuntary transformation remove individual phenomena from their familiar context, juxtapose them in bewildering contrasts, and reveal them as other than we believe to know them. As a means of historical analysis, Benjamin's method defies the categories of traditional scholarship and brings to mind Aby Warburg's psycho-historical view.[7] The peripeteia of the First World War, which paralysed the art historian with a shock of insight, equipped Benjamin with a penetrating and arresting gaze.

As an historian of the 19th century Benjamin analyses not so much what went on, but what went wrong. The demise of his own class and his precarious existence as a Jewish exile in Paris prevented him from a wistful cultivation of roots and continuities in the shelter of scholarship. His search was for the rifts in tradition, for the fatal breaks and repressions. His own experiences cast a light back into the 19th century; a raking light which deepens the shadows of even the slightest cracks and seems capable of penetrating the shallow surface of appearances. It is again the 'history of impact' (*Wirkungsgeschichte*) which yields to Benjamin's questioning of the 19th century a 20th-century answer:

'Balzac was the first to speak of the ruins of the bourgeoisie. But only Surrealism exposed them to view. The development of the forces of production reduced the wish symbols of the previous century to rubble even before the monuments representing them had crumbled. In the 19th century this development emancipated constructive forms from art ...'[8]

The development of structural and constructional techniques and the introduction of artificial building materials—chiefly iron and glass—was to change architecture as it had never been changed before. Eighteenth-century Classicism projected continuities from the primitive origins of architecture into its modern forms, but these speculative continuities snapped once and for all with the adoption of the new structural means furnished by industry. Over the span of a century, the new materials which had entered the realm of architecture in disguise slowly shed their masks and their skeletons displaced the architectural bodies of the past. If *'construction filled [originally] the role of the unconscious,'*[9] it achieved ego status and identity in the totally denuded projects of Le Corbusier's Dom-ino House and in Mies van der Rohe's Friedrichstrasse Towers. As structural schemes these projects put forward as architecture only that which was *not* a visible part of building before.

Benjamin perceived the historical events that led to this point within a framework for which he was indebted to Alois Riegl and to the early accounts of construction with iron and glass. He acknowledged the conceptual importance of Riegl's anonymous history of late antique art which touched in its very title (*Spätrömische Kunstindustrie*) on the impersonal force of historical change: industry. To be sure, Benjamin was also familiar with the history of modern building techniques; he never forgot Alfred Meyer's *Eisenbauten* (Iron Construction)

Entrance to the Passage des Panoramas from Boulevard Montmartre on the right, with the Théâtre des Variétés on the left (from J F Geist, *Passagen*, Munich, Prestel, 1969)

and he followed Giedion's early writings closely.[10] But he did not adopt Giedion's tenor of technocratic optimism, nor the metaphysical abstraction of Riegl's uniform *Kunstwollen* ('Will to Form').

Benjamin cleared the terrain of aesthetic destiny in favour of a dialectic mediation of form between the advance of industry and commerce on the one hand, and their transfiguration in ideology on the other. He avoided a reductionist view of culture and never implied that architecture and art merely 'reflect' their conditions as such. His reading of the urban palimpsest takes the fragmentary state of his evidence into account and his interpretation of certain types of construction never loses sight of their role in the cultural household of the epoch. The role of arcades, exhibitions and panoramas is fulfilled by the crowds in pursuit of commodities. Without the crowds they die, as indeed they did within an amazingly short time. Today, when some of their elements are preciously reintroduced into modern shopping centres—19th-century ornamental disguise of structure serving as an emblem of commercial kitsch in the 1970s, as a figment of tradition precisely where that tradition had originally been abolished—arcades of the last century have become the subject of industrial archaeology. Their principal investigator, Friedrich Geist,[11] starts out with the acknowledgement that his encyclopaedic work was triggered by the few sentences of Benjamin's *Fourier, or the Arcades*.[12]

In the 19th century, the ephemeral nature of arcades and panoramas, like their anonymity, resulted from their role: *'They are residues of a dream world,'* wrote Benjamin; and concluded that *'the realisation of dream elements in waking is the textbook example of dialectical thinking. For this reason dialectical thinking is the organ of historical awakening.'*[13] Within this analytical framework of commercial motivation and ideological transfiguration, the architecture of arcades, exhibition buildings, and panoramas assumes a far greater significance than their mere presence would warrant. They provide the sites of changing consciousness, and in the fulfillment of their role, they mark the historical passage of culture. All of them are containers of a particular sort, both empty and equipped in highly specialised ways. In this respect they recall one of the most ephemeral categories of building in recent centuries, theatres, where engineering was marshalled early and completely for the production of a dream world. But the dream worlds erected in Parisian arcades and at World exhibitions are not the stuff harmless fancy is made of. On the contrary, as Benjamin prophesied: *'each epoch not only dreams the next, but also, in dreaming, strives toward the moment of waking.'*[14]

Notes
1. W Benjamin, *Gesammelte Schriften*, Frankfurt M, 1972, III, p 543. Part of a review of Gisèlle Freund's *La photographie en France au dix-neuvième siècle*, which Benjamin wrote in 1938; author's translation.
2. Walter Benjamin, *Reflections; Essays, Aphorisms, Autobiographical Writings*, transl E Jephcott (New York and London, 1978), p 157.
3. The six chapters of *Paris, Capital of the Nineteenth Century*, have so far been published only in outline form, presumably as Benjamin submitted them to the *Institut für Sozialforschung*, then in New York. The extensive materials and manuscript versions of parts of this vast project, known as the *Passagenwerk* have yet to appear in the *Gesammelte Schriften*, ed by R Tiedemann and H Schweppenhäuser, Frankfurt/M.
4. *Reflections, op cit*, p 155.
5. *Ibid*, p 156.
6. See Benjamin's fundamental essay 'On Language as Such and on the Language of Man' in *Reflections, op cit*, pp 314–332.
7. Cf K W Forster, 'Aby Warburg's History of Art: Collective Memory and the Social Mediation of Images,' *Daedalus*, Vol 105, No 1, Winter 1976, pp 169–176.
8. *Reflections, op cit*, p 161.
9. *Ibid*, p 148.
10. Compare, eg Benjamin's reviews of these and other relevant publications in *Gesammelte Schriften*, III, 169f, 363, *passim*.
11. Friedrich Geist, *Passagen, ein Bautyp des 19 Jahrhunderts*, Munich, 1969.
12. The impact of Benjamin's thinking has been especially strong on Manfredo Tafuri and the younger scholars at the Venetian school of architecture; stronger than in Germany where the subtleties of Adorno's Frankfurt School lost ground rather precipitously to a single- (and often simple-) minded determinism.
13. *Reflections, op cit*, p 162.
14. *Ibid*, p 162.

Monument to the Third International
In Loud Voice
VIKTOR ŠKLOVSKIJ
b 1893

One day follows another like wagons heaped with strange and sundry carts, cannons, crowds crying who knows what. Days thunder like steam hammers, blow upon blow, they are already fused together and no longer take notice, just as men living along the sea no longer hear the crash of waves. The blows thud in our hearts, beneath our level of consciousness.

We live in the silence of an uproar.

Into this asphalt air an iron spiral was born, a project for a monument twice the height of St Isaac's Cathedral.

The spiral falls against one side and is supported by a strong inclining form.

Such is the fundamental structure of the Monument to the Third International, work of the painter Tatlin.

The swirls of the spiral are held together by a web of leaning structure; three geometric bodies rotate in its transparent core. At the bottom, a cylinder moves at a speed of one complete rotation per year; the pyramid above it does so once a month, the uppermost sphere revolves round itself once every 24 hours. Waves emanating from a radio transmitter at its summit extend the monument into the heavens.

For the first time, iron has taken wing and searches for its own artistic expression.

In the age of cranes, as beautiful as the wisest of Martians, iron has every right to fly into a passion, to remind people that since the time of Ovid our 'age' has not been called 'iron' in vain, even though we had no iron art.

One could discuss this monument at length. The bodies rotating within its body are small and light, a contrast to the immensity of the total volume. Rotation hardly changes its appearance: it seems more like an exercise than a realised form. The monument is permeated by a strange utilitarianism; even though it wasn't meant to be a paying piece of property, it is always in use.

According to the plan, the Soviet of the People's Commissary of the Whole World should rotate in the lower cylinder while the seat of ROSTA would be in the upper sphere.

In poetry, a word is not merely a word: it carries dozens, thousands of associations. This work is as soaked with associations as Petersburg air is soaked with snow in the middle of a blizzard.

The painter or author of 'counter-reliefs' is not free to block the anguish of associations which surge through the canvas of a painting or among the supports of an iron spiral. These works have semantics of their own.

It seems to me that Tatlin embraced the Soviet of the People's Commissary and ROSTA as new, usable artistic material from which to forge a new artistic form.

The monument is made of iron, glass and revolution.

Viktor Šklovskij, 'Monument to the Third International', *Chod Konja* (*The Knight's Move*), Moscow-Berlin, 1923.

Whenever I have to write a review, I always feel a bit like that state seal used by Tom, when he was king of England, to crack walnuts at Mark Twain's whim.

One really shouldn't jot things down about theatre or art in general: rather one should do thorough research, work in groups, in scholarly societies, and speak only when the foundations of a scientific poetry have been discovered – but then one must shout.

All the same, nuts still have to be broken.

One must write, if only to keep others from doing so and torturing you with their wit.

With such reservations, I shall discuss the production of a 'Mystery' underneath the portico of the Bourse.

I was only present at the dress rehearsal. I must discuss it in a disjointed manner.

I liked a good number of things about the direction. Most of all, it was lovely to see a parade brought into the 'Mystery' as an organic part of its structure. It gave rise to a very interesting division. A mass movement defined 'artistically', according to aesthetic laws, representing an oppressed people in revolt is equated to a 'prosaic' movement, one based on the utilitarian laws of an army. This use of extra-aesthetic material in a work of art struck me far more than the numerical size of the masses involved in the mystery.

The whole thing was dreamt up with a certain talent.

That's how art can be created. But it would be even more daring to juxtapose; to find an aesthetic relationship not between one aesthetic object and one that is not, but between two extra-aesthetic objects, directly relating two things that belong to the real world.

I think a work of art could be created by juxtaposing the northern part of a city with the southern.

The assault at the 'Kingdom of Liberty' gate is the most successful, the most powerful part of the entire production. The tension produced by the 'circensian chorus of the king' was far weaker.

To juxtapose a human body to a crowd of humans, is making it somehow heroic, or treating it with greater respect than we usually do.

The proportions of the production were good; they will be splendid when, as I was told, flood lights are brought in from the fortress of Peter and Paul. It's beautiful when stretches of water and city can take part in a performance. Perhaps the scale could still be increased and the composition extended into the whole city, including St Isaac's Square and the balloon floating above Urickij Square.

Even the cranes on the Neva, precursors of my friends, H G Wells' Martians, should act in such productions. A single spot light could conduct all the orchestras of the town and the drum roll of the cannons.

I envy the directors of the 'Mysteries'.

People with a loud voice like to speak out loud.

Viktor Šklovskij, 'In Loud Voice', *Chod Konja* (*The Knight's Move*), Moscow-Berlin, 1923.

VIKTOR ŠKLOVSKIJ was born in Petrograd in 1893. He was a founding member of the *Opojaz* group, a literary society focusing on the study of poetical language. Šklovskij soon became the most active member of this group and his theoretical thought influenced the Cubo-futurist circles of the time extensively. In 1922–23, while in Berlin for political reasons, Šklovskij published *Chod Konja* (*The Knight's Move*) and *Zoo*. In 1925 he published his masterpiece on Formalist theory entitled *O Teorii Prozy* (The Theory of Prose).

The Uncertainties of Formalism: Viktor Šklovskij and the Denuding of Art
MANFREDO TAFURI
b 1935

To re-assess one's own relationship with the instruments of criticism is – in my view – similar to examining the role played by those instruments in the various historical situations which conditioned their very origin and development. Surely, it is not 'method' as such that I refer to here. In a sense, the object of analysis itself determines the method or methods; that is to say, the results of analysis decide the fruitfulness of the method or methods chosen. When I stress – as I have done in the past – the need for an *infinite* analysis, this is precisely what I have in mind: the possibility of interrogating everything afresh, always using analytical tools of a different kind.[1]

But this is not our problem at the moment. In any case, analysis has its instruments; I think, however, that they themselves should be subjected to analysis if only to be freed from ideological contaminations. Which is to say that the instruments of criticism need to be sharpened periodically; they need to be taken back to their origins. Or rather: the *genesis* of our instruments of criticism must always be reconstructed anew.

In this essay, I have chosen a problematical area: I address the language of transgression codified by the *avant-garde*. What are the limits within which form is analysable in its own specificity? Is it possible to put forward hypotheses about the transformation of artistic languages without recourse to their internal laws? Once we have recognised that there exist no linear relations between forms and socio-economic contexts (which do nonetheless condition their existence), how can one write *history* on the basis of the vicissitudes of form alone? These are some of the questions which trouble today's historian, faced as he is with artistic experiments which are symbolic of an attitude that favours language rather than participation in the practical world.

Instead of offering abstract answers, I will retrace some guidelines laid down by Russian Formalism, the school of criticism which has focused most rigorously on the organisation of formal material. The reference to Russian Formalism is so implicit in contemporary thought that many contemporary analyses – perhaps unconsciously – have utilised Russian Formalism's specific procedures or categories; making direct historical comparisons, therefore, inevitable. It should be stressed, however, that Formalist analysis of the 1920s proved most successful in the examination of literary works; many of the structures, therefore, recognised as specific to poetic language cannot be transferred to non-verbal structures of communication. The Formalists themselves, when considering the language of the cinema, demonstrated that they were well

Tatlin and some assistants working on the model of the monument to the Third International, 1920. *Left to right* Sophia Dymshits-Tolstoya (Alexey Tolstoy's wife) sandpapering a joint, Tatlin, Shapiro nailing, Meyerson cutting out fittings (from Výtvarné Umění no 8–9, Prague, 1967)

MANFREDO TAFURI was born in Rome in 1935 and received his degree in architecture in 1960. Since 1968 he has been Professor of Architectural History at the Instituto Universitario di Architettura di Venezia, where he is director of the Department of Critical and Historical Analyses. He is a member of the 'Andrea Palladio' International Centre Committee, and he is editor of a series of books on art history by Officina publishers in Rome. He has lectured extensively in European universities, the Soviet Union and the United States, and his numerous articles have appeared in the main international journals of history, art and architecture. His books include *Progetto e utopia* (1973), translated as *Architecture and Utopia* (1976); *Jacopo Sansovino* (1972); *Teorie e storia dell'architettura* (1976), translated as *Theories and History of Architecture* (1980); *Architettura Contemporanea*, with F Dal Co (1979), translated as *Modern Architecture* (1980); *La sfera e il labirinto. Avanguardie e architettura da Piranesi agli '70.* (1980).

aware of such 'untranslatable-ness'.²

It is precisely in its relations with the *avant-garde* that Russian Formalism reveals its own ambiguities.³ Allied to the techniques of composition of the emerging artistic *avant-garde*, Russian Formalism proposed instruments of interpretation which tended to attribute to the past those very victories won by the *avant garde* itself. Paradoxically enough, transgression legitimises that very tradition it destroys. It is this realisation which makes it possible (that is, intelligible) to analyse the thought of Viktor Šklovskij, the most extremist of the adherents of the *Opojaz* group. It is this realisation which makes it possible to consider the development of his research as a coherent whole, despite the torments and crises it suffered from 1926 onwards.

In this essay, I will concern myself with the early writings of Šklovskij, from 1914 to *O teorii prozy* of 1925.⁴ This is not only because in the essays of the young Šklovskij the main preoccupations of the Formalist school appear the clearest, but also because the excesses which Šklovskij consciously indulges in prove to be – like all excesses – illuminating. They also reveal Formalism's most disturbing characteristic: the rigorous exclusion of all non-aesthetic meaning from the analysis of the work. It is well known that Šklovskij, Eichenbaum and Jacobson have defended jealously the specificity of the aesthetic message from any 'external' contamination. For them, the work of art is an autonomous universe, a concrete whole, a set of signs which refer only to themselves. This attitude, of course, had been characteristic of the Kantian and post-Kantian aesthetic tradition, but, as we shall see, in the case of Russian Formalism, the results were to be completely original. [...] It was between 1916 and 1917 that Lev Jakubinskij, Borish Kušner, Osip Brik, and Šklovskij contributed, among others, to the two volumes which mark the beginning of the mature phase of Formalist theory and of the polemic against the symbolist Potebnija.⁵ Formalism devoted itself to the exclusive study of the structures of poetic language. This extremism had an inevitable consequence: after the October Revolution, it occasioned the content-oriented criticisms of Lunačarskij and Trockij, which gave rise to crises, reflections and reconsiderations amidst the members of the Formalist group.

It does not seem fruitful, however, to trace the criticism which the Soviet culture of the 1920s directed against Formalism. Instead, it may be more profitable if we concentrate on the implications that the Formalist technique of analysis has had. Such analysis of Formalism must surely seem fruitful today, exactly when art and architecture so obstinately claim semantic roles or insist on rescuing their own specificity. One thing is certain: the *Opojaz* theoreticians locked poetic language in a laboratory; it remains to be seen whether that laboratory was simply glazed around or surrounded with impenetrable walls.

'In my theoretical work' [wrote Šklovskij in the preface to his 'O teorii prozy'], *'I have been concerned with the internal laws of literature. To use an industrial metaphor: I am not interested in the cotton world market or in the policies of the trusts, but solely in the type of yarn and in weaving techniques.'*⁶

This impenetrable wall erected by Šklovskij around the market place of poetic language has been interpreted as paradoxical and destined to crumble sooner or later. Thus, two of his statements have been quoted together gleefully: the first from his *Ulla, Ulla Marziani*, 1919 (later in *Chod Konja*, 1923); the second from an essay on Dante written in the late 1950s. *'Art has been always emancipated from life, and its colour has never reflected the colour of the flag which waved over the fortress of the city.'*⁷ Only to contradict himself 40 years later: *'in poetry, the colour of the flag is the colour of the soul, and the soul has a second incarnation: art.'* The contradiction, however, is only apparent. Recently, recalling his own formative years, Šklovskij wrote of Lev Jakibinskij (a pupil of de Courteney): *'the word (of practical language) has become a signal ... a coloured flag.'*⁸

Thus, what has changed is the *function* of the signal. The flag is coloured by its own light and rejects all other reflections in order to develop its own unique role: that of becoming a vehicle for *recognition*. Not simply in the sense of Mandel'stam, for whom poetry is the 'swelling joy of *recognition.*'⁹ Above all, it is the unveiling of the process of formation of a work of art which in itself constitutes a 'recognition'; in this sense, Šklovskij is the ally of Rodčenko, of Krinskij and of the left-wing of INCHUK. There seems to be some affinity between Šklovskij's unveiling of the process of formation of a work of art and what Benjamin calls the 'exposition value' of art as moulded by the technological universe. But it was Jan Mukařovský who, in 1934, made the connection between Šklovskij's delimitation of the aesthetic object and Herbart's formalism. Mukařovský realised that Herbartian formalism had served for Šklovskij as a 'launching pad' from which he could then aim beyond formalism.¹⁰ Concerning Šklovskij's 'composition', Mukařovský coined the following definition: *'what is meant by composition is the sum total of all the devices which make a poetic work into a meaningful whole.'* Thus 'meaning' reappears. The structuralism of the 1930s – like Šklovskij himself in his autobiographical book *Tret'ja fabrika*, 1926 – attempted to reconcile the internal dynamics of the artistic structure with the context in which it is set; with the *'weaving techniques'*, to use Šklovskij's own metaphor.

I am more concerned, however, with showing how Formalist theory understood the concept of the *priëm*, of the *ostranenie*, of the so-called *semantic shift*.

It is well known that for the theoreticians of the *Opojaz*, the poetic use of the image lies in the act of *estrangement*; that is, in the act of extracting an object from its habitual context by force, in order to situate it, artificially, on a different plane of reality. In this way, the 'distorted form' breaks the chain of habitual associations as well as the verbal or perceptual automatism. This is the shock effect in which Benjamin was to see the socialisation of the psychic reactions occasioned by the assembly line, by the 'surreality' of Max Bense, or by the semantic value attributed to the 'pre-established disorder' so dear in modern information theory. It is clear that, particularly for the early Šklovskij, the theory of the semantic shift is closely linked to the first manifestoes of Russian Futurism, like Kručënych's *zaum*, Klèbnikov's alliterations, or the assemblages of the Cubo-Futurist paintings. But the extending of the theory of *ostranenie* to areas outside the *avant-garde* – to the fiction of Tolstoij or Puškin – makes Formalist analysis an instrument which, in a sense, is dangerous for the *avant-garde* itself. If *every* work of art is the fruit of artificial devices, it is necessary to explain how such artificial devices can give rise to a totality called the 'work'.

'A work of literature,' maintained Šklovskij in 1921,[11] *'is the sum total of all stylistic devices employed in it.'* This formula is not so much mechanistic – as Erlich thinks[12] – but is linked to the technique of the a-logical montage characteristic of the pre-revolutionary Russian *avant-garde*. Furthermore, it is precisely such a conception of form as an agglomeration of devices which was to permit Šklovskij to comprehend the 'reliefs and counter-reliefs' of Tatlin, the paintings of Malevič and Ivan Puni, or the 'trans-mental' poetry of Kručenych. In fact, the concept of agglomeration was to lead to the technique of montage. It was no coincidence that in 1923 Šklovskij applied Formalism to the analysis of the techniques of cinematography.[13] What counts in 'montage' is the choice of the basic elements brought together and the method of achieving their harmony or clash; the emphasis is placed on the *materials* (the constituent elements) making up the montage and on the *procedure* of their assemblage.

By allowing the concepts of *materials* and *procedure* to emerge as substitutes for the traditional notions of *form* and *content*, Šklovskij underlined the *construction* of the work. The primacy of subject matter (*sjužet*) over narrative structure (*fabula*) reduced the *fabula* itself to a justification of the technical and formal procedure. The *priëm* which concerns the material not only deprives it of its sacred quality, it actually constitutes an instrument which communicates independently. The 'surprise' brought about the the *ostranenie* distorts the materials. Thus Šklovskij aims at determining the specific techniques which structure the semantic shift: to him, narration appears to be constructed by means of procedures like retardation or deceleration, ladder construction, framing or parallelism.

As Eichenbaum observed, in Šklovskij, the non-aesthetic materials, particularly those of a moral, social and political kind, are incorporated into the work as *justifications for the technique*; that is, as a way of satisfying the psychological craving for 'verisimilitude'. The materials, in other words, are bonded to the procedure only in so far as ideology and image adopt precise functions which give credence to the techniques of composition selected. This means that the materials are granted a life of their own: *art absorbs them and thereby stresses their autonomy*. The conventionality of art, its sidling gait, like the *'knight's oblique move'*, is in fact the reverse of a statement of freedom. In the 1923 preface to *Chod Konja*, Šklovskij compared procedure to the knight's oblique progress in chess. He wrote: *'the knight is not free; he moves obliquely for he is forbidden to follow a straight path.'*[14]

Something forces art, therefore, to travel oblique paths. The obstacles put up by the figments of the real are sidestepped so that they can be observed from unusual positions. The adventure into which art is forced is conditioned by 'revelations'. This implies a displacement of the time and space internal to the work vis-à-vis those of real life. This 'estrangement' operates on the co-ordinates of the artistic structure by distorting them. Distortion, dislocation, transgression – Klebnikov speaks of the *'splendid childish transgression'* – *show* the real as outer limit, giving it a solidity precisely by virtue of being 'other'. Art does not speak of this 'other'; therefore, this 'other' is its alternative subject.

'The literary work,' [wrote Šklovskij] *'is pure form. It is not an object nor a material, but a relationship between materials. And like any relationship, this one also has no dimension ... Humorous or tragic works, universal or particular ones, those contrasting one world with another, like contrasting a cat with a stone ... all are identical among themselves.'* And further: *'The selection of the material for a work of art is also made on the basis of formal criteria. Meaningful, perceptible dimensions are chosen. Each age has its own index, its own list of forbidden themes which are outworn.'*[15]

This does not mean that the *'forbidden themes'* do not continue to exist and operate: they surface continually, overcoming institutional censure *'just as repressed desires are always present in the psyche and appear in dreams from time to time, out of the blue.'* Šklovskij's interest in the *'forbidden themes'* takes us back to the question of *'materials'*: for even though they are devalued they still manage to have a valency, since the *'explosion'* which semantises the clash of forms cannot altogether fail to acknowledge the intrinsic power which each of them possesses. And further: once chosen, the materials constitute a *limit* for the work. The materials themselves create the obstacles which prevent the knight from moving in a straight line. In short: *the work itself puts up its own limits*; *it* alone arranges the obstacles it wishes to circumvent; it puts up barriers for itself of which it will never speak but which it will succeed in 'showing'. It is this very 'showing' which must be emphasised. Indirectly, we have returned to our initial problem: what is the significant stratum that is 'revealed' by the distortion of materials, by the *priëm*, by the act of 'estrangement'?

'We live in an enclosed and petty world,' [Šklovskij wrote in 1923]. *'We do not feel the world in which we live just as we do not feel the garments we wear. We fly through the world like Jules Verne's heroes, "through cosmic space in the belly of a rocket". But our rocket has no windows. The Pythagorians claim that we do not hear the music of the spheres because it rings all the time. Similarly, those who live by the seashore are so used to the sound of the waves, that they no longer hear it. We rarely hear the words we utter. We speak a poor language, the words of which are not thoroughly spoken. We look at each other, but we do not see each other. Our perception of the world has dried up and all we are left with is the faculty to recognise objects. We do not say "good morning", we say ... "morning". The whole world through which we move, the buildings we do not notice, the chairs on which we sit, the woman with whom we walk arm in arm, all mumble ... "morning".'*[16]

For Šklovskij, the 'disordering of objects' becomes imperative if language is to be made to speak. Everyday language has been trivialised. We are not told who or what has reduced the structure of communication to a series of aphasiac signals. What is certain is that everyday language is incapable of giving out articulate messages, despite the fact that the 'content' (even of the most privileged message, ie, the artistic message) lies exclusively in the organised arrangement of its elements.

But it is possible to read something more into Šklovskij's propositions. For him, words have become impotent because of a sort of historically determined 'semantic exhaustion'; because of an alienation which has struck at its roots the source from which communication arises. This implies that both for things and concepts there exists an original meaning which, nonetheless, is hidden by the reification of language and behaviour.

To test such an observation, it may be useful to refer back to one of Šklovskij's first theoretical texts. In his *Resurrection of the Word*, 1914, Šklovskij has not denied Potebnija's symbolist theories yet, and his propositions therefore become particularly important if compared with the clearly symbolic roots of Futurism (both Russian and Italian alike).

'When words are being used by our thought process in place of general concepts,' [wrote Šklovskij in 1914] *'and serve, so to speak, as algebraic symbols which need to be devoid of imagery, when they are used in everyday speech and are not completely enunciated or completely heard, then, they become familiar, and their internal (image) and external (sound) forms cannot be sensed. We do not sense the familiar, we do not see it, but simply recognise it. We do not see the walls of our rooms, it is so hard for us to spot a misprint in a proof – particularly if the language is well known to us.'*[17]

The word has suffered a loss. To be revitalised, it must be juxtaposed next to an adjective which will revive the word's 'figurative nature'. There is, therefore, no definite gap between the article of 1914 and that of 1923, even though in the second, semantic distortion has taken the position previously reserved for the adjective. In any case, the *priëm* emerges as an instrument which disalienates, a device which makes it possible to salvage the 'natural' relationship between name and thing, an act of violence done to convention so as to arrive at a primeval nucleus of meaning which is pre-existing but hidden somewhere under the floor of a 'sunken cathedral'.

But if Šklovskij's semantic distortion is a project of 're-cuperation', can his Formalism still be seen as deriving from the thought of Herbart or that of Fiedler? In his *Aphorisms on Art*, 1914, Fiedler wrote: *'Only the person who has recognised visible nature as something not completely stable and lacking in any absolute reality can understand the task of the work of art; just as the problem of knowing can be grasped only by someone who has realised that things have no absolute reality but only the form which they assume through it.'* This is the same Fiedler who, a few years earlier, had written that *'language is not an expression of being but a form of being.'* For Fiedler, art *constructs* new realities; for Šklovskij, art causes original meanings to resurface. Here, the relationship between the theories of Šklovskij and early Russian Futurism become clear. In the manifesto of February 1913 (signed by David Burljuk, N Burljuk, Elena Caro, Majakovskij, Nizen, Chlebnikov, Livsiž and Kručënych) which prefaces the book *Sadok sudej II*, we read: *'We consider the word a creator of myth; when the word dies, it gives birth to a myth and vice-versa.'*[18] Even the name *Gileja* chosen by the Burljuk brothers to designate the first Russian Futurist group, alluded to the primitivism of a search for roots. In the fifth paragraph of the *Declaration*, published by Kručënych in the summer of 1913, we read:

'Words die, the world is eternally young. The artist looks at the world with new eyes and, like Adam, gives to every thing its own name. The lily is beautiful, but the word "lily" has been

Malevich, *Arithmetic*, 1913, lithograph

sullied by fingers and defiled. Therefore, I call the lily euy *and, thus, its original purity is restored.'*[19]

This search for original etymons we find also in the 1913–15 paintings by Malevič; in the architecture of the *Živskulptarch* group; in Golosov's project for the Far East Pavilion at the 1923 Agricultural Exhibition of Moscow; or in Mel'nikov's peasant houses as well as in his 1923 Palace of Labour.[20] One might refer also to the pioneering contributions of Vladimir Mankov-Matveis who supported the St Petersburg painters of the *Union of Youth* (from 1913 onwards in association with the *Hylaea* group) and who, in the June 1912 issue of the Union's review, compared the laws of art with those of the game of chess; a probable source, as Nakov has noted, for Šklovskij's famous metaphor.[21]

Formalist theory now seemed to stand amidst a confusing number of literary attitudes. Šklovskij, when writing narrative prose (I have in mind the *Zoo* and *Sentimental Journey*, both of 1923[22]) experiments directly with highly metaphorical constructions, breaking up and dislocating real time, or incorporating portions of diaries and documentary material in order to obtain an effect of dovetailing and retardation. Both *Zoo* and *Sentimental Journey* were written in Berlin during a brief period of exile. The Alja who forces the writer to compose 'letters not of love' is only initially Elsa Triolet; ultimately, the 'cruel woman' for whom the letters are written, *is* Berlin culture. More exactly: the real subject to which the work refers is never spoken about. In *Sentimental Journey*, Šklovskij wrote:

'Art is basically ironic and destructive. It revives the world. Its task is to create deformity through confrontation.'

Irony takes the place formerly reserved for pathos. In its turn, criticism takes over the instruments hitherto belonging to the object of its analysis. It is not only the two volumes of 1923 which reveal the mastery with which Šklovskij uses the metaphor and technique of 'shift', but also the book which he dedicated to Majakovskij in 1940.[23] This would imply that analysis itself is imbued with structures similar to those of the artistic work it analyses. If irony shapes criticism, it is because criticism also constructs by destroying.

For instance, one might consider how Šklovskij describes Tatlin's spatial sculptures in *Chod Konja*.

'The rough version of a "counter-relief" is a sketch made with pieces of a certain personal paradise where there are neither names nor voids; where life does not resemble our missile flight, our way of existing by stages, from moment to moment like a journey along a road which one no longer notices. The new world must be a world without interruptions.'

With affectionate sarcasm, Šklovskij reminds Tatlin that the fragments of tin and iron which are the materials of the *'counter-relief'*, are *'pieces of a certain paradise'*; they make it possible to *'move away from painting'* but also to reconstruct metaphorically the unbroken continuum of a mythical Eden. A *'miracle'* would be needed for it to become part of the world, writes Šklovskij. The *'counter-relief'* is thus condemned to *'tend towards'*, to remain – like Lisickij's 'Proun' – pure aspiration, to live enclosed in a dream: analysis draws away from the artistic work through an excess of involvement. It is this very involvement which enables Šklovskij to understand the meaning of Tatlin's Monument to the Third International; born, as it were, *'in a paved air'*, the fruit of *'the silence of the uproar'*. A monument the materials of which are *'iron, glass and revolution'*, and which occasions *'tens, thousands of associations.'* The short article on Tatlin's monument is one of Šklovskij's few texts on architecture and the figurative arts. It makes clear, however, the kind of contribution Formalism was in a position to make to the analysis of non-verbal language. It should be noted that the *'revolution'* is placed alongside iron and glass as *'material'*. The *'Revolution'* is also a fragment of an ideal paradise which has no voids; it participates in the play of shifts which renders the object semantic. Assembled together, iron, glass and revolution create an 'other' universe in which space and time lose their weight. This makes the play of associations metaphorical and capable of infinite multiplication.

Admittedly, in such an interpretation the Tatlin monument is indeed a *'useless machine'*. As an object of propaganda, it does not work. But Šklovskij reminds us that it is paradoxical to *'hammer nails with a samovar'*. In *Chod Konja* he wrote:

'I do not wish to defend art in the name of art, but propaganda in the name of propaganda ... The "agitation" that was in the air, and with which the waters of the Neva were alive, can no longer be felt. A sort of vaccination has occurred against it, an immunity ... In the name of "agitation", take it out of art.'

In the 1920s and 1930s, Russian art and architecture could exist only by maintaining the tension between the defence of their own specific fields and the desire to go beyond their own limits. In the meantime, Šklovskij's analysis sketched a theory of art which excluded all poetic aesthetics. The real city can be experienced only *'stage by stage, from stopping-place to stopping-place.'* Form, closed within its own systems of self-examination, does not have the power to 'link'. The poetic word, all by itself, speaks also of the political word, which is equally alone. The knight's move is not the result of sophisticated cunning but of necessity. A reflection which we might find useful; we, the disenchanted players.

Notes
1 The term 'infinite' analysis is a reference to the text of Sigmund Freud, *Die Endliche und die unendliche Analyse*, in *Gesammelte werke*, XVI. On the possibility of using Freud's text for 'analytical work' in connection with artistic structures, cf Franco Rella, 'Introduzione', in *La critica freudiana*, Milan, 1977, pp 45 ff. Also see Manfredo Tafuri, *La sfera e il labirinto; Avanguardie e architettura da Piranesi agli anni '70*, Turin, 1980, pp 13 ff.
2 Cf the anthology, edited by Giorgio Kraiski, *I formalisti russi nel cinema*, Milan 1971, with texts by Eichenbaum, Tynianov, Brik and Šklovskij.
3 On Russian Formalism cf Victor Erlich, *The Russian Formalism*, The Hague 1954, 1964; Ignazio Ambrogio, *Formalismo e avanguardia*, Rome, 1968; Krystyna Pomorska, *Russian Formalist Theory and its Poetic Ambiance*, The Hague-Paris, 1968; Stephen S Bann and John E Bowlt, *Russian Formalism*, New York, 1973. On the relations between Formalism and the Russian and Soviet *avant-garde*, cf M Tafuri, 'Formalismo e avanguardia fra la NEP e il primo piano quinquennale' in *URSS 1917–1978. La città, l'architettura*, Rome-Paris, 1979, pp 17–65. A perceptive interpretation of Šklovskij's thought is to be found in the essay by Cesare Segre, 'Viktor Šklovskij e le strutture della pietà', in *Paragone* 1966, No 200. For a complete bibliography of works by and on Šklovskij, see Richard Sheldon, *Victor Šklovskij: an International Bibliography*, Ann Arbor, 1977.
4 V Šklovskij, *Voskrošenie slova* (*The Resurrection of the Word*), St Petersburg, 1914.
5 Cf *Sborniki po Teorii Poeticeskogo Jazika*, ed Osip Brik, Petrograd, Vypusk I 1916, Vypusk II 1917; for this cf, among others, Richard Sherwood, 'Victor Šklovskij and the development of early Formalist Theory on Prose Literature', in Bann and Bowlt, *Russian Formalism, op cit*, pp 26–40.
6 V Šklovskij, *O teorii prozy*, Moscow 1925, 1929.
7 V Šklovskij, 'Ulla ulla Marziani!' in *Iskusstvo Kommuny*, 1919, No 17, then in *Chod Konja* (*The Knight's move*) Moscow-Berlin, 1923, p 39, (Quoted in Erlich, *op cit*, p 57).
8 V Šklovskij, *Chudožestvennaja proza*, Moscow, 1961. Cf I Ambrogio, *Ideologie e tecniche letterarie*, Rome, 1974, for the chapter on Šklovskij, see pp 98–107.
9 Šklovskij, in a recent interview, recalled Mandel'stam's words, and stated shortly afterwards: *'The world exists, a world with which we struggle, always and for ever, just as Robinson Crusoe struggles with nature on a desert island. We fight with the world, we do not see it ... Art is continual amazement. A new perception of the world is born from amazement, and regains possession of it.'* V Šklovskij, *Testimone di un'epoca: Conversazioni con Serena Vitale*, Rome, 1979, for Mandel'stam's quotation see p 41; also see pp 51–52.
10 Jan Mukařovský, *Teoria della prosa di Viktor Šklovskij*, 1934, Italian translation in appendix to *O teorii prozy*, Einaudi, Turin, 1976, pp 303–312.
11 V Šklovskij, *Rozanov*, St Petersburg, 1921, p 15, (quoted in Erlich, *op cit*, p 70).
12 V Erlich, *Op cit*, p 70.
13 V Šklovskij, *Literatura i kinematograf*, Berlin, 1923.
14 V Šklovskij, *Chod Konja, op cit*.
15 *Ibid*.
16 V Šklovskij, *Literatura i Kinematograf, op cit*, p 11.
17 V Šklovskij, *Voskrešenie slova, op cit*. Quoted from the English translation in Bann and Bowlt, *Russian Formalism, op cit*, pp 41–42.
18 *Sadok sudej II*, St Petersburg, 1913, point 11 of 'The New Principles of Creation'. On the *Gileja* group, cf Vladimir Markov, *Russian Futurism: a History*, Berkeley-Los Angeles, 1968, chapter 2; also Vahan D Barooshian, *Russian Cubo-Futurism: 1910–1930. A study in Avant-Gardism*, The Hague-Paris, 1974.
19 Aleksej Eliseevič Kručënych, *Deklaracija slova kak takovogo*, pamphlet (lost), then printed in the scroll *Gramoty i deklaracii russkich futuristov*, 1913. Cf V Markov, *op cit*, chapter 4.
20 Cf Milka Bliznakov, 'The rationalist movement in Soviet architecture of the 1920s' in Bann and Bowlt, *op cit* pp 147–161; also Chan-Magomedov, 'Nikolaj Ladovskij' in *Lotus International* No 20, 1978, pp 104–124. On the spiritualist roots of Malevič, cf the introductory essay by Andrei B Nakov in K Malevič, *Ecrits*, Paris 1974.
21 A B Nakov, *op cit* p 67 of the Italian edition of Malevič's *Scritti*, Milan, 1977.
22 V Šklovskij, *Zoo ili pis'ma o neljuvj*, Moscow-Berlin, 1923; and *Sentimental'noe putešestvie*, Moscow-Berlin, 1923.
23 V Šklovskij, *O Majakovskom*, Moscow, 1940.

Translated from the original Italian by Judith Landry

Architecture and Ideology
GIULIO CARLO ARGAN
b 1909

Leon Krier, *Art, Architecture, Construction*

GIULIO CARLO ARGAN, born in Turin in 1909, has contributed greatly to the furthering of the arts and art scholarship. Graduating from the University of Turin in 1930, he began working for the Commission of Fine Arts in 1939, remaining there until 1955. But his administrative role never drew him away from his work as critic, historian, writer and teacher. A professor of medieval and modern art history, he is author of the important two volume work, the *History of Italian Art*. Other principal works include *Pre-Romanesque and Romanesque Architecture in Italy, Architecture of the Duecento and Trecento in Italy, Henry Moore, Walter Gropius and the Bauhaus, Borromini, Breuer, Baroque Architecture* and many others. In 1976, he was elected mayor of Rome.

After the experience of the Second World War, it was only too easy to criticise the cultural condition which had produced and fostered 'rationalist' achitecture. Certainly that culture's limitation was not in its marked politicisation, but in the insufficient clarity and resolution of its political vocation. In the same fashion, the fact that democracy had been over-nourished in many countries and that it was in a state of crisis everywhere did not mean that democracy was a politically incorrect or absurd solution, but only that it hadn't resolved all its internal contradictions nor attained sufficient strength to bear up against external attacks. It is certainly true that abstraction and utopianism were not only a part of architecture's social programme but part of a whole cultural condition. It is also true that the failure or insufficient success of the substantial contributions made by European intellectuals to the political struggle during the first post-war period was due to such abstraction and utopianism. But in the end, what else could modern architects have hoped to learn from that bitter experience if not that technical qualification, carried to its highest level by the 'rationalists', was not in itself a sufficient political qualification?

In the context of the recent bad experience, the attempt to de-politicise art, and architecture in particular, which is still going on today, is humanly comprehensible. However, it ceases to be so when, through excessive zeal, 'rationalist' architecture is claimed to be a kind of *sub specie aeternitatis*—not because of its political commitment, but worse yet, because its purpose is seen to rest on its relationship to technical and industrial progress and not on its relationship to the dramatic historical situation to which it had tried to react. Even the juxtaposition of the 'organic' formula to the 'rational' is humanly comprehensible as a dialectic attempt to break open a blocked situation. One mustn't forget that the 'organic' and the 'rational' are parallel phenomena, both requiring a historical situation which is substantially the same. The ideal of the nostalgic return to a 'natural' society is no less utopian than the ideal of a 'rational' society, nor is the theory of the 'intuitive' any less abstract than the theory of 'logic'. Rather, they are both clear indications of societies in crisis, even though the former marks a less acute and less imminent crisis than the one 'rationalist' architecture was facing.

Now that the crisis is expressing itself all over the world, it is necessary and appropriate to include the experiences of Wright and Aalto as essential data to the problem. Still, the data cannot be taken as the solution, nor is there any reason to remove a certain historical determination from Wright's or Aalto's work, even though it would invariably involve political evaluation. It is easy to recognise that these two masters were searching for the imaginative freedom of pure poetry in the fullness of plastic invention or perhaps, even in the happy re-discovery of forgotten nature. It cannot be denied that even the 'rationalism' of a Gropius, a Le Corbusier or a Mies van der Rohe, was born from a desire to attain a state of freedom, if not from the ultimate illusion of immunity carried to the heart of the struggle. Since the time that freedom was no longer an unbounded effusion in the immense domain of nature, but a moral elective to be conquered against internal and external obstacles, the world has not known a freedom that was not achieved through suffering and sometimes, tragic liberation. Every liberty is a liberty *from* something: the definition of that *from* is the most difficult moment on the road to freedom. It is very probable that European and American architects in the first half of this century defined that *from* imperfectly. Hopefully, architects today will dedicate themselves to going beyond the experience of earlier architecture, surpassing the limits or inhibitions that had kept others from realising their programmes without losing sight of their most authentic and vital moral impulses.

Giulio Carlo Argan, 'Architettura e ideologia' (1957), *Progetto e destine*, Il Saggiatore, Milan, 1977, pp 89–90.

The State of Defiance
MAURICE CULOT and PHILIPPE LEFEBVRE
b 1941 and b 1949

The thesis of this paper has been developed during the course of urban action and theoretical work on the city and can be summed up in the following three points.

Premise: An advanced industrial society inevitably engenders a process of total physical and social destruction of both the city and the country; just as it destroys history and thereby liberty.

Anti-industrial resistance: Resistance to this destructive process can be understood only as an act of defiance. Such an act of defiance can prove useful only if it is accompanied by a project of social significance; isolated architectural exemplars chosen from the history of architecture can be of no help here.

The practice of architecture: Architectural practice does not aim at creating an alternative to contemporary modes of production; it rather participates in the definition of a much greater project which integrates the preoccupations of the age. It is only in that sense that architectural practice gains historical significance and is, thereby, linked with reality.

In his essay *Architecture and Ideology*, Argan arrives at the conclusion that one should not repudiate the stimulating and authentic content animating the moral imperatives of the architects of the first half of this century; instead, since liberty is necessarily liberation *from something*, one should attempt to arrive at a clear definition of this *something*. It is not a question therefore of dismissing the influence of Wright or Gropius, but of evaluating their contributions in the light of a historical conjuncture that is inseparable from political criteria. With a lucidity almost scandalous for those years of economic optimism, Argan demands that all reflection on the future of Modern architecture should be allied no longer to technico-industrial progress, but rather to the dramatic historical situation against which it had so often reacted.

Some 20 years have passed since this thesis was first put forward; and yet, even the most rudimentary report on the state of contemporary European architecture reveals how inordinate was the optimism of the Mayor of Rome. Not because Italy and the other European countries were, in 1958, unaware of the degradation of cities and of the destruction of both urban and rural land, but rather because, at the time, everybody still hoped for change; that is, everybody thought that the systems of production could be channeled towards more or less 'happy' spatial and social solutions.

Certainly, today, Tokyo, London or Pittsburgh suffer less from atmospheric pollution than they did 20 or 50 years ago. And yet, the physical and social deterioration of urban and rural structures has accelerated and spread to such an extent

Sefik Birkiye, *La maison des fêtes*, 1979

MAURICE CULOT was born in Spain in 1941. He studied architecture at the La Cambre school in Brussels (1958–64). He worked at Frank Lloyd Wright's office (1964–65) and at Paolo Soleri's office in Arizona (1965–66). He is the founder and director of the Archives of Modern Architecture (Brussels, 1968) and the co-founder of the group ARAU (Atelier de Recherche et d'Action Urbaine, Brussels, 1968). From 1970 he taught at La Cambre, until the school's closure in 1979. He is an editor of the journal *AAM*. Since 1980 he is a director of the Institut Francais d'Architecture, Paris. His published work includes: *Rational Architecture* (1978); *Henri Sauvage*; *Lille, 1830–1930*; *The Landscape of Industry*: *Brussels 1900*; *Mallet-Stevens, Van de Velde*; *La Cambre, 1928–1978*; *La Tour Ferrée*.

PHILIPPE LEFEBVRE was born in Anvers in 1949. He studied architecture and urbanism at La Cambre school in Brussels, where he became Maurice Culot's assistant in 1975. His research has centred on urban renovation, and he has written and produced cabaret sketches about the city and its architecture today. A regular contributor to *Archives d'Architecture Moderne*, he is now preparing a book on conformity and public space.

that the average European takes it for granted that he has to walk wearing his 'blinkers', that is, seeing only what he wants to register positively, in the manner of these disciplined Japanese tourists.

Our daily environment has been so greatly altered that the irreversible nature of such destruction is evident to anyone with eyes to see: widespread pollution, fragmented countryside, dislocated urban networks, abusive priority given to private transport, etc. Such destruction is taking place in a definitive way and with no hope for return. The tower blocks of city centres are often badly built and their facades will cease to be fashionable, but they are there for ever. In an attempt to disguise this tragic fatality, Modernist architects insist that architecture should be ephemeral and adaptable to the 'changing rhythm of progress'. The virtue of the 'ephemeral' is doled out in massive doses: the hard drug of the avid consumer.

Instead, the concept of resistance implies that intelligence is not used to avoid answers, but to confront them. In other words, one should recognise that the process of total destruction *is* inescapable and irreversible: first, because the infrastructures already built are gigantic, necessitating excessive security measures which involve police authority and repression; second, because industrial societies have allowed themselves to be virtually blackmailed by the make-believe of 'progress'.

In view of such territorial devastation, Argan's proposition now seems a derisive critical tool. Just as, in the last few years, the focus of architecture has shifted from professional practice to academic reflection, so it is now moving from the historian's table to the realm of resistance. From back to front. The validity of the traditional links between Academia and the profession—that is, between the formation of authors of new projects and the actual production of architecture—has been shattered. In the same way, one ought to question the ties which bind the history of architecture to the so-called 'Modern' architecture; that is to say, to all contemporary production, and more precisely to post-World War II production.

Pessimism is necessary so that we advance beyond a reality which is today totally ensnared by cynicism and confusion. To admit the inescapable logic of total destruction, to realise that the guiding thread of history—tradition—has been broken and lost for ever, does not make one a deserter; rather, it shows one how to avoid the pitfalls of fragmentation, encouraging one to undertake a project which highlights the philosophical aspects of life. Such a project would attempt to integrate the knowledge acquired from the numerous struggles of inhabitants; it would address the utopian dimension of a city where functions are no longer isolated from each other; where the *quartier* offers simultaneously habitation, entertainment and work; where the emphasis is on communication between people and not on pointless mobility; where the formal division of labour has disappeared. Such a project would refuse to scrap the Model T-Ford after 20 years of production; it would not consider absurd the beating of egg-whites with a whisk; it would refuse to recognise big glazed apertures with aluminium frames as windows.

Such a project would also refuse to take responsibility for the economic strategy of favouring capital to the detriment of pleasurable work. Let us illustrate the effects of this strategy by means of an example taken from everyday life. We shall then see, that we are at the very heart of architectural criticism.

For several years now, the policy of public transport in Brussels consisted of replacing the traditional narrow-gauge tram lines with subterranean infrastructures and large carriages. According to the administrators, this policy has greatly improved the conditions of public transport in the Belgian capital. For the inhabitants of the city, however, this policy has proven a total failure. While the large carriages facilitate the daily exodus between the city and the suburbs, the public transport of the city proper is totally inefficient: train schedules have become infrequent and stations have moved away from the busy areas. Furthermore, the large carriages and tunnels have necessitated the construction of gigantic infrastructures which are in glaring opposition to the morphology of the actual town. The technicians, entrenched in specialist arguments, have effectively reduced the complexity of daily travel to a quantitative abstraction. In fact, engineering giantism ultimately aims not at the comfort of the inhabitants but at creating and maintaining speculative ventures. The transportation network in Brussels would have, thus, been better off if it was based on many little, comfortable trams which would run frequently at all hours of the day and night. For the city dweller, frequency is more important than speed. In other words, lots of little trams running all the time in every part of the city.

To adopt such a policy, of course, would presuppose that all suburbs and the consequent exodus of the inhabitants are eliminated. Furthermore, the production of thousands of little trams—for which the old models would prove worthy of creative imitation—would have encouraged an industry which, based on a highly specialised local work force, could have given expression to an inventive know-how, far more stimulating than the futility of contemporary 'design'.

Resistance, therefore, is much more than an emotional state and altogether different from a sense of *élan*; it is above all a state of non-acceptance which is immediately expressed in the form of a project. No attitude of reconstruction can exist outside this state of defiance. An analysis of contemporary conditions of construction shows the inability of the building industry to re-invent the past, whether in the millions of 'Phénix' maisonettes or the 'Gallaratese'. Exemplary buildings can only be false.

The political significance of a project conceived as a state of resistance does not reside in its eventual realisation: it is not a question of an architect in search of a site and a promoter. Furthermore, such a project is neither an alternative to present-day production, nor a modern version of the social utopias of the 19th century. Instead, it is the project's non-realisation that underlines its political value. This is not to say, of course, that the project is abstract or unrealistic; it simply means that it is rooted in tradition, or better, in the memory of tradition.

Categorisations like 'left' or 'right' do not prove useful here. Professional architects, whether with commercial or avant-garde interests, all seem to adopt the same attitude towards non-realisation: they all refuse to consider it even as a simple working hypothesis. Understandably so: for to accept utopia as a working hypothesis would mean admitting that they are

Leon Krier, Sefik Birkiye, *The Lake*

themselves the tools of a self-destructive society and not the creative artists they have dreamt of becoming. It is no longer a question of building 'commercially' or 'progressively', but of *building* or *abstaining from building*. This is not a strategy of doubt before an 'apocalypse'; it is not that certain emotional people risk disturbing the certainties of cynical practitioners. Contemporary doubt is by no means that of Descartes: it is not a method which leads to knowledge, but rather the expression of a collective fear *'as if we were living in and struggling with a protean universe where, at any moment, anything could be transformed into anything'*.[1]

Resistance is not, and has never been, a game: it presupposes continuity and the observance of rules; it is a 'security measure' conceived and practiced on an every-day scale; it is the heroism of those who reflect on the role the city could play in the development of democracy. Thus, when we contrast the strategy of doubt to the dictatorship of education, it is—in the words of Michel Bosquet—in order to provoke our interlocutor and ask him: *'are you ready to take upon yourself as an autonomous subject your own revolutionary choice?'*[2] Compliance to resistance is, therefore, not simply a matter of authority, but rather of authority and liberty at the same time. One of the principal objectives of resistance is to avoid the pitfalls of fragmentation by supporting those who fight for the preservation of the city and its historical components as tools of development; in other words, to participate in the struggle against the structures of industrial production.

In a revolutionary perspective, the avant-garde can only look towards history; partly because its projects should be familiar with it, but primarily because only the force of history can save us from futility. Just as a normal human being has a head, a trunk, two arms and two legs—and tailors do not make mistakes—so the city can only exist in its traditional form.

But are we not too naive to rely on the tenuous thread of tradition as an effective opposition to industrial production? Are we not underestimating the weight of current systems of production, the demands of trade-unionists or the attractions that the stimuli of consumption offer? Surely, these are all true; but there is no other way. One could attempt to re-establish our links with history at that very point where industrial capitalism has severed them: such an attempt would have been a seductive proposition were it not for the regressive hiatus which the 'destruction of memory' has already accomplished. Moreover, we should add that we have neither the courage, nor the time, nor the inclination to reconstruct a lost wisdom; our weaknesses are nostalgia and pleasure in things which last.

Just as a child builds a castle by piling up building blocks one after the other, similarly, knowledge can once again be acquired only through the utilisation of archaic methods. Archaism is here conceived as a rudimentary process of construction and as an aquaintance with the constituent elements of city building. This is an archaism which always proceeds from imitation: its models, however, are not defined by any heritage but are selected by the programme for the ideal city, as that emerges through research and urban struggle.

There is more to learn from the social project which animates the struggles in the working-class districts of, say, Brussels or Barcelona, than from the complete monographs of Wright, Le Corbusier, Gropius, or Aalto. They, along with all the other 'pioneers of Modern architecture' find their proper place in historiographic studies which are not likely to modify the course of history.

Argan's proposition that *'liberty is the liberation from something'* takes on a new meaning: this *something* no longer springs from ideology or metaphysics; it *is* the dominant mode of industrial and cultural production. We know what it is that we want to be liberated from; but also—and there lies our determination—we know *how*. The rest is merely a question of strategy.

Notes
1 H Arendt, *La Crise de la Culture*.
2 Michel Bosquet, 'Herbert Marcuse, professeur de liberté', *Le nouvel observateur*, August 6, 1979.

Architecture and Utopia
MANFREDO TAFURI
b 1935

Man Ray, *L'A*, 1941

MANFREDO TAFURI was born in Rome in 1935 and received his degree in architecture in 1960. Since 1968 he has been Professor of Architectural History at the Instituto Universitario di Architettura di Venezia, where he is director of the Department of Critical and Historical Analyses. He is a member of the 'Andrea Palladio' International Centre Committee, and he is editor of a series of books on art history by Officina publishers in Rome. He has lectured extensively in European universities, the Soviet Union and the United States, and his numerous articles have appeared in the main international journals of history, art and architecture. His books include *Progetto e utopia* (1973), translated as *Architecture and Utopia* (1976), *Jacopo Sansovino* (1972); *Teorie e storia dell'architettura* (1976), translated as *Theories and History of Architecture* (1980); *Architettura Contemporanea*, with F Dal Co (1979), translated as *Modern Architecture* (1980); *La sfera e il labirinto. Avanguardie e architettura da Piranesi agli '70.* (1980).

To ward off anguish by understanding and absorbing its causes would seem to be one of the principal ethical exigencies of bourgeois art. It matters little if the conflicts, contradictions, and lacerations that generate this anguish are temporarily reconciled by means of a complex mechanism, or if, through contemplative sublimation, catharsis is achieved.

The whole phenomenology of bourgeois anguish lies in the 'free' contemplation of destiny. It is impossible not to be confronted continually with the perspectives opened up by that freedom. In this tragic confrontation it is impossible not to perpetuate the experience of shock. The shock derived from the experience of the metropolis ... is in itself a way of rendering anguish 'active'. Munch's *Scream* already expressed the necessity of a *bridge* between the absolute 'emptiness' of the individual, capable of expressing himself only by a contracted phoneme, and the passivity of collective behaviour.

It is not just by chance that the metropolis, the place of absolute alienation, is at the very centre of concern of the avant-garde. From the time the capitalist system first needed to represent its own anguish—in order to continue to function, reassuring itself with that 'virile objectivity' discussed by Max Weber—ideology was able to bridge the gap between the exigencies of the bourgeois ethic and the universe of Necessity. [...]

The bourgeois intellectual's obligation to exist can be seen in the imperativeness his function assumes as a 'social' mission. Among the members of the intellectual 'avant-garde' there exists a sort of tacit understanding concerning their position, and the mere attempt to expose it arouses a chorus of indignant protests. Indeed, culture has identified its own function as mediator in such ideological terms that—all individual good faith aside—its cunning has reached the point where it imposes the forms of disputation and protest upon its own products. The higher the sublimation of the conflicts on a formal plane, the more hidden the cultural and social structures actually expressed by that sublimation.

Attacking the subject of architectural ideology from this point of view means trying to explain why the apparently most functional proposals for the reorganisation of this sector of capitalist development have had to suffer the most humiliating frustrations—why they can be presented even today as purely objective proposals devoid of any class connotation, or as mere 'alternatives', or even as points of direct clash between intellectuals and capital.

It should be stated immediately that I do not believe it to be by mere chance that many of the new and recent ideas on architecture have been gleaned from an accurate reexamination of the origins of the historical avant-garde movements. Going back to these origins, situated precisely in that period when bourgeois ideology and intellectual anticipation were intimately connected, the entire cycle of modern architecture can be viewed as a unitary development. This makes it possible to consider globally the formation of architectural ideologies and, in particular, their implications for the city.

But it will be necessary to recognise also the unitary character of the cycle undergone by bourgeois culture. In other words, it will be necessary to continually bear in mind the entire picture of its development.

It is significant that systematic research on Enlightenment architecture has been able to identify, on a purely ideological level, a great many of the contradictions that in diverse forms accompany the course of contemporary art.

The formation of the architect as an ideologist of society; the individualisation of the areas of intervention proper to city planning; the persuasive role of form in regard to the public, and the self-critical role of form in regard to its own problems and development; the interrelationship and opposition—at the level of formal research—between architectural 'object' and urban organisation: these are the constantly recurrent themes of the 'Enlightenment dialectic' on architecture.

Manfredo Tafuri, *Architecture and Utopia, Design and Capitalist Development*, transl. B L La Penta, London, MIT Press, 1976, chapter 1, pp 1–3.

Manfredo Tafuri: Neo-Avant-Garde and History
TOMAS LLORENS
b 1936

E quel che odi, non sai se ascolti
Da vir di neve in fuga un canto o un vento
O e in te e dilaga e parla la sorgente
Cupa tua, l'onda vaga tua del niente.[1]
                                    Franco Fortini

Among the forces which, over the last ten or fifteen years, have presided over the birth of the new avant-garde, none perhaps is more intriguing than the emergence of a new and problematic awareness of history. Nowhere has this awareness been more intense than in Italy. During the immediate postwar period, the anxiety to gain distance from the Fascist years seemed to demand a clean break with the past as well as a fundamentalist assertion of the future. Within the intellectual circles, this anxiety favoured a re-enactment of classical avant-garde attitudes. This urge was heightened by the memory of an Italian avant-gardist past and was made even more radical by the awareness that something had gone wrong in the relations between the avant-garde and Fascism.

R Poggioli has popularised the contrast between 'positive' and 'negative' avant-garde attitudes. Under different names this distinction was already implicit in the views on 20th-century art which were current in Italy immediately after the Second World War. In the first place, such a distinction was useful as a means of classifying the different avant-garde movements of our century into two clear-cut categories: on the one hand Expressionism, Surrealism, Dadaism, etc; and on the other, Cubism, Constructivism, De Stijl, Bauhaus, etc. Furthermore, it provided a means of conceptualising the two kinds of abstraction which seemed to embody – from the point of view of Italian art criticism in the 1950s – the ultimate stage of modern art: on the one hand 'informal', 'gestural', 'expressive' abstraction; on the other, 'geometrical', 'experimental' abstraction.[2] It is interesting to note that this double use presupposed an understanding of the immediate present in the light of historical precedent. Furthermore, the criterion upon which such a dichotomy was based, presupposed the question of how the avant-garde could best accomplish its mission in the face of history, that is, how it could best progress.

It is also necessary to note that the 'positive' category was sometimes called 'constructivist', revealing a sort of synecdochal extension of the avant-garde movement which had prevailed in Russia after the Revolution. This protracted validity of the concept suggested that, beyond its use as a classificatory criterion, the dichotomy 'negative/constructive' referred to two 'moments' which could be considered as

Paul Klee, *Air-Tsu-dni*, 1917 (Industria written back to front)

TOMAS LLORENS was born in 1936. He received his degree in law from the University of Madrid in 1958 and his degree in philosophy from the University of Valencia in 1964. From 1969 to 1972 he lectured on aesthetics at the School of Architecture of Valencia. From 1972 until 1977 he was Research Fellow at the Portsmouth School of Architecture, England, where he is currently a lecturer. During 1977–80 he was a visiting lecturer at the School of Architecture of Barcelona. He has been an active art critic in Spain and has published extensively in art-historical and philosophical journals like *Metro, Op Cit, Versus, Lotus International, Arquitecturas Bis* and others. He is currently a member of the editorial board of *Arquitecturas Bis* and has edited the book *Arquitectura, Historia y Teoria de los signos*, Gaya Ciencia, Barcelona, 1974.

logical components of the very *concept* of avant-garde. Thus, the re-enactment of the classical avant-garde could claim the historical inheritance of both lines, while their mutual logical implication validated such re-enactment in the light of the necessities of the postwar situation.

Finally, the very term 'constructivist' could be associated with two different meanings. 'Constructive' can mean, as in ordinary language, bringing about a new thing in the real world. But in certain contexts, as when speaking of 'constructive logic', it can also mean *defining* according to a system of rules and in such a manner that, from the point of view of the system itself, the definition creates its own object, quite independently from wordly events. During the 1920s, under the influence of logical positivism, or, more broadly, of epistemological formalism, these two meanings were frequently conflated into one single, special meaning; this conflation between 'cause-effect processes' and 'rule-governed relationships' was a characteristic feature of those avant-garde attitudes which could be classified as 'constructivist'. Indeed, such conflation of meanings was indispensable to anyone who hoped to endow the formal definition of an avant-garde system with the effectiveness of revolution in real historical terms. Although the Italian Modernists of the 1940s and 1950s may not have been aware of it, this conflation of meanings was implicit in their appeal to the spirit of the classical avant-garde. And conversely, since this conflation of meanings could be transferred symmetrically from the 'constructive' to the 'negative' component, the avant-garde attitude could also refer to the clean break with the past (the years of Fascism) which post-war Italian reality demanded.

Italian post-war reality, however, was more complex than that. Given the circumstances, a rejection of the ambiguous modernity of the Nationalist (Fascist) past in favour of pure avant-garde implied faith in internationalism. At the time, Italy was being integrated in social, political and economic terms into the domain of post-war capitalism. In such an international context, of course, classical avant-garde attitudes were to lose their meaning. Thus, while the Modern Movement was slowly drifting towards an international context, the problem of defining an avant-garde became much more pressing for Italy than for the rest of Europe or America. In fact, it was in Italy that concern for the 'crisis' of the Modern Movement first appeared; the obsessive intensity of such concern still haunts architectural culture today. Since the formal avant-garde could no longer be immediately equated with real social change, the conflation between the two senses of the 'constructive' side of avant-garde attitudes no longer held water; the mutual relationship between the 'constructive' and the 'negative' sides became questionable, and this opened the door to the problematic of the relationship between the avant-garde and history.

Two trends could then be distinguished, contrasting in their assessment of the dialectics between history and modernity. One, under the direction of Zevi and with the intellectual patronage of Argan, interpreted the changes that had taken place in international architecture after the Second World War as a sign that the Modern Movement was alive and well – just coming of age. Continuity with the classical avant-garde, with changes that were only a matter of degree or of enrichment, perhaps, was what history demanded. The other trend, led initially by Quaroni and Rogers – although with recognisable differences between them – engaged in a process of reassessment tainted with disbelief and heterodoxy with respect to the principal tenets of the Modern Movement. For them the re-examination of history implied a change of orientation; the research they proposed aimed at re-establishing the basic principles which history had validated in the past, before the break brought about by the classical avant-garde.

Both parties called thus upon history to legitimise the peculiar kind of modernity each of them proposed. Both addressed history in order to fill the gap between the 'negative' and 'constructive' sides of the avant-garde attitude. Both stigmatised the compromise of Modern architecture with tradition – particularly during the last years of the Fascist regime – as a betrayal: not only of the avant-garde, but of history itself. It was argued that the demagogic use of forms from the past, favoured by Fascism, deprived these forms of their original and authentic *raison d'être*.

The former trend conceived of history as a sort of natural force which could be beneficial only when not hindered by a deliberate consciousness of the past. The latter, denying the possibility of a smooth continuity with the Modern Movement, looked deliberately into the past for a renewed definition of the boundaries of architecture itself – *il territorio dell'architettura*, to use Gregotti's successful expression – in the belief that such a definition was the necessary prerequisite for validating any new creative move.

When, in the early 1960s the young Tafuri joined the second party, its views had already become the predominant force in Italian architectural culture. The journal *Casabella* was its main publishing vehicle. In the works of Albini and Gardella, it had produced examples which were followed throughout Italy and also Spain – particularly in the domain of Catalan architecture. A younger group – mainly Gregotti, Rossi and Canella – engaged in the task of defining the theoretical foundations and the didactic tools of the movement.

Tafuri's first book was on Quaroni.[3] It made an important contribution to the theoretical programme of the movement for it assessed the role of one of its founding fathers. And, even within the limitations of a genre imposed by the publisher's programme, Tafuri found a way to organise his second book around three themes: the design process and its methodology; the city as the context which provides architecture with its meaning; and 'architectural language as a means of symbolic communication'.[4] These themes echoed the positions frequently advocated in the pages of *Casabella* during the late 1950s and early 1960s.

Design methodology – *metodologia della progetazione*[5] – seemed to be, at the time, the most important of these three themes: first, because it belonged more properly within the field of competence of the architect; second, because it promised tangible results in its application to teaching in Schools of Architecture. It was in fact, a series of lectures organised by Giuseppe Samonà during the 1964–65 academic year at the Venice Istituto Universitario de Architectura which marked the peak of Tafuri's integration within the former Casabella group.[6] The central theme was labelled '*teoria della progettazione architettonica*', and Tafuri's contribution was to fulfil the role of the professional architectural historian within the common enterprise.

At that time Tafuri must have been finishing his third book, *L'Architettura del Manierismo*,[7] which focuses, for its main argument, on the conflict between the moral and civic ideals of the *quattrocento* and the demands for scientific and rational efficiency associated with the rise of the Machiavellian States of the *cinquecento*. Although this argument anticipates others developed later by the author, the emphasis in this book was different from that of his later work. The young Tafuri does not yet seem to have seriously attempted to break his links with the tradition (pervasive in Italy) of idealist Art History. 'Humanist ethics' and 'Rational scientism', as he discusses them, still partake of the nature of Hegelian ideas.

It was precisely this idealistic component that provided the hint for the match between history and *'metodologia della progettazione'*. In his contribution to the Venice course,[8] Tafuri's key concept was what he called 'control parameters' (*parametri di controllo*). According to this concept, the set of 'control parameters' (the general principles controlling the design process) constitutes the 'symbolical form' that presides over a certain historical period. Tafuri seems to be thinking of historical periods in terms of the stylistic cycles of conventional Art History. Although he does not quote Cassirer, he explicitly refers to Panofsky's *Perspective as a Symbolical Form*. But Tafuri's interest was not so much in the interplay of these symbolical forms with the general conceptual framework of society as a whole, as in their *formative* action within the creative process of design itself.[9]

This tendency to test the operative potential of general historical concepts on the drawing board of the artist or architect permeates Tafuri's writings throughout these years. For instance his two first articles on Borromini end by stating the lessons which, the author suggests, should be learnt by contemporary architects.[10] And although Tafuri explicitly abandoned this criterion around 1969, it still appears in two other books of his which were also published in 1969.[11] More surprisingly, it constitutes yet again the central argument of another study on Borromini which was published as late as 1972.[12]

The same criterion also permeates *Teorie e Storia dell'architettura*,[13] the book which crowns Tafuri's effort to give an answer to the architect who addresses himself to history in search of a programme or, at least, of some theoretical guidance. In the same book, however, Tafuri attacks those who believe that historical analysis can be put at the service of design.

Chapter after chapter, the book challenges the reader who tries to make out the author's thesis on such questions as whether or not history was a constitutive element of the Modern Movement; whether or not experimentalism (including typological research) can raise itself to the status of a theoretical critique (or, more radically, whether or not theoretical critique can raise itself to the status of a 'true' critique, breaking the circle of solipsism); whether semantic analysis (under which heading the author ranges almost everything, from Riegl to recent structuralism and semiology) penetrates, or whether, on the contrary, it mystifies the true historical meaning of architectural forms; whether awareness of history smooths or hinders the ways of revolution (or of the avant-garde, or, indeed, whether the avant-garde has anything to do with revolution).

In my opinion *Teorie e Storia*... should be approached as a palimpsest,[14] a document where the successive and often contradictory discourses of a crisis are superimposed rather than fused. This is the crisis that European culture, and particularly Marxist thought, underwent around 1968. It also coincides with the end of a cycle of modernism (which one may call post-avant-garde in its chronology and humanist in its orientation) as well as with the victory of the neo-avant-garde attitudes in every field of the arts as well as in architecture. In Italy, where this cycle of humanist Modernism had begun sharply in 1945, and where intellectuals had been involved in the organisation of the parties of the left, both aspects (ie the crisis of humanist marxism and modernism and the development of neo-avant-garde attitudes) were felt very intensely[15] and became crucial to an understanding of the change in Tafuri's thought.

This change can be placed in 1969, between the first and the second edition of his *Teorie e Storia*..., and the author refers explicitly to it in his prefatory 'Note' to the latter. *'We are speaking here about architecture, the* whole *of it, that is to say, about architecture as an institution. This implies (something which has been carefully concealed by current soft versions of official 'marxism' – from Fisher to Goldmann or della Volpe – as well as by the Marcusian school – Mitscherlich and his disciples – by Hauser's 'vulgar' sociologism, and by 'progressive' architects, whether American or European, in their recent flirtations with the left) that*, just as it is not possible to establish a class Political Economy, but only a class critique of Political Economy, neither is it possible to "anticipate" a "class architecture" (that is, an architecture for a "liberated society") but only a class critique of architecture'.

As an argument, the analogy could hardly be weaker. Why not extend it to a 'class critique' of, say, mathematics? In a sense, it could also hardly be less marxist, since it is essential for a marxist theory of history to attribute to the critique of economy a unique epistemological status, which cannot be transferred, without change, to the other levels of social and cultural reality.

The objection could be dissolved, however, or attenuated if the critique (as 'class-critique') of architecture were made to consist of tracing architectural conceptions to some basic kernel in the economic domain. In 1969 Tafuri could hardly do it by reworking *Teorie e Storia*... into a completely different book for the second edition; but he undertook this approach that same year in a separate essay, 'Per una critica dell 'ideologia architettonica', which was later to become, in an enlarged version, *Progetto e Utopia*, the book that still remains his major theoretical statement to date.[16]

The basic argument in the article, as in the book, is that the history of architectural ideas (of architecture as ideology) can be traced down to the development of economic rationality – the latter seen as the model of capitalist society. The relations between architectural ideology and capitalist rationality however do not follow a smooth linear path. Ideology projects and distorts the needs of economic development into the realm of illusion, and this creates a tension between the two levels that produces apparent contradictions, both between ideology and rationality and between alternative conceptions that seem to conflict with each other. Thus there comes a point in time at which ideology (or certain ideological formations) becomes a hindrance rather than a help to the development of bourgeois economy. According to Tafuri, this is also the case with architecture (he does not however indicate any particular period in which this transformation took place; rather, it seems that it is a sort of endemic threat inherent to the nature of architecture itself). The area in which the ideological link between architecture and capitalist rationality is most open to analysis lies in its dependence upon the city. Although Tafuri does not explain the reasons for this assumption, it seems permissible to imagine that they consist of, on the one hand, his acceptance of the Weberian view of the city as the cradle and paradigm of bourgeois society and, on the other, his continued allegiance to the *Casabella* positions, according to which the city was both the prerequisite for the existence of architecture and the ultimate scope of its striving for form. Along with the discussion of the history of the concept of urban form, Tafuri analyses the path of the avant-garde of our century (and its crisis). Since, as I have said, Tafuri does not specify any particular point in time for this process, one has to infer that the Enlightenment (the period at which the author starts his historical account) already contained the seeds for the avant-garde (and its crisis) as well as the symptoms of the degeneration of architecture into an ideological obstacle for the development of economic rationality.

These two themes provide Tafuri with the argument for his analysis of architecture as ideology. The conclusion seems to be that architecture, as such, is doomed. It no longer serves the interests of capitalism, which in its present stage of reason-as-mere-practicality bypasses it, and it cannot bear any honest promise for any eventual new (non-capitalist) society, since its substance was in the first place only ideology, ie 'false consciousness' induced by capitalism itself in its early stages of development.

But before discussing this conclusion, I would like to say a little more about the argument itself and the assumptions it entails. The initial step had already been encapsulated by Tafuri in the passage quoted above from his preface to the second edition of *Teorie e Storia...*; namely, that in order to make a complete analysis of 'the whole of architecture' (which by implication demands a 'class critique' of architecture) it is necessary to look at architecture 'as institution'.

The specific claim made in that statement may not be apparent at first sight. There are aspects of architecture, namely in its professional practice, for which the statement merely seems a truism. But these are not the aspects discussed in *Progetto e Utopia* or *Teorie e Storia...* The polemical purport aims primarily at the *theory* of architecture, that is, at the concepts and ideas that make up architectural doctrines. (These may be related, in an ultimate analysis, to professional practice; but the links Tafuri contemplates in that direction are, if any, extremely abstract and unspecific.)

There are several senses in which it can be said that concepts and ideas are 'institutions', or, to be more precise, that they partake of the nature of institutions. In a sense this statement can be related to the marxist principle that ideas are to be understood ultimately by the role they play in forming social reality. But this is not a claim exclusive to marxism. Other currents in modern thought have put forward propositions that entail a somewhat similar principle. For instance structuralism, particularly of the Lévy-Strauss kind, assumes that ideas, beliefs and social phenomena in a given society all describe the same underlying system of formal relationships. Although the emphasis seems to be, for most structuralists, at the opposite pole to marxism (they seem to be saying that it is social institutions that partake of the nature of ideas – in their logical form), this may not be taken as an irreducible opposition, since neither marxism nor structuralism consider the explicit content of ideas (or institutions) to be determinant; thus they shift their analysis to the *functions* that link them to a certain global frame (social reality for marxism; 'structure' for structuralism). On the other hand it has not been common, within the marxist tradition, to talk of 'institutions' as the basic constituents of society (or of its superstructure); classical authors, who never made a special concept of it, used the term in the ordinary restricted sense in which it was being used by most historians and social scientists, namely to refer to those frames of organised social interaction which are objectively defined by a set of explicit norms (whether written or customary), such as political institutions of civil law, etc. However, a certain trend within western marxism developed in the late 1960s, and tended to enlarge the concept so that it also embraced other superstructural phenomena, such as religious beliefs, art doctrines, and the basic concepts or categories of scientific thought. This approach reflected the impact of traditions extraneous to marxism: structuralism, because of its concern for the law-like aspect of cultural phenomena; Durkheimian sociology and anthropology, because of its emphasis on the specificity of social phenomena; and psychoanalysis, because it considers psychological consciousness as the result of an all-embracing polarity between 'inner' – natural – impulses and 'outer' – artificial – norms. All these traditions have in common the assumption of a strong ontological dualism between reality and appearance, and the more or less neo-kantian principle that reality can only be approached as an *a priori*.[17] Around and after 1968, leftist intellectuals tended to amalgamate these different approaches with marxism in order to arrive at 'methods' for the discovery of the hidden political meaning of cultural phenomena that were apparently not political (or for the discovery of the hidden political meaning of phenomena whose political appearance was deceitful, like the conduct of social democratic and communist parties).

This is the intellectual atmosphere which constituted the background to Tafuri's change of position. But in order to find its influence, it is necessary to see in more detail the content of *Progetto e Utopia*. The term 'institution' no longer appeared in the book; perhaps because the author felt now that its use by functionalist positivist sociology had made it irretrievable. But the concept itself (and the approach from which it derived, namely that of the German sociology of the classical period) still constituted the main focus for the argument. Tafuri intended to show how the attitudes that were to evolve into the doctrines of the avant-garde related to the social character of the bourgeois city, which was, in its turn, the privileged *locus* for the revelation of the spirit of capitalist economy. This entailed the problematic of the relationship between economic structure, 'ways of life', attitudes, cultural objects and spiritual phenomena; a problematic that had been extensively discussed at the end of the 19th century and the beginning of the 20th in the works of German social philosophers, such as Tönnies, Sombart, Simmel, Scheler, the two Webers, Spengler and Mannheim. This body of literature, to which Tafuri now addressed himself in search of analytical concepts, also held for him an additional promise, since two of its more recurrent themes had eventually become the two central ideas in the doctrine of the architectural avant-garde in Germany, especially after the war. These themes were, first, the assumption that the city (or more precisely the 'metropolis') was the stage chosen by history to play the drama of the birth of modern man; and second, the view that intellectual élites were called upon to play the role of disclosing and facilitating the forces of history – a view that had helped to shape the concept of avant-garde in artistic circles. It must be added that, for Tafuri, the fate of the architectural avant-garde in the Weimar Republic encapsulated the fate of the Modern Movement as a whole, because there and then, within the framework of pressing economic needs and progressive political attitudes (largely determined by the weight of the Social Democratic Party), Modern architecture had to face the first and most decisive test for its claims to represent the spirit of Modern society.

The rise and development of avant-garde architecture in Germany, therefore, together with the study of the Russian avant-garde (which took only a second place, and was in any case related), became for Tafuri and his collaborators the main subject of research soon after he took the direction of the Istituto di Storia dell'Architettura in Venice. Their increasing interest in the ideas of the social philosophers who had so influenced the cultural atmosphere of the Weimar Republic is reflected in the additions that turned the 1969 article 'Per una critica dell' ideologia architettonica' into the 1973 book *Progetto e Utopia*. In particular, chapter three (with the title of 'Ideologia e Utopia'), which is, from the point of view of theory, the more substantial of these additions, consists entirely of a discussion of the German social philosophy of the classical period. But the contents of *Progetto e Utopia* give an incomplete picture of this shift, which was achieved, as the author says in the preface, thanks to the collective research of the Istituto. In this research, the important contribution of Massimo Cacciari, Tafuri's younger collaborator, must be credited in particular.[18]

Since the programme attempted to explain the dialectics of the avant-garde in the light of the development of capitalist rationality, the main problem was how to account for the 'negative' side of the avant-garde. The 'cleanest' approach to this problem – 'cleanest' in that it was extreme, direct and free from 'vulgar' marxism – was Cacciari's essay 'Note sulla dialectica del negativo nell'epoca della metropoli (Saggie su Georg Simmel)'.[19]

Cacciari summarises Simmel's explanation of the relationship between the development of a 'metroplitan' way of life and that of (bourgeois) rationality.[20] Both entail a process of *Vergeistigung* ('spiritualisation' or 'mentalisation' in the sense of Hegel's 'mind'). Just as money establishes a system of formal relationships between the exchange value of things which excludes their qualitative differences, rational thought establishes systems of formal relationships between the contents of experience which exclude their qualitative uniqueness as psychological impressions. This process of *Vergeistigung* is a necessary prerequisite for the development of rational action, since the latter implies foresight and the reduction of surprise; but on the other hand the process of *Vergeistigung* presupposes the resistance to reason that characterises those psychological impressions, or stimuli, upon which it feeds, just as the exchange values which constitute the monetary system presuppose and feed upon the qualitatively different use, or consumption values, of concrete things. The 'metropolis', which is the *locus* for the exchange and circulation of 'mental' economic value (ie money) is also the locus for the mind, for the development of rational systems of thought. But this achievement depends on a continuous process of dialectic interaction between rationality and irrationality, foresight and surprise, abstract homogeneous exchange value and actual embodiment in qualitatively different, unique, acts of use or consumption, a life of planned action and a life of intensified psychological impressions. This is the 'nervous way of life' (*Nervenleben*) of modern metropolis, the way of life of the *blasé* type, as exemplified by Baudelaire. The *blasé* type, torn between superficiality and passion, between ever deeper indifference and ever higher stimulation, between a studious search for surprise and the elegance of methodic and highly formalised routines, is the subjective counterpart of the objective system of monetary economy.

Thus the *Vergeistigung* process entails a profanation of the uniqueness of concrete experience; at the deepest levels, a dissolution of personality and a dissolution of *religio* (the transcendent bond between a personal unique subject and a unique personal God)[21] which accounts for the typical cosmopolitanism – indifference to place and community of origin – the denial of transcendence and sacredness, and, with that, the fading of the forms of ancient culture in the consciousness of modern man. Cacciari agrees with Simmel up to this point. He sees in his analysis the first stage of a radical criticism of (bourgeois) rationality, and an important contribution to the development of 'negative thought' (*pensiero negativo*): '*The fundamental aspect in Simmel, with respect to contemporary bourgeois ideology, consists in the fact that he admitted the company of the negative principle throughout a decisive part of his way*'. It must be said at this point, however, that Cacciari does not set himself to identify what he calls 'negative thought'. According to Cacciari the next stage after Simmel would be Walter Benjamin; but it seems that this would apply only to the topic of the metropolis. In the discussion that follows in the next section of his essay, Cacciari refers to Nietzsche, and it seems reasonable to assume that the concrete historical embodiment of Cacciari's *pensiero negativo* is close to the philosophy of Nietzsche-Heidegger and the influence of Nietzsche's philosophy on avant-garde circles in our century.

It is in the name of that 'negative thought' that Cacciari criticises the conclusions Simmel derives from his analysis. Namely, that for the individual the other side of the *Vergeistigung* process consists in regaining the subjectivity he had lost as an externally defined personality; the latter being the result of the loosening of all bonds of transcendence which linked him to the hierarchically structured cosmos of pre-bourgeois culture as well as to the religious. Cacciari sees here in Simmel an ideological reinstatement of hope at the last minute. He considers these conclusions to be unwarranted by the analysis of the metropolitan culture. The logic of 'negative thought' precluded the hope of a new subjectivity; it pointed rather, according to Cacciari, towards that radical disenchantment which haunts the theme of the metropolis and which Benjamin found expressed in Baudelaire and the subsequent development of modern poetry. Since the function of monetary economy is to make class domination possible in its capitalist form, the *Vergeistigung* process cannot leave any 'positive' residuum in the form of pure freedom. Its result, after the destruction of every qualitative value, can only be the dissolution of the inner bonds of the self. This is the truth perceived by 'negative thought'; the image of metropolis as an inescapable machine of destruction expresses in its most naked form the essence of rationality (the bourgeois *Geist*) as pure power and domination.

But from this point on, Cacciari's argument becomes less clear. Explaining the background of Simmel's new subjectivity he refers to the mutual implications between the concepts of self (going back to the Cartesian *ego*) and rationality (in both aspects considered by Kant: scientific rationality and ethic, the latter based on the concept of pure duty). The rise of 'negative thought' would bear witness to the dissolution of that central kernel of bourgeois ideology. Nietzsche's attack on the concept of duty, Max Weber's relativisation of the concept of value, and de Saussure's exclusion of the concept of meaning (as an extra-linguistic bond between language and the world) from his analysis of language would be the exponents of that trend. Hoffman, Poe and lastly Kafka would express, in the domain of narrative, the successive stages of that same process of destruction of the bourgeois self. The thematic of sentimental irony in Romantic literature throughout the 19th century would determine the failure of the bourgeois drama to reach the level of classical tragedy – as Nietzsche had explained. The impossibility of tragedy in the modern world derives from the impossibility of reconciling the plane of life and the plane of form into one single certitude. Thus the intrinsic impossibility of Goethe's classical ideal, which Simmel (the first representative of those German intellectuals who, from the standpoint of a decadent bourgeois culture at the doors of the First World War, looked nostalgically back towards Goethe) would take as a model for his attempted synthesis of the new subjectivity.

In dealing with all these subjects Cacciari is more indebted to Lacan and Derrida than he cares to tell by way of open quotation. But the shift from Benjamin to the *maîtres à penser* of the French neo-avant-garde leaves him in an uneasy position and makes the essay strangely inconclusive. Cacciari states that Benjamin does not measure up to the radicality of 'negative thought' in its ultimate consequences. Benjamin, Cacciari maintains, conceives of it in terms of rebellion, and thus fails to obtain a *'clear vision of how the negative principle really represents that powerful criticism which alone can dissolve the privileged status of the Ego, of Duty, of Value, of the transcendent bond between words and things; and it is upon such criticism that the foundations of Metropolis are established'*. On the other hand, since the synthesis attempted by Simmel was impossible, Cacciari sees in his new subjectivity a mere 'compromise' with the humanist tradition of early German Romanticism. Without such a compromise the essential negativity of metropolis would have been historically untenable. Ultimately, Simmel's new subjectivity would not entail any ontological claim, it would merely respond to a need for 'consolation'; to that effect Cacciari quotes Simmel: *'Der Mensch ist ein Trostsuchendes Wesen'* ('man is a being in search of consolation').[22] Therefore, Cacciari seems to suggest that the new synthesis of Goethe's classical humanist ideal attempted by Simmel is really a form of disenchanted neo-classicism,[23] and, in its effective silence about transcendence, is truer to the spirit of 'negative thought' than Benjamin's attempt to express it. But if there are hints at such a position in several passages, Cacciari never states it explicitly, and the essay ends in a rather inconclusive manner.[24]

In spite of all its ingenuity, Cacciari's view that the concept of new subjectivity as pure freedom and interiority was, on the part of Simmel, a 'compromise' involves a good deal of distortion. For Simmel's concept of 'soul' (*Seele*) is inseparable from his concept of 'mind' (*Geist*), while both are ontologically posited as results of the same process of *Vergeistigung*. *'Whatever is a product of mind (*Geist*), whatever the life process expels from its interiority and exteriorises as 'result', assumes, with respect to that living and creative reality, the character of something that is inert, prematurely moulded... It is curious that these really poor fragments, in which there is no room for the plentitude of subjective life, are, on the other hand, whatever there is of perfection.'*[25] This is why *'the intrinsic contents of life become ever more intrinsic and impersonal, so that whatever is not liable to transaction may become ever and ever more personal, an indisputable patrimony of the self.'*[26]

There can be little doubt that Simmel's 'mind' and 'soul' are respectively functions of Dilthey's 'culture' and *'Erlebnis'*. Both are exponents of a 'philosophy of life' which attempted to develop at an empirical level – 'empirical' as opposed to 'logical', and used here in the sense of subjective experience – the polarity 'exteriority'/'interiority' posited by Hegel in his *Phenomenologie des Geistes*.

Underlying this distortion, which betrays his desire to streamline Simmel[27] in order to fit him into the schema of a developing 'negative thought', there is in Cacciari a fundamental ambiguity about how to approach the cultural phenomena he studies; namely, whether he takes them as *symptoms* of the fate of bourgeois culture, or as analytical explanations of such a fate. In other words, Cacciari seems to have set out to analyse the concept of metropolis as ideology – ie 'as false consciousness' – and then, having found at its core the schema of 'negative thought', he concludes that there is no true alternative, and therefore places his own search for truth under the aegis of that same schema. There is an element of self-contradiction here which cannot but affect the conclusion drawn from the analysis. This is also, as we shall see, the central difficulty underlying Tafuri's analysis of architecture as ideology.

For a truly dialectical approach, this contradiction could resolve itself into an increased richness. The 'symptoms' of a certain stage of consciousness can be recovered as partial self-disclosures of truth at a further stage. But a dialectical approach of this sort, ensuring a transition between 'symptoms' and 'consciousness', between the epistemological and the ontological realms, demands that such a further stage be 'positively' posited. And Cacciari denies himself that possibility. What he posits in the place of such a further stage of consciousness is a projection of what he calls 'negative thought', which can only deny any (ontological) substance to those 'symptoms', while it depends on them in that they constitute its own (epistemological) substance. Instead of engaging in a dialectical interplay, 'consciousness' and 'being' become entangled in a formal contradiction. Or else, there is no possible transition between them. In both cases the outcome can only be 'silence'. No wonder 'silence' has such positive connotations in the terminology of both Cacciari and Tafuri.

These questions are never discussed either by Cacciari or Tafuri. They use the term 'dialectics' (Cacciari speaks of the 'dialectics of the metropolis' as the *locus* for the epiphany of 'negative thought'),[28] but they belong entirely within that trend of *'marxism without dialectics'*[29] which in the 1960s under the influence of disguised neo-kantism reverted to the postulate of an unbridgeable gap between the epistemological and the ontological realms (and degenerated eventually into the 'negation' of substance for any sort of consciousness).

The fruits that could be expected of such a *'marxism without dialectics'* in the domain of cultural history can be appreciated in Tafuri's *Progetto e Utopia* even better than in Cacciari's 'Note sulla dialectica del negativo . . . '. While Cacciari focuses on the genesis of negativity, Tafuri – who wants to account for the whole panorama of avant-garde attitudes – focuses on the moment at which negativity is 'positivised', so that it gives rise to 'utopia'. Tafuri looks at this process at a very general level: from Simmel to Max Weber and Manheim (or to Keynes and Schumpeter); from dadaism and surrealism to constructivism (or Russian formalism); from the 'leftist communists of the early 1920s[30] to the social-democratic (and by implication sovietic) doctrines of planification. This may help to explain the fact that Tafuri's arguments are more confused than those of Cacciari.

But a more fundamental reason seems to be inherent to the nature of his problem. It is a safe (and trivial) principle to state that capitalist rationality *may* give rise to immature manifestations in the form of 'utopias'. On the other hand, to state that a given particular instance of 'utopia' (or any other cultural phenomenon involving an utopistic element, as is often the case with architectural doctrines) *is* – and in which degree or capacity – such a manifestation of ideology at work is entirely a matter of historical judgment, not a matter of principle. But Tafuri's problem was more difficult, because he was dealing with the whole complex of avant-garde attitudes; and further, he was convinced, now, that these avant-garde attitudes entailed an essential component of 'negative thought'. Taking as his point of departure the thesis – adopted by Cacciari – that 'negative thought' represented the most advanced moment of capitalist ideology, Tafuri had to show not only that such 'negative thought' could be 'positivised', but also the manner in which this was done.[31]

I wonder whether it is possible to make sense of the problem thus stated. Tafuri certainly does not. Apart from the vagueness and confusion of his examples (which is a matter of proper historical information and plausible judgment), the kernel of his argument is inconsistent.

Tafuri starts by saying that 'negative thought' had a role to play, as an ideological force at the service of capitalist rationality; namely that of getting rid of the ancient values of bourgeois culture: *'In order to survive, ideology had to negate itself as such, break its own crystallised forms and throw itself entirely into the "construction of the future"'*. Max Weber is called upon as first witness: his postulate of a value-free scientific approach to social reality makes him the heir of Nietzsche and constitutes the first step towards such a 'utopian' 'construction of the future' as was demanded by capitalist rationality. Then, as second witness, comes Mannheim. About him Tafuri has this to say: *'This is why [ie why after Weber had cleared the way, capitalist rationality was still pressing on its demands] Mannheim was obliged to offer a rather mystified version of the functioning and reality of 'utopia'*. The reader, who wonders why and in which sense Mannheim's concept of utopia is mystifying, is referred to a long explanatory footnote, which starts thus: *'I refer in particular to Mannheim's distinction between "progressive" and "conservative" thought . . . '*, and goes on with quotations from Mannheim in order to illustrate this distinction. The quotations, which come from an early essay by Mannheim ('Das konservative Denken', 1927), are not perhaps very well chosen, but if the reader has also read Mannheim he may remember that for him 'utopias' are, in early stages, the necessary form of expression of progressive thought, while they become 'ideologies' in those stages where the thought they express or determine plays a socially conservative function. So far, Tafuri is merely trying to explain what Mannheim understood as 'utopias'; but he has not said a word to explain why he (Tafuri) considers his conception to be 'mystifying'. This comes as if as an afterthought: *'But see also idem, Ideologie und Utopie, (3rd ed, Frankfurt 1953)*[32] *which treats fully the theory of utopia as a tendency realisable in itself, capable of breaking the confines of existing reality "to leave it free to develop itself in the direction of the successive order"* (Op cit, p 201)'. This must be the reason why, according to Tafuri, Mannheim's concept of 'utopia' is 'mystifying'. Tafuri thinks that according to a 'non-mystified' conception, utopia is not *'capable of breaking the confines of existing reality to leave it free to develop itself in the direction of the successive order'*. A very sensible remark, after all, the reader may think. But then the reader also realises that the spirit of capitalist rationality – which is what Tafuri is concerned about – must be a rather stupid spirit. It needed, in the first place, to clear the ground of social reality, ie of those values of the old bourgeois culture which were becoming a hindrance. It needed, in other words, to *'break its own crystallised forms'*, in that they *'defined the confines of existing social reality'*, as Tafuri puts it. And it had Nietzsche and Weber to do the job. In the second place, it needed to *'throw itself entirely into the construction of the future'*, and thus it 'positivised' that 'negative thought' (of which Nietzsche and Weber were the exponents) into 'utopia'. But then, 'utopias' being what they *really* are, they were *unfit* to do what the spirit of capitalist rationality had appointed them to do. In the third place, it had Mannheim to invent the *mystifying* notion that utopias could, after all, do the job. What for? If they could not, they could not, and Mannheim's *saying* the contrary would not change their *real* nature. But it is precisely this irreconcilable duality between 'saying' and 'doing', between 'reality' and 'appearance' that lies at the heart of Tafuri's approach and causes the trouble.

So far the reader has reached the third page of Chapter

three of *Progetto e Utopia* and the author has told him, in a footnote, what utopias are *not* capable of. He has not said a word about what they really are, nor about the function that they really fulfil (apart from the general notion that they are instruments for the spirit of capitalist rationality), nor about the particular circumstances, historical or otherwise, under which they were, are, or may be called upon to fulfil this unknown function. For the rest of the chapter (and the book) these questions remain unanswered; but the spirit goes on playing its incomprehensible games of positivity, negativity, equivalence and transmutation. With an Olympian disrespect for conventional notions (and chronology) the spirit has Weber positivising what was 'still' not so in Mannheim (p 54 English edition). It has the dadaists championing a *'new type of rationality'* and releasing *'the valve of an unlimited potential for development'* (p 56, *ibid*). It has Keynesianism ridding free market economy of the ghost of interventionism (p 61, *ibid*). It has Šklovskij defending the absolute autonomy of artistic creation against Mayakovskij's demand for propaganda art, and it has André Breton stating the mathematical identity of these two positions so that artists might comply with Henry Ford's demand that they engage in industrial production (pp 64–67, *ibid*). And so on. The spirit – the author seems to be pressing the point – may be stupid and impotent, but at least it is not lacking in imagination. Not that all these fireworks of games with history throw any light onto the question of its nature. On the contrary, as the display goes on, the games become, more and more, variations on a sort of identity game. The spirit of capitalist rationality may not be, after all, the ideology of capitalism. At least not in the ordinary marxist sense of being related to the capitalist mode of production. It is the spirit of the Plan (the capital is Tafuri's) and its abodes are in sovietic and capitalist grounds alike.³³ Its logic, however – as Tafuri unequivocally suggests in several passages – is that of the interests of intellectuals and artists as a 'class' struggling for its own survival.³⁴ Whether the 'ideology of the capitalist bourgeoisie', the 'ideology of the Plan' and 'the ideology of the intellectuals', are manifestations of one same spirit remains a mystery which the reader is never allowed to penetrate.

Lurking behind every episode – 'positive' or not – there is Cacciari's 'negative thought', which tends to invert everything by pulling it inside out, so to speak. But if this is the logic of history, as Tafuri sees it, it is also the logic he wants to have for his own analysis. It was already mentioned in the motto chosen for *Teorie e Storia*...: *'One has to pull oneself out of the ditch/from one's own hair/pull oneself inside out/and see everything with new eyes'*.³⁵ But whereas this epistemological position led Cacciari to leave his essay without conclusions, Tafuri wanted to have conclusions at all costs. One might see it as a consequence of the nature of his object of study. Where Cacciari studied the 'dialectics of negativity', Tafuri was concerned with the 'dialectics of utopia'. Thus where Cacciari could still claim an ultimate self-consistency by resorting to the ecstatic position of the voyeur, such a consolation was denied to Tafuri.

One might also see it biographically, as a struggle to get rid of his position as *the* guide – in moral and theoretical terms – of a generation of Italian architects (in order to become the guide for the next generation). The conclusion of *Progetto e Utopia* is, as I have remarked above, the doom of architecture. This was particularly poignant, given Tafuri's previous role of making history contribute to the *'metodologia della progettazione'*. In Italy, the 'doom of architecture' was resented to such an extent that Tafuri had to protest that he was being misunderstood: *'The way was found to consider my essay an apocalyptic prophecy, "the expression of renunciation", the ultimate pronouncement of the "death of architecture."'*³⁶ But he was not interested in prophecies or prescriptions, Tafuri said, only in a diagnosis which, stemming from a marxist critique of ideology, would make the judgment about architecture the expression of a judgment about society.

But apart from the fact that – as Tafuri himself shows – judgments about architecture have consistently been associated in our century with judgments about society, it is difficult not to see Tafuri's diagnosis in the light of similar diagnoses which, formulated around and after 1968, bespoke the death of film, of painting, of psychiatry, of books, and eventually of marxism itself. Tafuri shares with this post-1968 climate a curious *détournement* of revolutionary puritanism against itself: *'To the deceptive attempts to give architecture an ideological dress* [by giving it 'revolutionary' aims – since these could only be 'utopias' and as such, not only ineffective but also deceptive] *I shall always prefer the sincerity of those who have the courage to speak of that silent and outdated "purity" even if this, too, still harbours an ideological inspiration, pathetic in its anachronism.'*³⁷

Although the concept of ideology as utopia implied here is in opposition to that of Mannheim, from a moral point of view, both Mannheim and Tafuri share the same assumptions as to the question of what ideology really is. They both start with the marxist principle that ideologies distort reality, and they both emphasise that this distortion is different from ordinary error in as much as it is not accidental, but determined by the social situation. Now, the central epistemological problem for any marxist theory of ideology is how to conceive of such 'distortion' without falling into the inconsistency of postulating an ideal, 'non-distorted' model of reality (which would not be socially determined). Mannheim skirts the issue by making a distinction between ordinary relativism and his own position, which he calls 'relationism'. The principle upon which the distinction rests is that the question of truth – which ordinary relativism begs by asserting the falsity of every view – is not relevant for a 'relationist' approach. Mannheim is not concerned with the specific content of ideas, but only with their relation to *'a certain mode of interpreting the world which, in turn, is ultimately related to a certain social structure which constitutes its situation'*.³⁸ He sees this approach as a generalisation of the marxist theory of ideologies, which goes beyond marxism – the 'generalisation' consists mainly in applying the theory to marxism itself as an ideological distortion of reality. And the differences are not difficult to detect. For instance, the formal use of the concept of *Weltanschauung* – translated in English as 'a certain mode of interpreting the world' – as an *a priori* frame for any 'content', is something Mannheim takes from the neo-kantians, particularly from Dilthey, just as he takes from Max Weber the concept of social structure as an abstract system of relationships between social groups. The main difference, however, consists in the fact that marxism cannot dismiss the question of truth as not relevant. The point has been made by marxist critics of Mannheim, such as Lukacs and Adorno,[39] and also by Mannheim himself, who sees in this the main reason why marxism can only achieve what he calls an incomplete theory of ideologies. The chief example Mannheim had in mind was, of course, Lukacs' *History and Class Consciousness*.

Although Tafuri does not discuss epistemology at such a general level, it is revealing that – probably without being aware of it – he joins Mannheim in criticising the positions held by Lukacs in the 1920s with an argument which is very much the same.[40] His concept of utopia as ideology is also very close to what Mannheim defines as 'total'; it is not so much concerned with the specific content of ideas as with their value as symptoms of the *'integrity of the mental structure'*.[41]

Tafuri fails to see the moral implications of this assumption, namely that, as Mannheim says *'the use of the term "ideology" cannot have moral or denunciatory interest'*. However, the implication underlies his position in such a manner that he cannot avoid being unwillingly affected by it: since the 'moral denunciation' brandished by the intellectual cannot penetrate the indissoluble, necessary (and amoral) bonds that link ideology with social structure, it hits him back and results in a guilt complex. The two opening words of *Progetto e Utopia*, *'allontanare l'angoscia...'* (to ward off anguish...) become a recurrent theme that pervades the book at every level: it is the motivation imputed to bourgeois ideology in its changing forms; it is the motivation imputed to intellectuals in as much as they develop a guilt complex out of their inability to comply with the demands of capitalist rationality; and, the reader guesses, it is also, for the opposite reason, the motivation behind Tafuri's own attitude towards his object of study in as much as the study itself *'cannot pretend to have any "revolutionary aim"'*;[42] it must also be the motivation behind his aesthetico-moral preference for pure formalism in architecture.

Like Mannheim's, Tafuri's conception of ideology entails an activist conception of knowledge; they both discount whatever in knowledge cannot be reduced to social action.[43] This is what was ultimately implied by the statement that architectural theories must be regarded from the point of view of architecture as institution.[44] When the distortion of reality in ideologies results from the radical effect of a 'distorted mental structure', the only criterion to make manifest the distortion is the principle that *'reality discloses itself only in actual practice'*.[45] It must be noted that the emphasis here is on 'actual', since according to Mannheim, any form of consciousness which exceeds the conditions of the immediately given present (either because it carries into it conditions of the past, or because it transcends it towards the future) is necessarily affected by ideological or utopian distortion. The consequence must be that all forms of consciousness are such, since nothing is given immediately, except in terms of pure practicality. And then, this 'dark gap' between consciousness and the demands of action has its counterpart in a conception of the moment of revolution as that 'dark moment' in which the leap into the future completely obliterates consciousness – as Marx remarked of Fichte's account of the French Revolution. The substitution of the criterion of truth by that of immediate adjustment and absorption into successful 'actual practice' has its counterpart in a radically immanent conception of action, which effectively precludes the anticipatory and representative function of projects. The final conclusion of Tafuri's diagnosis, that it *'precludes'* the survival of any anachronistic *'hopes in design'*[46] was already fully contained in the premises of his approach. While the criterion of adjustment implies a conception of social reality as modelled on a completely integrated structure, the substitution of the criterion of truth by that of successful action puts this structure in terms of power. The approach is representative of that sort of diffuse Darwinism in social history which found its most popular version in Spengler. While Tafuri refers frequently to 'capitalist rationality', there are no indications in *Progetto e Utopia* as to the concrete economic substance which corresponds to that expression.[47] On the other hand, by avoiding the concept of alienation Tafuri misses the essential marxist nexus between the concrete conditions of economic production and the *dividing* effect of consciousness upon social structure.[48] Thus, 'social structure' becomes an abstract totality which determines consciousness by acting upon it from without; and since the dual root of social structure – ie the interaction between consciousness and the concrete historical conditions of man's material transformation of the world – is ignored, there is no suggestion as to what that structure may be. It is a category which the researcher has to posit as an *a priori*, according to affinities which are only recognisable from his *particular* point of view and intellectual interests. As Mannheim says, *'the radius of diffusion of a certain thought-model'* must be explained according to *'the peculiar affinity it has to the social situation of given groups and their manner of interpreting the world'*. Once that correlation of 'affinities' between *Weltanschauung* and 'social structure' has been established, the research has exhausted its aims, as Tafuri's *Progetto e Utopia* illustrates very well. Mannheim's remark that *'By these groups we mean not merely classes, as a dogmatic type of Marxism*[49] *would have it, but also generations, status groups, sects, occupational groups, schools, etc'*,[50] paves the way for Tafuri's typical oscillation between the concept of 'capitalist ideology' and that of 'ideology of architects'.

Concerning the reduction of social structure to a set of power relationships, there is, however, a difference between Tafuri and Mannheim. While *Progetto e Utopia* is entirely pervaded by what one might call a 'polemologist' conception of class-struggle, one that is redolent of military imagery and in which the whole question seems to be one of domination or shaking off domination,[51] such a view plays a secondary role in Mannheim.[52] This difference can be related to the more obvious and explicit difference I have mentioned above, namely that Tafuri rejects Mannheim's distinction between (conservative) ideologies and (futuristic) utopias.[53] In this, Tafuri seems more consistent than Mannheim, since, if reason does not enter as a criterion, there is no way to tell the future, and therefore no basis for distinguishing between ideologies and utopias. To put it in terms of German Romantic philosophy, this can only be a function of the will, and the assessment of ideologies by the 'social situation' must be made entirely in terms of power. It seems indeed that the argument by which Mannheim reinstates the concept of utopia at the end of his discussion is no more than an instance of wishful thinking, whereby the author shrinks away from the consequences of his own approach: *'The complete elimination of reality-transcending elements from our world leads us to a matter-of-factness which ultimately would mean the decay of the human will [...] The disappearance of utopia brings about a static state of affairs in which man himself becomes no more than a thing. He would be faced then with the greatest paradox imaginable, namely that man, who has achieved the highest degree of rational mastery of existence, left without ideals, becomes a mere creature of impulses. Thus, after a long, torturous, but heroic development, just at the highest stage of awareness, when history is ceasing to be blind fate and is becoming more and more man's own creation, with the relinquishment of utopias man would lose his will to shape history and therewith his ability to understand it'*.[54]

However there is more than mere surrender to traditional humanism in this. What Mannheim really attempts is the salvaging of the formal consistency of his approach. In the conflict between utopias and ideologies, the triumph of the former is warranted by their eventual success in shaping the reality of the future; but then such a triumph implies 'adjustment' and therefore the disappearance of the utopia itself. *'It is nevertheless inevitable that here too* [Mannheim is discussing the succession of his sociology of knowledge, as scientific knowledge, to the marxist theory of ideologies] *the utopian element, through its many different forms, has completely (in politics at least) annihilated itself. If one attempts to follow through tendencies which are already in existence, and to project them into the future, Gottfried Keller's prophecy – "The ultimate triumph of freedom will be barren" – begins to assume, for us at least, an ominous meaning'*.[55] Although Mannheim suggests that this self-cancellation of utopia is a trend to be found by empirical observation in history, it is not difficult to realise that he is really talking about a difficulty in his theory.

The difficulty has a double face. First, it is a formal difficulty which lies in the definition of utopias as (a) 'distorted' views of the world, which (b) 'correspond' to future forms of social reality. The definition is ambiguous since it does not specify what that 'correspondence' with future states of affairs means. The difficulty, as Mannheim sees it, concerns the manner of correspondence: it is certainly not so 'distorted' that utopias can eventually 'correspond' to anything. Whenever the second *definiens* is actualised, the first cannot logically be in force; and *vice versa*, whenever the first applies, the second can only be *virtual*. In other words, for the definition to make sense, one has to presuppose that the (virtual) correspondence (with future social conditions) affects the nature of the 'distortion', so as to permit a distinction, between those cases in which 'distorted' views of the world are 'utopias' and those cases in which they are not.

The second side of the difficulty is epistemological. It concerns the following question: what is it that can give foundation to our (or Mannheim's) claim that anything can be known at all about global frames of mind such as utopias and ideologies? Again, for the assumption to make sense it has to refer to an epistemological position *outside* the global frame in question. But since all knowledge – by definition for Mannheim – is bound to a certain global frame, we can only speak *about* and *from within* an *actual* frame by referring to another frame, which can only be *virtual*. Thus the two sides of the problem correspond to each other.

In reconstructing Mannheim's problem in this manner I have somehow 'hegelianised' it; but his solution is kantian or rather, neo-kantian. 'Distorted' utopian statements and statements *about* 'distortion' (whether 'utopian' or 'ideological' distortion, including those of Mannheim's 'sociology of knowledge') partake of the same epistemological nature. In a kantian sense, they are transcendental, in that they go beyond what is immediately given, and in that they 'name' what, properly speaking, cannot be 'named' (ie social structure). They can do it because they escape the global frame of mind – *Weltanschauung* – determined by the actual social structure by evoking a different frame of mind which corresponds to a different (virtual) social structure. While utopian statements still claim a material content for this virtual social structure (this content has to be unreal[56] accounting, therefore for their 'distorted' character), Mannheim's sociology of knowledge recognises the proper status of that virtual structure as a pure epistemological *a priori*. It is precisely by means of this that they can make the *actual* social structure *totally* transparent (while utopian statements can only make it partially transparent); in a sense (ie from a purely formal point of view) they create it as *structure*.[57]

Assuming a purely 'activist' conception of knowledge,[58] this is how Mannheim achieved an epistemologically consistent theory of ideology. The consistency demanded the *concept* of 'utopia', since it implied the possibility of virtual frames of mind capable of transcending the adjustment of knowledge to its actual social situation – without implying such a possibility Mannheim's own sociology of knowledge could have no epistemological basis. More important, it demanded that while each utopia could conceive of (virtual) social structure in material terms, the *concept* of utopia (and therefore the epistemological basis for the sociology of knowledge) could admit no conception of social structure unless in an *a priori* form [...]

In reproducing the elements of Mannheim's approach while dismissing (as he may have thought, 'critically') these two demands of epistemological consistency, Tafuri put himself into an epistemologically impossible position. For if every attempt to transcend the social situation – as given in terms of actual practice – is 'ideological', and if reason has to resign its pretences at penetrating the 'dark gap' that surrounds it, this of course applies to Tafuri's own approach as well. The absurdity that impairs its basis also pervades the body of Tafuri's account of modern culture, reducing it to an endless succession of episodes which are functional (for the conservation of social structure as it exists) and yet ineffective, necessary and yet futile. While aiming at a theory of ideology which claims to be more substantial and at the same time more general (even) than that of Mannheim (and of the whole of classical German sociology), Tafuri achieves only a duplicate where, as in a mirror image, the component parts float weightless.

The figure of the mirror image is also appropriate in placing Tafuri in the context of other cultural phenomena and art movements which, in the late 1960s and early 1970s, exhibited similar intellectual influences. To a varying degree, these art movements showed a fascination for their precedents in the classical avant-garde. Seen now from the perspective of a few years, their duplications also seem to be haloed by the 'weightlessness' typical of mirror images. As to their mood, these neo-avant-gardes certainly belong to the antipodes of the classical avant-gardes; where the classical were programmatic and optimistic, the neo-avant-gardes are speculative and pessimistic (openly or by implication). The gesture that was once thrown against historic time both as a break and as a new start is now, through endless repetition, brought to a perfection which is more untimely than timeless.

This change of mood is very noticeable in Tafuri. In a reversal somehow similar to that of recent architectural neo-avant-gardes, Tafuri, fascinated by the *Sachlichkeit* of Weber and Mannheim, pushes his search for the mechanisms of ideological determination well beyond the limits of epistemological plausibility. He thus imparts to historical analysis the halo of a dream where mythified abstract characters (who bear a resemblance, but only that, to the concrete historical phenomena with which we are familiar) play, according to fixed rules, an incomprehensible game.

In the case of Mannheim, the interchangeability of roles between the epistemological transcendence of his 'sociology of knowledge' and the material transcendence of 'utopias' bears witness to that conflation between rule-governed definitions (in his case the definition of a new and higher stage of knowledge) and effective transformation of the world (which I have described above as characteristic of the classical avant-garde). In contrast, Tafuri's approach is characterised by a moral mistrust of any intention towards effective social transformation, and by an emphasis on the rule-governed status of cultural phenomena.

While the 'humanist' intellectual left of the 1950s and the early 1960s had decided to accept history as a mediating factor, the neo-avant-gardists, who rebelled against both the 'humanism' and the 'historicism' of their predecessors, have succeeded in repeating that classical avant-garde gesture against time, but at the cost of confining it to the domain of the *a priori* which they see divorced from the real world. Their attitude is not only anti-historicist – in that they deny to historical knowledge the dimension of operativity, which is essential to all historicism – but it is also one that make historical research epistemologically impossible, since the *a priori* as such can have no history. The neo-kantians of the classical avant-garde, at least, postulated that the *a priori* transcended the empirical world producing its phenomenal structure. Instead, the neo-avant-gardists conceive of the *a priori* as overlapping the empirical world in such a manner that, to all epistemological effect, it obliterates it. As Tafuri's *Progetto e Utopia* illustrates, the attempt to narrate such a world results necessarily in a discourse where all shapes and figures are erased by the monotonous repetition of the same judgment; a judgment which always uses the same concept as a predicate, namely that everything amounts to 'silence'.

Just as the attempt to give a radical twist to the *Sachlichkeit* of the classical avant-garde results in subjectivism, Tafuri's attempt to radicalise neo-kantian epistemology leads back to a form of Berkeleyan idealism. And then having confined himself (and reason) within his own solipsistic sphere, the historian can no longer hear the voices of history (of those who *made* history), or discern them from *'the perennial chatter of the spring, dark inside him, the vague dark wave of nothingness'*.

Notes

1 And in that sound you can't discern the song/Of flying snow in vanishing ways or winds/From the perennial chatter of the spring/Dark inside you, that vague dark wave of nothingness.
2 Cf G Dorfles, *Il divenire delle arti*.
3 *Ludovico Quaroni e lo sviluppo dell'architettura moderna in Italia*, Milan, Comunità, 1964.
4 *L'architettura moderna in Giappone*, Bologna, Cappelli, 1965. Surprising as it may seem today, Tafuri had then judged that modern Japanese architecture was working along the lines of those three themes, and that it was a positive answer to the crisis of the Modern Movement *'because of the vigour with which it asserts its civic ideals and social contents at every level of the planning process'*.
5 The concept of *'metodologia della progettazzione'*– or *'teoria della progettazione'* as it was also called – was developed in Italy at a time coinciding roughly with the rise of the concept of 'design methods' in English speaking countries, but it had little in common with the latter. The most conspicuous difference consisted in the fact that the Italians kept mainly within the field of architecture (with marginal, though not insignificant exceptions, such as domestic furniture). Other important differences may also be mentioned: a) for the 'design methods' view, the key criterion was 'fit', and the design process was basically envisaged as practical 'problem solving'; for that of *'metodologia della progettazione'*, the design process was considered in the light of cultural (artistic) creativity, and the key criterion could be defined as something like 'exemplariness'; b) the paradigm the Italians had in mind for the practice of design was that of the individual architect; for the 'design methods' view the paradigm was implicitly the supra-individual organisation – public or private – aiming at maximum efficiency; c) for its doctrinal content 'design methods' addressed itself towards managerial 'sciences;' *'metodologia della progettazione'* towards history (which, for the Italians, implied an important proportion of sociological and political theory).
This list of differences could be extended further. But for a proper explanation it would be necessary to enter into a discussion of the different ways under which some fundamental categories, such as those of 'politics' or 'culture', were seen respectively in the Italian and the Anglo-American context; but this is not a proper place for such a discussion. It must be said, however, that the Italians followed with attention the development of 'design methods' during the 1960s. And the assumption that a certain convergence was possible, however problematic, was implicit in the late positions of the HfG at Ulm, under the direction of Tomas Maldonado.
6 The lecturers included Canella, Coppa, Gregotti, Rossi, Samonà (Alberto), Scimemi, Semerani and Tafuri. The texts were published as book, with G Samonà acting as editor, under the title *Teoria della progettazione architettonica*, Milan, Dedalo, 1968.
7 Roma, Officina, 1966. By then Tafuri had also published two important articles about Borromini (see note 10).
8 'Le strutture del linguaggio nella storia dell'architettura moderna', in G, Samonà (ed), *op cit*, pp 12–30.
9 Tafuri does not quote Pareyson here, but his debt, if perhaps unspecific, is obvious. Pareyson's concept of *formatività* can be characterised as a synthesis of Riegl's concept of 'style' and Fiedler's 'pure visibility'; but Pareyson analysed and discussed explicitly the kantian roots of these concepts, and focused more deliberately on the phenomenology of artistic creation. The influence of Pareyson was pervasive in Italy, and it would be difficult without it to understand the links which, within the *'metodologia della progettazione'* group, held together positions as different from each other as, for example, those of Gregotti and Tafuri.
10 'Borromini e l'esperienza della storia,' in *Comunità*, 129, 1965, and 'La poetica borrominiana: mito, simbolo e ragione', in *Palatino*, 3/4 1966.
11 In *L'architettura dell'Umanesimo*, Bari, Laterza, 1969, Tafuri for instance characterises Brunelleschi as attempting to confine the problematic of urban space within the bounds of architectural form; it is not difficult to find in this interpretation the echoes of concepts developed by Rossi as belonging to the field of the *'metodologia della progettazione'*. The same theme pervades *Jacopo Sansovino e l'architettura del '500 a Venezia*, Padova, Marsilio, 1969. In this second book, however, Tafuri interprets negatively Sansovino's surrender to the (ideological) rhetorical demands of the Venetian State; a historical attitude that seems little different from what he praises in *L'architettura dell'Umanesimo* as Brunelleschi's 'pragmatic realism'.
12 'Il metodo di progettazione nel Borromini', in Accademia di San Luca (ed) *Studi sul Borromini*, vol II, Roma, 1972. See the conclusion: '[*for Borromini*], *the crisis of typology is compensated by the problematic of the city as a set of fragments; the crisis of (the conception of the building as) organism is tempered by the recovery of partial typologies, by means of geometrical control, formal types and geometrical figures reflect each other in the polysemic communication of symbolical systems'*. Practically every term in this paragraph refers to a concept that was a current topic in the literature of *'metodologia della progettazione'*. The first sentence echoes Rossi's positions. The concept of building as an organism (not to be confused with Zevi's advocation of 'organicist' architecture) refers to the indissoluble synthesis between the different levels (technology, conception of space, stylistic features, social and symbolic function, etc) at which architecture relates to its social and cultural context; as such it again echoes Rossi, but also other authors, for example Gregotti. The concept of figurativity (and particularly geometric figurativity) in architecture recurs frequently in the vocabulary of critics and historians in *Casabella* during the late 1950s and throughout the 1960s; it also occurs when the design process is discussed (Gregotti for instance speaks of 'la figura del territorio'). The concept of 'polysemy' had been developed by della Volpe, and was immensely influential in art and architectural criticism throughout the 1960s. It is amazing to see how Tafuri manages to find all these themes in Borromini.
13 Laterza, Bari, 1968, 1970. I have used the Spanish translation of the second Italian edition, Barcelona, Laia, 1972.
14 This applies, I think, to the whole of Tafuri's work. His writing seems like the flow of a river that preserves in its waters fragments and trophies from whatever regions it has traversed. Themes and arguments which had their origin in his early publications are carried through, intact, ten years later, in spite of the radical change in direction that the author underwent around 1969. And not only in the content, but in the letter as well. It seems as if Tafuri's method of writing reproduced, in a most extreme manner, the method Barthes once described as his own. It is as if he extracted from his readings in history, sociology, philosophy and journalism a continuous stream of notes and kept them in a range of assorted shoe boxes, ready to be used; given the occasion, he would sketch quickly

the outline of an article or book, flesh in this pre-written material, and then return it all to the shoe boxes for further use. The reader expecting the linear exposition of an argument will be defeated. He should take each paragraph not as a link in a chain, but rather as a shot in a series aiming at a distant and not always discernible target. What is extraordinary about this is not so much the procedure in itself as the distinct impression one has, after reading several of his works, that the author has never thrown away one item of his collection of pre-written material. See note 16 for a striking example of this procedure.

15 And particularly so in Venice, where Tafuri received the chair of history of architecture in 1968. The confrontations between the police and the students, intellectuals and artists who had occupied not only the Biennale buildings and gardens but also the Piazza San Marco, made Venice, shortly after Paris, an important stage in the emergence, on an international basis, of leftist groups composed mainly of students and intellectuals. In Italy the PCI later managed to attract a fraction of these groups with the prospects of an internal reassessment and a radical change in orientation. During the first half of the 1970s, it was possible for PCI membership, radical gauchisme and neo-avant-garde cultural attitudes to be compatible. This explains the position of intellectuals like Tafuri, who after 1969 systematically attacked 'official' marxism from gauchist positions, while actively continuing to be a member of the PCI.

16 *Progetto e Utopia*, Bari, Laterza, 1973; translated into English as *Architecture and Utopia*, Cambridge, Mass MIT Press, 1976. Tafuri tells in the preface that the book *'is the result of a reworking and sizable enlargement'* of the previous article, 'Per una critica dell'ideologia architettonica', originally published in *Contropiano*, 1, 1969. I have compared this article with the book and have found, to my surprise, that not a single word of the former has been lost or discarded in the latter. The 'reworking and enlargement' consists solely of the interpolation of new paragraphs or series of paragraphs within the original text of the article; sometimes causing in it striking changes of meaning, due to the new context. If the patient reader counts and takes off, for instance, paragraphs 70 to 99 in the first chapter of the book he will obtain a literal transcription of the corresponding part in the article. (For stylistic reasons, the English translator has sometimes modified the paragraph distribution, thus in the MIT edition the interpolation consists of paragraphs 69 to 98 up to the first stop). In this chapter the author discusses, in general terms, the evolution of concepts in urban planning since the 18th century. In paragraph 69 (68 in the English edition) he states: *'Between [the fascination for chaos and the picturesque implicit in] Laugier's [conception of the city as] forest and Antolini's aristocratic reserve [in his neoclassicist plan for 19th-century Milan], there existed a third road, destined to lead to a new way of operating upon and controlling urban form.* L'Enfant's *plan for Washington* [. . .] *use[s] means that were new with respect to European models.'* This was followed, in the 1969 article, by paragraph 100 in the book (paragraph 98, from the first stop to the end, in the English edition) in which the author refers to urban planning proposals for New York since 1811 as a *further* example of such a third road. The nature of this third road, the reader learns from the text, would be that of a pragmatic American rationalism, radically different from either European neo-classicism or picturesque, in that the latter would be both culturally and ideologically motivated, rather than pragmatically. The interpolation, however, changes the meaning of the examples, and therefore, in an implied manner, the purport of the argument. In the added passage, Tafuri discusses his Washington example at length by tracing links between L'Enfant (and Jefferson) and the European polemics of classicism versus naturalism (or picturesque). At the end, in order to link up with the (pre-written, and indeed published three years before) paragraphs devoted to New York, he concludes: *'But just the* opposite *of the case of Washington is that of New York'.* (In the Italian edition this constitutes the whole of paragraph 99, in the English edition it is the first sentence of paragraph 98). It is obvious that this contradicts the statement in paragraph 69 (when read in the context of the 1969 article) that L'Enfant's plan for Washington *was an example* of the mentioned American 'third road'. In the new context, the reader who approaches the book without knowing the article will probably conclude that the author considers Washington as a case to be interpreted in relation to the European dichotomy (classicism versus picturesque), and New York as the *only* example of the American 'third road'. But the reader who compares the article with the book can no longer decide whether this was the author's last intention or whether it was to suggest the case of Washington as an instance of perhaps a 'fourth road'; one which would be different from the European dichotomy (as stated in paragraph 69) and 'the opposite' of the American pragmatic 'third road' illustrated by New York (as paragraph 99 states).

17 The common neo-kantian ascent of the intellectual trends that were to prevail in Europe, mainly in France, after the decline of existentialism is not generally realised. However, it is not too difficult to trace. Durkheim's *Règles de la Méthode Sociologique*, which constitutes the undisputed background for the sort of social theory that became academically established in Paris after the Second World War, implied a close familiarity with German neo-kantian epistemology, particularly that of the Marburg school. Saussurian linguistics, which became the paradigm for structuralism, derives from the same epistemological matrix, and was certainly influenced by Durkheim's example. In the case of psychoanalysis, the connections are more distant. But C Schorske in *Vienna, Fin de Siècle*, (New York, Knopf, 1979) has shown that the diffuse influence of German neo-kantianism amongst the intellectual milieux of Vienna constitutes a significant background for the formulation of Freud's psychoanalytical method. The combination of psychoanalysis with structuralism in France during the 1960s undoubtedly strengthened this epistemological component.

18 Apart from the discussion contained as already mentioned in chapter three, Tafuri quotes Cacciari in several passages of the book. Furthermore, some of his more important judgments – and, more significantly, those which constituted additions with respect to the 1969 article – seem to derive from an extension of the lines of Cacciari's analysis, for instance, Tafuri's opinion that Mendelsohn's architecture was *'aimed at that* intensification of sensory stimulation (Nervenleben) *that Georg Simmel* [. . .] *recognized as the typical effect of the metropolis on the "metropolitann individual."* It should not be forgotten that for Simmel, as for *Mendelsohn, this intensification of stimuli was only a premise for the achievement of a superior rationality'* (note 68, p 102; p 112 of the English edition). An even more important example is the passage in the last pages of chapter five, where Tafuri considers the anti-urban doctrines of the 20th century to be reactionary because they all revert to the nostalgic ideal of Tönnies' *Gemeinschaft*. This reflects a general statement to that effect in the last section of Cacciari's 'Note sulla dialectica del negativo nell'epoca della metropoli'.

19 In *Angelus Novus*, 21, 1971. But Cacciari developed a similar argument in a simplified (and less convincing) form, in 'Sulla genesi del pensiero negativo', published in *Contropiano*, 1, 1969, (the same issue in which Tafuri published his 'Per una critica dell'ideologia architettonica').

20 Cacciari refers only to a late essay by Simmel 'Die Grossstädte und das Geisteslebens', but the classic source is his book *Die Philosophie des Geldes*.

21 For this aspect cf Simmel's *Die Religion*, Frankfurt, 1906. Cacciari does not refer explicitly to Simmel's analysis of the role of religion within his analysis of the *Vergeistigung*; but it played a prominent role in Simmel's thought, especially in his late work, and it is an essential component to take into consideration for a proper understanding of the concept of new subjectivity which Cacciari criticises.

22 It is very revealing of the mood of young leftist intellectuals, like Cacciari, in the 1970s that they should take 'negatively', (as a symptom of self-defeat) the value of 'consolation', the positive assertion of which has been one of the high points of the humanist tradition.

23 Although this is a special case – Simmel would show 'neo-classicism' with respect to Goethe's 'classicism' – it is an early instance of the typically Tafurian theme of 'neo-classicism as silence' (and therefore fundamentally true to 'negative thought'). This theme, which can be related to the more general one of 'formalism as silence', has become very popular amongst Tafuri's admirers, and has played some part in triggering the fashion for neo-classicism current now in the architectural neo-avant-garde. It has also helped to provide a sort of *a contrario* reinterpretation of the kind of classicism generally associated with late Fascist architecture. Tafuri himself has also recently contributed towards this: his article 'The Subject and the Mask: and Introduction to Terragni' (*Lotus*, 20, 1978), although subtler than most, is still a variation of the same theme.

24 The attitude of Cacciari towards Benjamin is ambiguous in more than one respect. Benjamin on Kafka becomes Max Bense on Kafka (!) – which opens the door to a footnote arguing that Benjamin (particularly because of his 'The work of art at the time of its technical reproducibility') was a forerunner of the 'technological aesthetics' of 'negative thought'. The reader is then left in doubt as to whether such a need to 'pacify' the Nietzschean mourning for the loss of tragedy, is comparable to Simmel's 'consolation', and as to which of these two positions is finally truer to 'negative thought'. Cacciari's view on Benjamin and Max Bense consists in the central argument of G Pasqualotto's *Avanguardia e Tecnologia: Walter Benjamin, Max Bense e i problemi dell'estetica tecnologica* (Rome, Officina, 1971). The author is one of the collaborators mentioned by Cacciari, and the book was number 4 in the series 'Collana di Architettura', edited by Tafuri. According to Pasqualotto, the logical outcome of Benjamin's 'utopia' (as well as Adorno's) would necessarily be Bense's 'technological utopia', ie his information-theory based aesthetics. He intends this to be a 'radical' criticism of the Frankfurt school as a whole. At the end of the book he refers to Tafuri ('Lavoro intelletuale e sviluppo capitalistico', in *Contropiano*, 2, 1970 – I have not read this article) for his own concluding paragraph: *'The technocratic project, with all its endowment of technological solutions for economic and social problems, can only be considered to be a generalised completion of Bense's discourse* [. . .]. *The whole of Bense's theory of ethical realisation and 'intentionality' must be considered as a primary ideology for this global project which aims at the constitution of a perfectly self-regulating system, endowed with the capacity to eliminate every contradiction by transforming it into the necessary energy for the accelerated development it needs for its own survival. Given such conditions, that every element in the system, from ethics to aesthetics, from physical science to sociology, from science to art, concurs to build the most absolute Integration [in English, and with capital I in the Italian original], the discourse of Benjamin can only be taken as* analysis *albeit extremely acute, of the technological phase of capitalist development, but can never be assumed as a political* proposition against *this development.'* Its tautological emptiness – *'Given such conditions that'* everything *'concurs to build the most absolute Integration'*; of course, everybody's discourse 'concurs' to that effect – makes this statement a particularly naïve example.

25 *Fragmente und Aufsätze*, Munich 1923, p 264.

26 *Philosophie des Geldes*, Munich, 1920, p 532.

27 One may think of the accidents of fragmentary thinking as well. Thus the role that Simmel attributes to religious experience is overlooked by Cacciari, who never refers to *Die Religion* (see note 21). But Simmel's painstaking polarity between the 'contents' (which belong to the *Geist* and are therefore 'inert') and the 'inner spring' of religious life (which belongs to the 'soul') is so central that it would have been difficult to discuss it without entailing a mutual implication between 'mind' and 'soul' which establishes them equally as ontological entities. This would contradict Cacciari's interpretation of Simmel as a true 'negative' thinker who 'compromises' with classical humanism.

28 Both Tafuri and Cacciari imply that the 'dialectics of negativity' is anti-hegelian, and they seem to refer to the famous 'inversion of Hegel' effected by Marx. But not every form of anti-hegelianism is marxist. Of course, the very concept of a 'dialectics of pure negativity' would be, in hegelian terms, unthinkable. The role of 'negation' in Hegel's dialectics is often misunderstood. Hegel made it correspond to the second of Kant's 'regulative principles of reason' (cf the appendix to the Transcendental Dialectics in the *Critique of Pure Reason*, and in particular A, 657–658; it is no accident if the neo-kantians have overlooked this aspect, since it provided the main link between Hegel and Kant). Kant referred to it as the principle of 'variety' or 'specification'; Hegel reformulated it as 'negation' (ie of 'homogeneity' or 'generality') or, more properly, 'determination'. It can be said that Marx 'inverted' Hegel by transferring this category from the epistemological to the ontological domain – or rather, by giving priority to the latter; in this sense he went further than Hegel in his criticism of Kant's anti-metaphysical stance. But for this interpretation to make sense, it is necessary that the original framework, ie the postulation of a *transition* between the epistemological and the ontological, be retained. This is precisely what makes it possible to speak of marxist *dialectics*. The 'dialectics of negativity' mentioned by Cacciari and Tafuri seems to refer rather to Nietzsche. Like Marx, Nietzsche 'inverted' Hegel by postulating the priority of the ontological. But unlike Marx he did so by breaking it free from the critical framework of epistemology. Therefore there is no transfer, in Nietzsche, of logical categories, and his 'negativity' is 'negation' in a pre-kantian, material sense. How one can then speak of dialectics – Hegelian or not – I do not understand.

29 The problematic considered by Cacciari and Tafuri had been treated not only by classical German sociology, but also by two outstanding marxist works which, in a sense, relate to that tradition; namely Lukacs' *History and Class Consciousness* and Adorno and Horkheimer's *Dialectics of the Enlightenment*. The fact that Cacciari and Tafuri are silent about them cannot be accidental. It is well known that both these works (leaving aside their important differences) triggered – in their respective times – a 'back-to-Hegel' trend within contemporary marxism. Nor can it be accidental that both put the concept of alienation at the centre of their analysis. Alienation, however, was a concept too 'soiled' with humanism for the neo-avant-garde marxists of the early 1970s.

30 Tafuri (note 45, p 68; note 46, p 73 in the English edition) mentions 'left-wing communism of the 1920s and the 1930s'. This is confusing. (In the history of German communism, there are two different episodes usually referred to as 'left communism': one belongs to the early 1920s, the other to the early 1930s and they have nothing in common.) However, it appears that Tafuri refers to what he calls the 'humanist marxism' of Lukacs (and Korsch and Löwith) in the early 1920s. (Lukacs was involved in both episodes – although he held a very different position in each – which may be the cause for Tafuri's confusion. On the other hand, Tafuri also mentions Brecht in this connection, which I find rather puzzling.)

31 The 'palimpsest' image I have used above may help to understand the additional difficulty of Tafuri's position. As I have already said *Progetto e Utopia* carries theses which derive from positions held by the author before his 1968–69 change, for instance, the view that Laugier's architectural rationalism relates to the ideology of bourgeois economic rationalism. The idea is plausible in itself, but hardly a contentious one (it could be subscribed to by an idealist historian of culture, such as Cassirer). The difficulty lies in Tafuri's attempt to make *new* sense of ideas like this, from the point of view of his new radical position.

32 The first edition, under the same title (although a shorter version) was published in 1929; since no important change of positions affected Mannheim between 1927 and 1929 – or even later – one wonders why this work, which is the standard source for Mannheim's concept of utopia was not quoted in the first place.

33 Of course this recalls what has been and still is an arduous problem for contemporary marxism: the nature of the mode of production and the role of ideology in those countries which have undergone a socialist revolution. Although there is probably more than one, the answer *cannot* be that it is identical to that of capitalist countries, no matter how advanced the capitalism of the latter.

34 Although Tafuri does not state explicitly that intellectuals constitute a social class of their own, he can hardly avoid the implication when he explains ideological phenomena as caused by their interest to survive – which besides evoking the ghost of the concept of a 'class' of intellectuals, implies a rather Darwinian twist to marxist theory. It must be added that this spurious concept has been one of the more powerful vectors in diffusing Tafuri's popularity amongst students and *jeunes turcs* of all sorts. The reason is that it feeds on some genuine social problems (typical of late capitalism), like the marginalisation of the liberal professions, and the functional disruptions associated with changes in the educational system (particularly with the increase in the number of students in higher education). The concept also entails (and abuses) a genuine conceptual problem in marxist theory, namely that of the relations between division of labour and the phenomena of culture. When reading Tafuri, one has the impression that the concept of 'ideology of intellectuals' is continuously on the verge of degenerating further into that of 'ideology of architects'. Curiously enough, many of Tafuri's followers find themselves in the company of those populist Anglo-American radicals advocating the abolition of the role of the architect in the design process. The concept has also made its impact in the field of architectural history. In Spain, for instance, young architectural historians have been arguing for the last three or four years that the *ideological* content of the neo-classical architecture patronised by the Francoist régime in the 1940s *consisted* ultimately in the corporative interest of

35 architects to survive as a 'class'. In its more typical Tafurian manner the argument is often expressed rhetorically: it is Architecture Herself who expresses, *via* architectural styles, doctrines or fashions, Her will to survive.
35 From Weiss, *The Prosecution and Assassination of Jean Paul Marat*. The quote helps to date the book.
36 *Progetto e Utopia*, op cit, preface. Tafuri refers to the reaction caused by his article 'Per una critica dell'ideologia architettonica'. During the four years that had elapsed between the article and the book, the very success of his theses within the younger generation may have convinced him of the need to qualify what was already becoming a cliché.
37 *Ibid*. In the early 1970s a similar sort of argument was used by M Gandelsonas to justify, in marxist terms, the formalism of the American architectural neo-avant-garde. Tafuri shares with other post-1968 European leftists or ex-leftists (like the French art critic M Pleynet) a fascination for America that leads him to endorse an aesthetic programme which is typically American in its conception of modern art. This conception (the formalism of which was intended as a weapon against the incipient leftism of American artists and intellectuals during the 1930s and the 1940s) has been supported from the 1950s onwards, within the context of a militant anti-marxism, by the major American centres of power in the domain of the arts, such as the MOMA.
38 K Mannheim, *Ideology and Utopia*, Routledge and Kegan Paul, London, 1936, paperback edition 1960, p 253.
39 See, Lukacs, *Die Zerstörung der Vernunft*; and Adorno's reply to K Popper in 'Adorno, Popper and others', *Der Positivismusstreit in der deutschen Soziologie*, Berlin, Luchterhand, 1969.
40 Note 45, in *Progetto e Utopia*. Tafuri even uses (probably without being aware of it) Mannheim's terminology. He describes Lukacs' defence of *Geist* – which implies the question of truth – as *'un'ulteriore utopia'*. (In the English edition this corresponds to note 46 and the translator has omitted the phrase.)
41 Mannheim, *Ideology and Utopia*, p 238.
42 *Progetto e Utopia*, preface.
43 Of course, this does not apply to knowledge which is independent of man's position in history. While Mannheim refers to mathematics for obvious examples of ideology-free knowledge, Tafuri does not mention this aspect of the problem. One may assume that pure formalism is for Tafuri the nearest equivalent in architecture to what mathematics is in the domain of scientific knowledge.
44 It may be remarked that the words of Marat quoted in the motto to *Teorie e Storia* . . . stand as the reply to a question put by Sade concerning 'what to do'.
45 Mannheim, *Ideology and Utopia*, p 87.
46 *Progetto e Utopia*, ad finem; 'hopes in design' translates poorly the original Italian *'speranza progettuale'*. The expression constitutes furthermore, a concealed reference to T Maldonado, *La speranza progettuale*, (Milan, Einaudi, 1970). which Tafuri chooses as the epitome of the architectural doctrines prevalent in Italy during the 1960s.
47 The expression 'capitalist rationality' is misleading as to the conception it represents for Tafuri. Since he discounts the criterion of truth, 'rationality' for him can only mean the ability to act with success. Thus he imputes 'capitalist rationality' even to the (apparently) more irrational attitudes (such as dadaism), on the basis that, according to him, they would help to trigger off economic development. Since Tafuri does not give any further specifications, success in the economic domain may relate, at best, to what is called, in marxist theory, 'productive forces'. As to the term 'capitalist', since he does not take into consideration any of the features that define capitalism as a mode of production, it can only be read as an identification tag. But, in terms of marxist theory, to speak of 'productive forces' alone does not make sense since it is assumed that they appear in economic reality only insofar as they are mediated by a specific mode of production. (This point has been made by Italian critics with respect to positions similar to that of Tafuri.) The real meaning of 'capitalist rationality' for Tafuri could be rephrased thus: 'mental conditions which (being imputable – in the Weberian sense – to "social structure") may contribute to the success of "economic development" (whatever this effect may be)'.
48 There is an essentially anti-marxist component in the flirting irrationality of Cacciari, Tafuri, and so many intellectuals of the post-1968 left. For Marx, without *reason* there would be no class struggle. The concept itself would be meaningless (and social violence would have only a biological meaning), since, contrary to the diagnosis that the logic of capitalism leads towards a progressively higher degree of social integration, Marx's own diagnosis was that the logic of capitalism led, *via* the ever changing conditions of economic exploitation, to the emergence of the proletariat as a social class which it was impossible to integrate functionally *because* it represented a new and higher level of reason.
49 That is, one that states that the concept of social class is *the* proper approach to understanding social structure. Mannheim uses 'dogmatic' here in the sense of the positivist tradition; ie as entailing an ontological commitment.
50 Mannheim, *Ideology and Utopia*, pp 247–48.
51 A constellation of influences was driving the intellectual left of the late 1960s and early 1970s in that direction: Neo-anarchism, of course, and, almost at the other end of the political spectrum, a certain diffuse trotskyism, and also less obviously political trends, like the revival of Nietzsche and contemporary versions of psychoanalysis. The real political correlates of these cultural fashions were the realities of colonial oppression and the new forms of revolutionary nationalism; but the understanding of these realities (Castro and maoism for instance) by western intellectuals were rather superficial and short-lived.
52 However Mannheim is often ambiguous in this respect. He writes for instance: *'We may regard competition as such a representative case, in which extra-theoretical processes affect the emergence and the direction of the development of knowledge. Competition not only controls both economic activity through the mechanisms of the market and the course of political and social events, but also provides the motor impulse behind diverse interpretations of the world which, when their social background is uncovered, reveal themselves as the intellectual expression of conflicting groups struggling for power.'* (*Ideology and Utopia*, p 241.) But although competition is mentioned here as merely one case of the determination of ideologies by social structure, Mannheim does not mention others. Furthermore he presents in its light the theory of ideologies itself (and his own theory to the rival formulation of marxist theory): *'In the development of a new point of view one party plays the pioneering role, while other parties, in order to cope with the advantage of their adversary in the competitive struggle, must of necessity make use of this point of view. This is the case with the notion of ideology.'* (*op cit*, p 67).
53 Tafuri adheres to a criticism of Mannheim that has become almost a cliché, namely that the *intelligentsia* cannot be the motor of historical change. For Tafuri this would be a consequence of rejecting the distinction between ideologies and utopias: the *intelligentsia* can only produce ideology and therefore plays a conservative role.
54 *Ideology and Utopia*, p 236. This is the conclusion to chapter IV in the English edition of 1936. Originally (in the 1929 German edition) it was the conclusion to the whole essay. But here it still plays the same role, since chapter V, added in the English edition, constitutes a systematic summary, at a general level, of the doctrine of the sociology of knowledge. Since it was written originally in 1931 as an article for a dictionary of sociology, it has, as such, no conclusion proper.
55 *Ibid*, p 225.
56 As, for Kant, metaphysical entities are unreal in that they result from claiming a material content for the conceptions of transcendental reason.
57 As, for Kant, the conceptions of transcendental reason, when taken in their pure epistemological status as *a priori* forms, can make the actual structure of the phenomenal world transparent and in a sense (purely formal) create its structure.
58 Which is a sort of Schopenhauerian version of Kant's purely empiricist conception of knowledge – as the neo-kantians saw it, stripping Kant bare of all 'metaphysics' (ie of the rationalistic and romantic elements of his philosophy).

Fischer von Erlach, Ideal reconstruction of the Phidian statue of Jupiter, from Pausania's description

Notes on a Method
DEMETRI PORPHYRIOS
b 1949

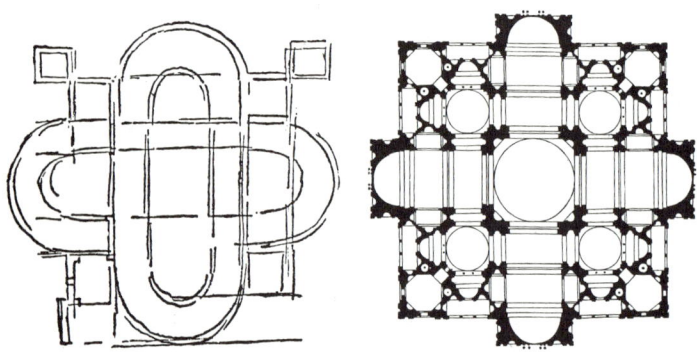

Left Leonardo da Vinci, sketch for a church on the Greek cross plan with angle towers, Paris Manuscript B *Right* Bramante's original plan for St Peter's, Rome, 1506

Michelangelo, *Victory*, detail from the sculpture for the tomb of Julius II, Palazzo Vecchio, Florence

DEMETRI PORPHYRIOS was born in Athens, Greece, in 1949. He received his M Arch and Ph D in the history and theory of architecture from Princeton University. During the years 1975 to 1976 he was a Graham Foundation Fellow researching the work of Alvar Aalto in Finland. He has published in the *Journal of the Society of Architectural Historians, Architectural Design, Controspazio, Lotus International, Oppositions* and *Architektonika Themata*. He has a private practice in Athens and has taught at the Architectural Association and the Royal College of Art. He is currently director of the History and Theory Studies in architecture at the Polytechnic of Central London. His book on Aalto, entitled *Sources of Modern Eclecticism*, is to be published in 1981 by Academy Editions.

Nearly all the important accomplishments of the history of art and architecture in the last hundred years or so have been achieved under the shadow of Hegel. The history of the history of architecture, from Strzygowski, Burckhardt, Riegl, Wölfflin, Frankl, Wittkower, Pevsner or Giedion, to contemporary scholarship, has been the story of re-interpreting the concepts of 'representation' and 'Idea', always remaining within the legacy of Hegelian Idealism.

Against the classical category of the 'imitation of nature', Hegel proposed that of the 'representation of the Idea'. The classical and Renaissance world firmly believed that the task of art was to imitate nature and that in fact artistic excellence lay in the masterly and proper imitation of nature.[1] Hegel's critique of the classical category of 'mimesis', as well as his critique of the Kantian theory of the disinterestedness of art, aimed at lifting art from the metaphysical realm within which it had been debated for centuries. Instead, Hegel attempted to situate art within culture. Hegel, thus, spoke of art as 'proceeding from the Absolute Idea', and assigned as its end 'the sensuous representation of the absolute itself'.[2] Hegel used the term 'Idea' to convey not simply some abstract Platonic image that has lodged itself in the mind as a constitutive *a priori*, but instead in order to mark a mode and an awareness of concrete reality.

In the preface to *The Phenomenology of Mind*, Hegel asserts that 'the true is the concrete', which means that all phenomena (material and/or conceptual) should always be viewed within their living (actual) cultural and social context and never in isolation. The study of a people's architecture, for example, should always be pursued within the context of a people's cultural life, since architecture, according to Hegel, represents that people's vision of the world. In fact, every civilisation is characterised by its peculiar and distinctive spirit, its *Zeitgeist*, the overwhelming power of which holds everyone in its spell. In his turn, the architect/artist, through the 'Idea', appropriates the external world, and in doing so he acquires a *Weltanschauung*. This *Weltanschauung* or worldview, lodged within the conscious or unconscious constitution of the humand mind, becomes the *modus operandi* of all social activity and production. Thus the architect/artist, in the very act of creating, simply represents the 'Idea' in sensuous form; that is, he expresses his *Weltanschauung* by means of sensuous, corporeal form.

This incessant mirroring of the 'I' and culture is not simply a synchronic operation. Hegel maintains that culture is in an incessant state of becoming; of being *aufgehoben*; of cancelling itself out yet preserving, through sublimation, its essentials in an always higher synthesis. In that sense, we are the products not only of the 'Spirit of our Age' but of the 'Spirit of all past Ages' in as much as, through history, a continuous, evolutionary and uninterrupted flow binds everything into a single and sovereign coherency.

THE HEGELIAN LEGACY OF ART AND ARCHITECTURAL HISTORY

The theoretical debt that art and architectural history owe to this legacy of Hegelian Idealism is truly immense. Behind the apparently unsystematic methodology of architectural history, behind its dispersed concepts, its uncodified rules, or its broad humanistic horizons of scholarship, lies in fact the Hegelian epistemology of history. It is on the terrain and within the boundaries of the Hegelian 'historicity of the Idea' that architectural history has unfolded its debates and has founded its disciplinary field. Let us describe, then, the implicit methodological principles with which research in the history of architecture has been—and, to a great extent, is still today—pursued.

First, the notion of the *Zeitgeist*, or the 'Spirit of the Age': it allows one to establish between the simultaneous or successive phenomena of a given era a commonality of sense, an incessant play of mirrors where everything is animated by the image of a collective consciousness. Pevsner, in his *An Outline of European Architecture*, writes: '*It is the spirit of an age that pervades [a period's] social life, its religion, its scholarship and its arts.*'[3] And since architecture is the product of '*the changing spirits of changing ages*',[4] Pevsner asserts categorically that '*the illuminated manuscripts of the Reichenau, the sculptures of Reims, or Giotto's frescoes were ... created because of ... a Zeitgeist expressing itself in religion, politics and philosophy, in guild and in workshop.*'[5] This collective consciousness, conceived as the spirit of a collective archetype against which all deviations or orthodoxies are measured, is always clear yet obscure, obvious yet hidden, everywhere yet nowhere. It is in that sense that for Frankl '*church architecture, sculpture and painting, religious poetry and scholasticism are connected with one another, here and there, by cross-connections ... permanently transfused with and vitalised by the same sap, because they have the same root.*'[6] Even Wölfflin, setting aside for the moment his strict adherence to the absolute autonomy of art, concludes that '*in a word, architecture expresses the* Lebensgefühl *of an epoch. As an art, it [gives] an ideal enhancement of this* Lebensgefühl; *in other words, it [expresses] man's aspirations.*'[7]

This conception of a *Zeitgeist*, expressing itself in the various disciplinary fields of human activity, presupposes that the notion of expression is given a specific relational meaning. Hence the notion of *influence*: it provides always a reason for the birth of an event, implying a causal relationship which alludes to a cause and effect binary determination. Its task is to mark kinships between chronologically successive phenomena by assigning them the role either of a chicken or of an egg. '*One of the tasks which particularly preoccupy the historian of art,*' writes Frankl, '*is to demonstrate the dependence of works of art on those that went before and the influence of different regions or schools on one another.*'[8] To be influenced means to be marked by borrowed traits, and to have one's roots in the land of one's fathers. According to Pevsner, '*Leonardo's Paris Manuscript B ... [consisting] of a combination of a major Greek cross with minor Greek crosses in the corners ... was to prove ... important for the future [of Bramante]. Bramante must [have] seen this, and remembered it years after he had left Milan and moved to Rome.*'[9] To be influenced, then, means to be catalogued according to the common features one shares with others, to be lexically or formally classified, grouped, cleansed of all impurities, charted, grafted, and thus given 'historical' intelligibility.

Art and architectural history have conceived of another kind of influence as well; this time not between individual artists or *écoles*, but between the ideas, beliefs or conceptions of distinct disciplines. In the period between 1130–40 and about 1270, Panofsky observes

'*a connection between Gothic art and scholasticism which is more concrete than a mere "parallelism" and yet more general than those individual—and very important—"influences" which are inevitably exerted on painters, sculptors or architects by erudite advisers. In contrast to a mere parallelism, the connection which I have in mind is a genuine cause-and-effect relation; but in contrast to an individual influence, this cause-and-effect relation comes about by diffusion rather than by direct import. It comes about by the spreading of what may be called, for want of a better term, a mental habit ... Such mental habits are at work in all and every civilisation.*'[10]

This *Zeitgeist*, expressing itself in everyday activity by influencing the artist/architect's *Weltanschauung*, by forming various group tendencies or *écoles*, or even by defining the mentality of an epoch, has always been conceived as a dynamic force that unfolds in History. Hence the notion of *evolution*: it allows one to group historical events by relating them to a sovereign principle of intelligibility, by discovering always a distant beginning and a principle of coherence which is savoured so that it may sketch the outline of historical development. In a similar manner, Frankl ascertains that the '*central thread of this book* [Gothic Architecture] *is the logical process by which the changes from Romanesque to the Gothic style, and those within the Gothic style until its fulfillment in the late Gothic phase, developed from one basic principle.*'[11] Such an understanding of a history of architecture is founded on two fundamental assumptions: first, that there exists an early origin in which lie dormant all the traits that the artistic phenomenon in its development will exhibit; and second, that the history of this phenomenon is nothing but its primordial traits now traced in their successive narrative trajectory called evolution.

'*In England, in France, in Italy, in Germany, in the Netherlands, in Spain,*' writes Pevsner, '*one coherent and unbroken development runs through the last thousand years and more ... Charlemagne restored a Roman Empire, and against his will, helped to raise the first youthful western spirit, the Cluniacs in France and the Saxon Emperors in Germany evolved the Romanesque style, in the Île de France ingenious masons devised the Gothic system, English, Spanish, German, Italian masons somewhat later modified it to suit their growing national consciousness, Italy revolted against it for a new purity, scientific order, and grace, then for a newer gravity and solemnity and then for a forced, self-tormenting artificiality, in*

Saint-Denis, abbey church, interior

her Early Renaissance, High Renaissance and Mannerism. [Such is the] mighty drama of the birth, adolescence, virile maturity, and first symptoms of ageing of the West . . .'[12]

But above all, the notions that allow architectural history to bracket into unities the material it investigates, are those of architecture as 'object' and of the architect as 'author'. These notions have an immediate, empirical and real existence in our lives: they establish their presence by their height, weight, their looks, the shadows that accompany them, the money with which they are involved, the bids, the contracts, the signatures, their birth and their death, or the photographs which stay long after they have vanished.

First, the notion of *architecture as 'object'*: it allows one to assign the building a unity defined by the boundaries of its physical existence; always assuming that the unity of the building is an instantaneous given, an immediate and homogeneous coherency. Conversely, this notion of architecture as 'object', founded on the assumption of a pre-given coherency lying dormant in the mortar of its joints, allows architectural history to set as its task the resurrection of such coherency. Thus, architectural history always neglects the contradictions present in the building and always silences its antimonies, so that the building's generalised thematic is extracted as the sovereign organiser. The consistencies of the building, therefore, grow stronger and are given the status of 'principles'.

Closely linked to the notion of architecture as 'object' is that of the *architect as 'author'*. In fact, the notion of the architect as 'author' explains why in everyday life we tend to think of architecture only in terms of physical objects. That is so since the coherency of the architectural object—its cleverly hidden consistency—is nothing else but the expressive projection of its actual, living architect. Such an architect/author, easily bracketed between two dates and empirically grasped by means of an exhaustive biography, is marked always by a deep individual coherency, by a unity of thought which rises to a charismatic uniqueness.

The architect/author, therefore, becomes the inventor of his order and his laws. The making of architecture is always a creative process. Creation is conceived as a genial epiphany that visits from time-to-time certain charismatic minds. It is such an architect/author, always incarnating, expressing, translating, reflecting, rendering, etc, his individual vision in the sensuous corporeality of the architectural object, thus endowing it with an analogical coherency, whom the architectural historian will set out to resurrect. Panofsky, in his *Studies in Iconology*, discussing the 'intrinsic meaning or content' of a work of art, writes: *'it [the intrinsic meaning or content] is apprehended by ascertaining those underlying principles which reveal the basic attitude of a nation, a period, a class, a religious or philosophical persuasion—unconsciously qualified by one personality and condensed into one work.'*[13]

With these analytical categories, architectural history has attempted to study its material: always searching to salvage from the opaque presence of the architectural object the hidden intention of the creative architect/author. *'When we try to understand it [da Vinci's 'Last Supper' and by extension an architectural object as well] as a document of Leonardo's personality, or of the civilisation of the Italian High Renaissance, or of a peculiar religious attitude,'* writes Panofsky, *'we deal with the work of art as a symptom of something else which expresses itself in a countless variety of other symptoms, and we interpret its compositional and iconographical features as more particularised evidence of this something else.'*[14] Thus, the idealist historian becomes the perpetually restoring conscience of another one hidden in the work itself. Such an understanding of architectural history rests on an allegorical operation: its objective is always to recover what is meant by that which is actually said. Such a history of architecture is always conceived as an 'interpretive commentary'. Panofsky writes: *'the discovery and interpretation of the "symbolical" values . . . is the object of what we may call iconography in the deeper sense . . .'*[15] Such a history loves being constitutive; it loves to resurrect the possible semantic values of the architectural object by tracing forgotten influences; it loves to formalise into principles the internal logic of the architectural object since such principles point once more to the coherency of the architect/author, the only one qualified to condense into his work the 'sap' of an age.

We witness, therefore, a history of ideas which is coupled with a history of the incarnation, expression, translation, reflection, transcription, etc, of ideas into sensuous form. Discussing the Neoplatonic movement and its reflection in the work of Michelangelo, Panofsky writes: *'to say that the sculptures of Michelangelo reflect a Neoplatonic world-view is to say or imply that there is some kind of similarity between the work of art and the world-view and that the latter has influenced the creation of the work of art.'*[16] Thus, the necessary and sufficient schema for the passage from ideas to sensuously given artistic or architectural objects is as follows:

if x = work of art, and y = world-view,
in order to claim that x reflects y,

it is necessary and sufficient that we show that:
(1) *x* and *y* are similar;
(2) *y* influenced *x*.

Influence and similarity are, therefore, necessary requirements for any art historical study. In fact, the world-view influences the artwork because the former, deeply rooted in the personality of the artist, determines the way he conceives and carries out his creations. Paying homage to the mediatory subjectivity of a constitutive consciousness, the investigation of the art and architectural historian is always a description of origins and effects; it is a description of conceptual unities as manifested in iconographic or stylistic unities; it is the tale of a thematic trajectory which constitutes the linear succession of historical development. We witness here a history of the Hegelian couple, Idea/Form. We witness, in other words, a history of successive developments, of influences, and of thematic or stylistic unities that describe concentric circles around the ontological primacy of the architectural 'object', making us therefore see what the 'object' itself hides, its profound message. The task of such a history of architecture is to perpetuate the ideological foundations of a 'humanist' anthropology of creation, which, in its turn, helps *re*-produce the dominant ideology of our conjunction: architecture as an 'object' for consumption.

NOTES ON A CRITICAL HISTORY OF ARCHITECTURE
(a) General. Let us, for a moment, suggest that we suspend the notions of *Weltanschauung*, *Zeitgeist*, influence, evolution, origins, architecture/object, architect/author, creation, and above all the understanding of history as an interpretive commentary, so that we may sketch the outline of 'another' history of architecture.

I will not discuss the reasons that make this 'other' history of architecture necessary. Surely, the issue of legitimacy or non-legitimacy of a theoretical model of history is an important one, yet its apodicticity is *not* a matter of proving or disproving its internal epistemological logic. Instead, the issue of the legitimacy or non-legitimacy of a theoretical model of history is, in the final analysis, a political issue. It sustains (or not) its status of 'truth' on the basis of the value and practical application it has in promoting (or not) the dominant ideology of a period. For the purposes of this essay, however, I will confine the discussion to a purely descriptive level.

Let us hastily sketch this 'other' history of architecture. It begins the moment *we* begin to suspect every teleology of reason, and instead when we conceive the historical relation between a result and its conditions of existence as a *relation of production* and *not of expression*. Once we grasp the relationship of architecture and society not as one of result/cause, effect/origins, form/content, representation/Idea, etc, but as one of production, then, we have freed ourselves from all the categories of the Hegelian model. We no longer need to fall back on the notions of *Weltanschauung*, *Zeitgeist*, influence, origins or evolution, for they presuppose the relationship of expression or representation.[17] We no longer need to fall back on the notions of creation or interpretive commentary, for they presuppose the unities of the artist and the *oeuvre*.[18]

We immediately confront, however, the problem of describing that peculiar coherency on the basis of which we can periodise history. Instead of bracketing historical unities on

Fontrevault, abbey church, interior looking south-east

the basis of calendar contemporaneity or on the basis of stylistic filiations, individual artists, or *écoles*, we will do something else. We will set out to identify the very assumptions on the basis of which a building's plan, section, elevation, space, decoration, materials, proportions, composition, etc, have been envisaged and conceptualised. In other words, we will ask whether the building was produced (that is, conceived, designed, executed and recognised in everyday life) within a field of knowledge that was characterised by its own rules, its own hierarchies, its own axiomatic and derivative principles, or its own classificatory and axiological criteria. We will, therefore, interrogate the building *not* on the level of its apparent thematics or stylistics, but on the level of the implicit rules which allowed its thematics and stylistics to be formulated, hierarchised, semanticised, given everyday credibility, and eventually institutionalised.

These formative rules, that make it possible for any building to be produced (that is, conceived, designed, executed, and recognised in everyday life), we will call its architectural *problematic*.

(b) The Concept of Problematic. The concept of *problematic*[19] introduces us to a fact peculiar to the very existence of any discourse. Any discourse (in our case architecture) '*can only pose problems on the terrain and within the horizon of a definite theoretical structure [in the case of architecture also figurative and syntactic structure], its problematic, which constitutes its absolute and definite condition of possibility, and hence the absolute determination of the forms in which all problems must be posed, at any given moment...*'[20] Althusser, in an effort to capture the specificity of knowledge that a

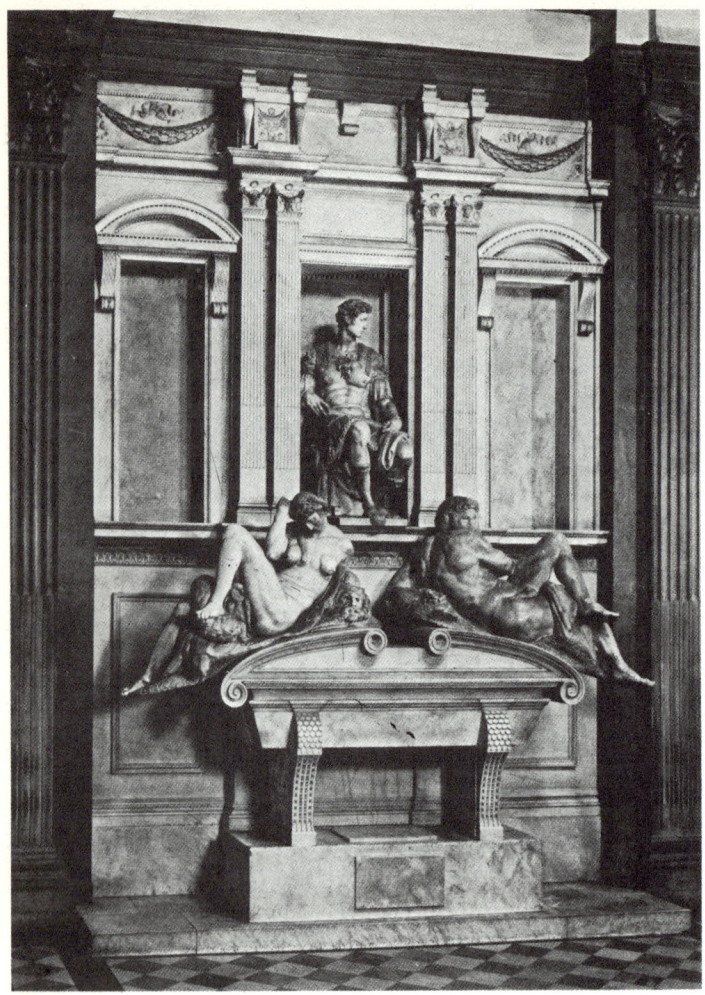

Michelangelo, Tomb of Giuliano de'Medici, New Sacristy, San Lorenzo, Florence

problematic inaugurates, has resorted to a spatial metaphor—adopted from Foucault's *Histoire de la Folie*. In his book *Reading Capital*, Althusser writes that the concept of the *problematic*

'*opens the way to an understanding of the determination of the visible as visible, and conjointly of the invisible as invisible, and of the link binding the invisible to the visible. Any object or problem situated on the terrain and within the horizon, i.e. in the definite structured field of the theoretical problematic of a given theoretical discipline, is visible. We must take these words literally . . . It is literally no longer the eye—the mind's eye—of a subject which sees what exists in the field defined by a theoretical problematic: it is this field itself which sees itself in the objects or problems it defines . . . The same connection that defines the visible also defines the invisible as its shadowy obverse. It is the field of the problematic that defines and structures the invisible as the defined excluded, excluded from the field of visibility and defined as excluded by the existence and peculiar structure of the field of the problematic . . . Here again, the invisible is no more a function of a subject's sighting than is the visible: the invisible is the theoretical problematic's non-vision of its non-objects, the invisible is the darkness, the blinded eye of the theoretical problematic's self-reflection when it scans its non-objects, its non-problems without seeing them, in order not to look at them.*'[21]

This is the case, for example, with the notion of *convenance*. To the 18th-century mind, *convenance* stood for propriety to customs and mores; to the 19th-century mind, instead, *convenance* stood for utility and convenience to use. For Ledoux, Boullée or Le Camus de Mézières, the looks of a building were chosen on the basis of its propriety to the social mores. Utility and convenience to use were invisible within the problematic of 18th-century *architecture parlante* because they were defined as excluded. Instead, for Viollet-le-Duc or Reynaud, the looks of a building were directly linked to its purposive utility and to its convenience to use and construction. Propriety to mores was invisible within the problematic of 19th-century Structural Moralists; instead, purposive utility was to hierarchise the century's field of architectural knowledge.

The scattered buildings, the fragile detail paper amassing on drawing boards, the slide-shows animating the lecture halls of accredited professional institutions, the hastily written lecture-notes that the 'master' conspicuously hides in his pocket on his itinerary around the world's most distinguished schools, all these different traces or people define their discourse not simply on the basis of their thematics, stylistic obsessions or transmitted messages. Above all, they define their discourse on the basis of the unity of their unconscious assumptions: the unity of their problematic. It is their problematic which defines the field of knowledge where they can eventually unfold their formal identities, their thematic continuities, their manifestoes, their working tools, or their polemical dialogues.

Thus, to study the problematic of an architectural discourse means to study, at a given moment, architecture's field of knowledge: that is, its constitutive axioms; the specific articulation and hierarchy of its concepts; the tensions which contradictory survivals introduce; or the boundaries within which the discourse exercises its debate, and which assure and define its specificity as a domain of knowledge.

To study an architectural discourse on the level of its problematic does *not* mean to analyse it on the level of its formalisation. The rules to which the concept of the problematic refers should not be confused with the rules of design which characterise a given architectural discourse. Instead of asking what design tools, methods, techniques or stylistic inventions characterise an architectural discourse, one has to ask a different question; namely, what are the rules which, once assumed, give to such design tools their posture as theoretical instruments and their credibility in everyday life as relevant or problem-solving methods?

For example, instead of asking what are the compositional principles (grid, rotation, procession, etc) which govern a given architectural work, we will ask a different question: say, what is the peculiar classificatory mode (for example, homotopic reasoning) which allows for the 'grid', 'procession', 'rotation', etc, to be conceived in the first place? In other words, we will periodise architectural history not according to styles, themes, ideologies, artists, *écoles*, or individual masterpieces, but instead on the basis of classificatory, ordering, significatory, etc, categories. Such a history of architecture, therefore, is interested not in categories that would describe a building, but in categories that would *describe the production* (that is, the conception, design, execution, and recognition) of a building.

(c) Relations between Architecture and other Discourses. We have seen that to study the problematic of an architectural discourse means to study the *field of knowledge* which allows for the thematics, design tools, techniques, stylistics, etc, to emerge in the first place. What we have described, therefore, is in no way similar to what we commonly understand by the term 'disciplinary field'. A discipline, according to the common use of the word, is totally ordered on the unity that its object of study establishes. A discipline, in that sense, defines the boundaries of its specificity on the basis of the object of its study. Thus, political economy, theology, architecture, the history of painting, the history of ideas, etc, comprise so many disciplines because they are interested in studying so many objects respectively: wealth, God, shelter, paintings, ideologies, etc.

The concept of problematic, however, allows the historian to cross the boundaries of such disciplines since the coherency he searches to describe is neither thematic nor semantic, but rather tropological. For example, confronted, on the one hand with Buffon's classification of the natural kingdom according to each object's characteristic *'size, colour, substance, or whatever other sensuous quality . . .'*[22] and on the other with Blondel's classification of architectural genres into *'light, elegant, delicate, rustic, etc . . .'*[23], we will not exclaim we have discovered the 'sources' which 'influenced' 18th-century architectural theory. Instead, we will note that architecture shares with natural science the same category of classificatory reasoning. We will examine whether the problematic of natural science has been displaced *en bloc* (that is, whether architecture has borrowed all the structuring categories of natural science), or whether such categorical interferences are fragmentary and episodic. We will map the possible changes that the various categories or concepts undergo when displaced from one discourse to another; we will also study their hierarchy in the internal economy of the respective disciplinary systems. We will not assign 'influences' depending on what came first: natural science or architecture? Instead, we will note that natural science functions as the 'overdetermining' ideological region, since its categories structure the problematic of almost all the other ideological regions in that given 'conjuncture' (philosophy, linguistics, architecture, etc). We are, therefore, interested in describing the relations of dependence that exist between the problematics of different discourses, so that we may discern the 'hegemonical' role played by one or another discourse and, thereby, the degree of effective intervention assigned to each one of them.

It should be stressed that these studies are not dependent on the existence of causal relationships between chronologically contemporary events. In that sense, we are not interested in synchrony. Similarly, these studies are not dependent on the existence of causal relationships between the old and the new or between the original and the derivative. In that sense, we are not interested in diachrony.

These studies do not aim at an interpretive commentary or a profound exegesis of the birth and death of architectural events. We study neither hidden messages nor arbitrarily encoded ones; our study is neither a hermeneutics nor a semiology. Instead, we study the rules which define—within a historical conjuncture—the field of knowledge on the basis of which the various discourses unfold their debates and thematics. Our interest in this field of knowledge stems from the realisation that the emergence and functioning of any symbolic language is, in the first instance, structured by those 'matter-of-fact truths' which constitute our historical *a prioris*.

Michelangelo, Tomb of Lorenzo de'Medici, New Sacristy, San Lorenzo, Florence

(d) Relations between Architecture and Economic-political Life. We are, thus, interested in a history of architecture which describes the functioning not of the thematics, formalisations, stylistics or ideologies surrounding architecture, but the functioning of the problematic which in the first place allows such thematics, formalisations, stylistics or ideologies to be formulated. We, further, said that such a history of architecture is interested also in describing the relations of dependence that exist between the problematic of an architectural discourse and those of the different other discourses. There still remains, however, the question of the relations that exist between an architectural discourse and all those non-discursive practices, like economic practice, political practice, or institutions. How could one think of the relationship between architectural discourse and economic activity? Between architectural discourse and the massive lines of unemployment? Between architectural discourse and the formalised obligatory University training, or the numerous rites that mark one's passage from studentship to professionalism?

It could be possible to present the economic and political

'atmosphere' of the period under study by referring to the widely accepted texts of political and economic history. Discussing the architecture of Michelangelo, Ackerman writes:

'In the early years of the 16th century the extraordinary power, wealth, and imagination of the Pope, Julius II della Rovere (1503–13) made Rome the artistic centre of Italy and of Europe and attracted there the most distinguished artists of his age. Chiefly for political reasons, the rise of Rome coincided with the decline of the great centres of 15th-century Italian culture: Florence, Milan and Urbino. The new 'capital' had no eminent painters, sculptors or architects of its own, so it had to import them ... This sudden change in the balance of Italian culture had a revolutionary effect on the arts ... No creative Renaissance artist could fail to be inspired and profoundly affected by the experience of encountering simultaneously the works of ancient architects ... and those of his greatest contemporaries.'[24]

One would, thus, link an architectural discourse with contemporary political and economic events solely on the basis of calendar-time. One would, in a sense, sanction the sovereignty of the 'essential section'[25], where history, when sliced, exhibits naked in its fresh and odorous section all the possible links that constitute the contemporaneity, simultaneity and spontaneity of Hegelian history.

Alternatively, it could be possible to consider the thematics, tools, techniques or stylistics of an architectural discourse as the reflection or expression of political, economic and institutional events or strategies. Hauser, attempting to relate politics, philosophy and Gothic architecture, writes:

'Realism was appropriate to an essentially undemocratic order of society, to a hierarchy in which only the peaks counted, to absolutist organisations which transcended the individual and confined life within the framework of church and feudality without allowing any freedom of movement. Nominalism, on the other hand, reflected the dissolution of authoritarian forms of community, and the triumph of a social life built out of individual gradations over one based on unconditional subordination of the individual ... [Accordingly,] Gothic breaks up the whole, which Romanesque art had at least pervaded by a decorative unity, into a number of partial compositions, each one in the main built up according to the classical principle of unity and subordination, but in total giving the effect of a rather indiscriminate conglomeration of subjects. Interest is now completely centred upon the individual and the characteristic.'[26]

One would, thus, link politics, philosophy and architecture on the assumption that there exists an 'analogical equivalency'[27] between discursive and non-discursive practices; that is, on the assumption that architecture, philosophy and politics have entered into a silent agreement of mutually reflecting or expressing each other, of constantly mirroring each other, of manifesting different sides of the same thing. In that sense, one would sanction an allegorical functioning of history where the sovereignty of a *Zeitgeist* is manifested analogically in the so many different activities of life, and then set out to decipher the symbolic precipitate couched in the very products of these activities.

Or, further, one could study the political or economic literature of a period tracing step-by-step the long lists of political disputes, crown successions, parliamentary debates, dissident rallies, the status of the emporium, the fluctuation of the price-index, the institutional codes, or the tastes and aspirations of the patrons. Wittkower writes:

In the 14th century, the rising middle class in cities like Ghent and Florence superseded the old aristocracy in political power and wealth and vied with it in social prestige. They soon began to aspire to a cultured style of living and required artists in growing numbers ... The new class patrons—wealthy burghers or nobles who had a bourgeois past—with their highly developed individualism, sense of liberty and enterprise, their progressive and competitive spirit ... imprinted in their artists an attitude towards life which they themselves cherished ...'[28]

One would, thus, assume that there exist causal relations between political changes, economic processes, institutional or patronage practices and architectural discourse, and that these causal relationships determine the consciousness of the 'architect/author', his world-view and his mentality. Such a history, however, is primarily a search for influences: it ascribes irrevocable causal hierarchies between political, economic and architectural events, through the mediation of a transcendental consciousness, the subjectivity of the architect/author.

The study we have in mind is situated on a different level. In attempting to grasp the relations between an architectural discourse and political practice, economic practice or institutions, we will not trace the simultaneity of context; we will not decipher the expressive, analogical or symbolic pacts between architecture and society; we will not account for the forces which influenced the consciousness, intention, or world-view of a constitutive subjectivity which (subjectivity), in its turn, expressed such a world-view in actual built form. Instead, we will ask a different question. We will ask whether, to what extent and in what manner, political practice, economic practice and institutions intervened in the formulation of the problematic of an architectural discourse. Instead of asking how political practice determines the thematics and the meaning of an architectural discourse, we will ask how and in what manner it takes part in delimiting the choices and the internal economy of the problematic of an architectural discourse. We will ask: does political practice, for example, allow a problematic to be recognised as legitimate in everyday life? How does it assign a problematic to a statutory position in everyday life? How does it reproduce or combat its implementation? How does it assure its revivals or transformations? How, in other words, does it allow a problematic to entertain the respectful title of updated knowledge?

Thus, we set out to show how an architectural discourse, concerned with its particular domain of interests, practiced by a number of professional and statutory figures, taught by a number of academically hallowed 'masters', and functioning in a specific manner within the production cycle of a society, is articulated on practices which are external to it and of a non-discursive nature. It is not a matter of showing that there is, for example, a 'communist' or 'capitalist' window, but of how political practice, economic practice, and their respective institutional codifications delimit the domain, functioning and everyday recognition of the

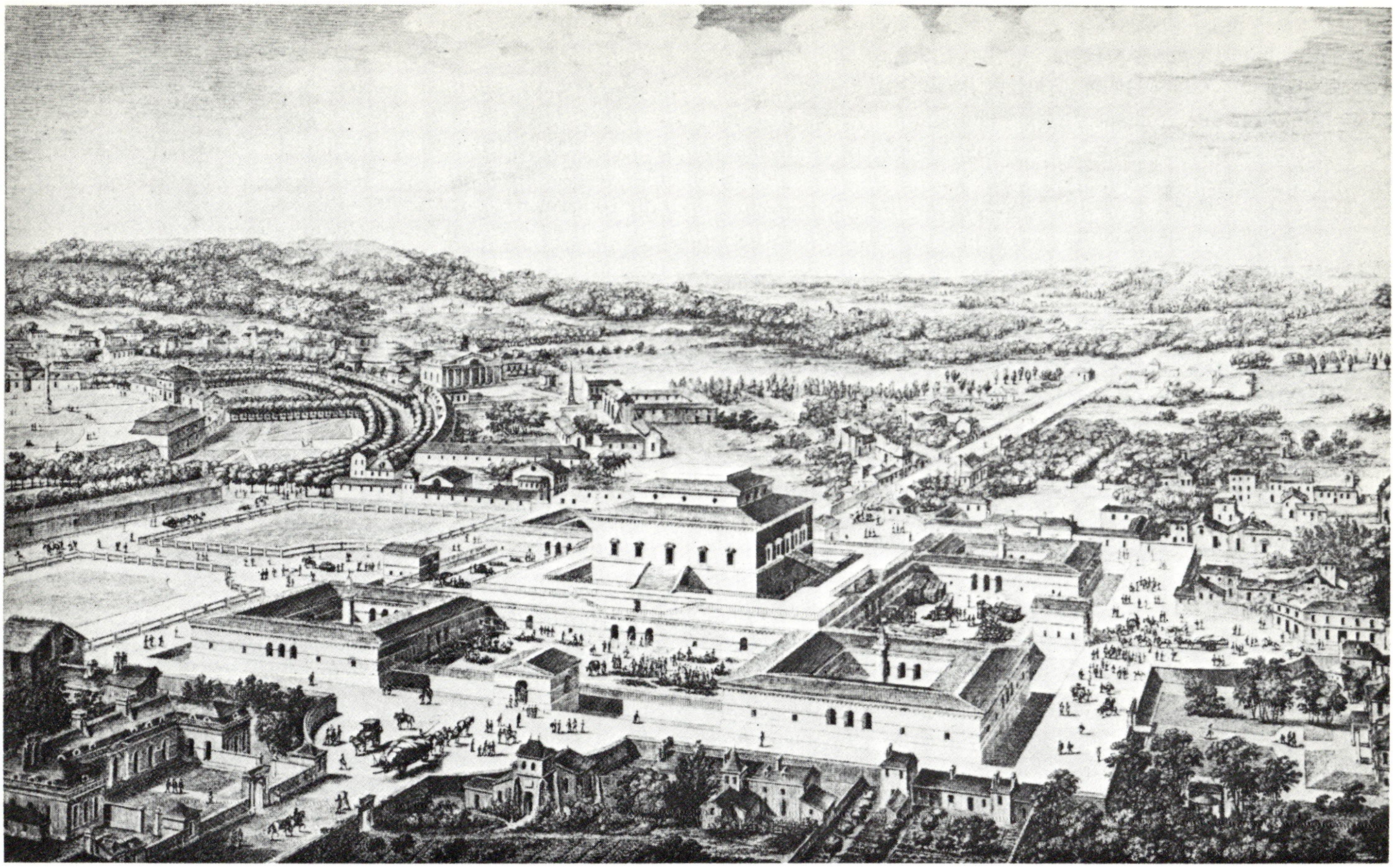

![Ledoux Marketplace]

C-N Ledoux, *Marketplace*, 1773–79, (from *Visionary Architects*, University of St Thomas, 1968)

G L F Laves, *Naturbrücke*, 1852–53, (from *Dortmunder Architekturhefte*, no 4, 1977)

C-N Ledoux, *Bridge on the Loue*, 1773–79 (from *Visionary Architects*, University of St Thomas, 1968)

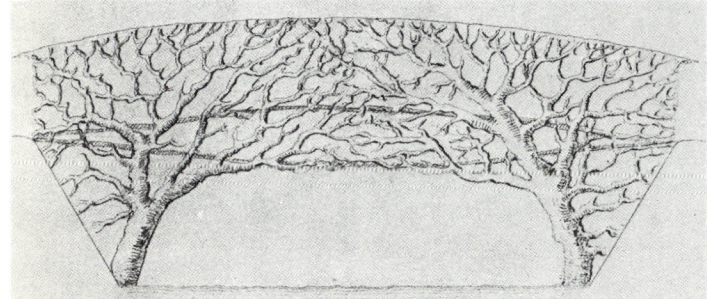

problematic of an architectural discourse.

Let us take an example. Comparing 18th-century and 19th-century architectural theory (ideology), one notices a shift in the meaning of the design principle of *convenance*. The 18th century, operating within the general problematic of engineering excellence, assigned to *convenance* the meaning of 'utility'. The notion of 'befitting', therefore, changes from that of 'socially befitting' to 'operationally or constructionally befitting'. Such an etymological shift marks the way in which the new architectural problematic is effective in legitimising the emerging technocratic ideologies of the engineer. At the same time we see a thorough re-organisation of the architectural problematic. New concepts appear (eg the grid as a design tool; imitation as *la similitude par identité* and not as *la ressemblance par image*; *ossature*; etc). Some concepts disappear (eg that of the expressive physiognomy of a building). Some old concepts are retained, but their role within the internal economy of the problematic is modified (eg decoration does not aim at beauty but at the legibility of the building type).

Faced with such shifts, exclusions and valorisations, the historian will have to study whether and to what extent they were instrumental in sanctioning the new methods of construction, assemblage, efficiency and economy. He will also have to study whether the disappearance of certain concepts facilitated (or not, and to what extent) the priorities of the new systems of production. As, for example, might be the case with mid-19th century Europe, where the priorities of industrial production discouraged physiognomic expressionism in buildings (since expressive individuality under-utilises mass-production techniques), and instead encouraged stylistic eclecticism as an alternative for individualising buildings (since style, when severed from construction, serves the aims of mass-production and consumption while maintaining the illusion of individuality). Further, the modifications in the internal hierarchy of 19th-century architectural discourse (eg the shift from decoration as beauty to decoration as communication) seem to have been related to the change in the status of the concept of style. It is in that sense, therefore, that economy, politics or institutions 'determine' architecture: never leaving a clear label of sovereignty but simply hinting at exclusions or valorisations.

I am aware of the oversimplification of these examples. Their sketchiness, however, points to the road to be traversed. Theories can only serve as starting points for concrete historical case studies. I am also aware that there can be no single normative model of historical study. In a sense, the historical material has to be 'conquered' by many 'contenders'. Of them, the one I have described here studies the way in which the problematic of an architectural discourse—by formulating the discourse's tasks, limits, exclusions, valorisations, hierarchies, concepts, design tools, instruments or techniques—functions effectively within the struggle of dominant and dominated ideologies by serving the interests of one or another.

It is not a matter of relating architecture and society in an effort to salvage the mythical footnote which would instantaneously sort out attributions, causes or influences. It is a matter of showing the effective emergence, insertion and functioning of architecture within society. And that since *'the peculiarity of art is to "make us see" ... the ideology from which it is born, in which it bathes, from which it detaches itself as art, and to which it alludes.'*[29]

Notes
This text is an edited version of a paper first presented at Princeton University in April 1975.

1. For a more detailed discussion on the history of the concept of 'imitation', see: W Tatarkiewicz, *History of Aesthetics*, (ed) J Harell, The Hague, Mouton, 1970; L Venturi, *History of Art Criticism*, Dutton, NY, 1964; N Pevsner, *Academies of Art Past and Present*, Cambridge, 1940; A Blunt, *Artistic Theory in Italy*, Oxford, 1956.
2. G W F Hegel, *Vorlesungen über die Aesthetik* (transl) B Bosanquet, as cited in *On Art, Religion, Philosophy*, (ed) Glen Gray, Harper Books, NY, 1970, pp 22–127. For a complete translation of the aesthetic writings of Hegel, see: *The Philosophy of Fine Art*, (transl) F P B Osmaston, Bell and Sons, London, 1920, Vol III, subsection I, deals specifically with architecture. For an acquaintance with Hegel's system of metaphysics, see: *The Phenomenology of Mind*, (transl) J B Baillie, (introd) G Lichtheim, Harper Books, 1967. For the specific views of Hegel on History, see: *The Philosophy of History*, (transl) J Sibree, NY, 1899, or the later edition with preface by J C Friedrich, NY, 1956.
3. N Pevsner, *An Outline of European Architecture*, Penguin Books, 1974, p 17.
4. *Ibid*, p 17.
5. N Pevsner, *Academies of Art Past and Present*, p 224.
6. Paul Frankl, *Gothic Architecture*, (ed) N Pevsner, Penguin Books, Baltimore-Maryland, 1962, p 268.
7. Heinrich Wölfflin, *Renaissance and Baroque*, (transl) Kathrin Simon, Cornell Univ Press, Ithaca, NY, 1966, p 78.
8. Paul Frankl, *op cit*, p xvi.
9. N Pevsner, *An Outline of European Architecture*, p 327.
10. Erwin Panofsky, *Gothic Architecture and Scholasticism*, The Archabbey Press, Latrobe, Pennsylvania, 1951, pp 20–21.
11. Paul Frankl, *op cit*, p xvi.
12. N Pevsner, *An Outline of European Architecture*, p 709.
13. Erwin Panofsky, *Studies in Iconology*, Oxford Univ Press, NY, 1939, p 7.
14. *Ibid*, p 8.
15. *Ibid*, p 8.
16. *Ibid*, pp 171–230.
17. The theoretical status of the relational notion of 'representation' has a long history. I cannot here trace its numerous nuances. Though of a purely Hegelian origin, it has often been used (with various shifts in meaning) in marxist literature (cf Hegel's '... the task of art is to represent the "Idea" to direct perception in sensuous form ... it follows, therefore, that the level of excellency of art in attaining a realisation adequate to its "Idea" must depend upon the grade of unity with which "Idea" and form(shape) display themselves as fused into one.' (ed Glen Gray, *op cit*, p 106.) A rigorous study is needed that would distinguish the categorical nuances of the 'relational aspect' of representation in its various aspects. It has been used, eg in its Classical or Renaissance notion of 'mimesis'; in the notion of 'mimesis' as a *simulacrum*; in the notion of 'mimesis' as an analogon, cf Quatremère de Quincy; in the notion of the Hegelian fusion; in the notion of the Lukaçsian typicality; in the notion of vulgar Machian economism; in the notion of marxist realism; in the notion of structuralist isomorphism; in the notion of the semiotic arbitrary connection between signifier/signified; in the notion of the Althusserian effectivity; in the notion of Marx's *Darstellung*; or in so many other understandings that I might not be familiar with. An excellent discussion on the notion of marxist realism as a mode of 'mimesis' can be found in Stefan Morawski's *Inquiries into the Fundamentals of Aesthetics*, M I T Press, Mass, 1974. For the Lukaçsian model see Georg Lukaçs, *The Theory of the Novel*, (transl) Anna Bostock, M I T Press, Mass, 1971. Also, *Realism in our Times*, (transl) John and Necke Mander, Harper Books, NY, 1971. For an extensive discussion of the Althusserian notion of 'effectivity', see his *For Marx*, (transl) Ben Brewster, Vintage Books, NY, 1970. Also, Louis Althusser and Étienne Balibar, *Reading Capital*, (transl) Ben Brewster, NLB edition, London 1972. For a related notion and its spatial metaphor of mirror/reflection see Pierre Macherey, *Pour une Théorie de la Production Littéraire*, Maspero, Paris, 1966. For the notion of structural isomorphism see Jean Piaget, *Structuralism*, (transl) Chaninah Mascher, Harper Books, NY, 1970. Marx's concept of *Darstellung* can be seen in a non-theoretical form in his *Capital*.
18. For an extensive discussion of the unities of 'artist' and '*oeuvre*' see Michel Foucault, *The Archaeology of Knowledge*, (transl) Sheridan Smith, Tavistock Publications, London, 1972. Also, Pierre Macherey, *op cit*.
19. '... the concept of a problematic ... designate[s] the particular unity of a theoretical formation ...', Louis Althusser, *For Marx*, p 32. See also Saul Kärsz, *Théorie et Politique: Louis Althusser*, Librairie Fayard, Paris, 1974, pp 34–38. A similar concept can be seen in the thought of Michel Foucault applied more generally to characterise that particular framework which allows any discursive practice (and not only scientific discourse) to draw the frontiers of its specificity within which it can unfold its debate. For a theoretical discussion of these and related issues, see Michel Foucault, *The Archaeology of Knowledge*, as well as Pierre Macherey *Pour une Théorie de la Production Littéraire*. For an application of these theoretical tools on concrete historical material, see Macherey's chapter 'Lenin as a Critic of Tolstoy', as well as the brilliant studies of Foucault: *Histoire de la Folie*, Librairie Plon, Paris, 1961; *Les Mots et les Choses*, Éditions Gallimard, Paris, 1966; *Naissance de la Clinique*, Presses Universitaires de France, Paris, 1972. Also see, Raymond Williams, *Marxism and Literature*, Oxford Univ Press, 1977; Terry Eagleton, *Criticism and Ideology*, New Left Books, London, 1976.
20. Louis Althusser, *Reading Capital, op cit*, p 25.
21. *Ibid*, pp 25–26.
22. Le Comte de Buffon, *Discours sur la Manière de Traiter l'Histoire Naturelle*, taken from *Oeuvres Complètes*, L'Imprimerie Royale, Paris, 1774, p 31.
23. Jacques François Blondel, *Cours d'Architecture*, chez Desaint, Paris, 1771, vol I, p 412.
24. James Ackerman, *The Architecture of Michelangelo*, Zwemmer, London, 1961, p xxxv.
25. Empiricist conceptions of history (Hegelian Idealism included) see in the contemporaneity of calendar-time the possibility of an analysable totality. This implies the intelligibility of a synchronic section of history assuming an even development of the various levels of social practice. On the contrary, Marx has spoken of the *uneven development* of the various levels of social practice, thus, underlying the 'peculiar time' of each level and, thus, its *not* necessarily calendar articulation with the historical totality.
26. Arnold Hauser, *The Social History of Art*, (transl) Stanley Godman, Vintage Books, NY, 1951, p 238.
27. Trying to think of the concept of influence or determination between art and society, Hauser adopts the notion of 'analogical equivalency' according to which the description of influences is the description of similarities. In that sense, Hauser, though starting with Marx's methodological guidelines of an overdetermined whole, cannot think of the nature of such a determination but within the Hegelian category of analogical similarity. In fact, such Hegelian survivals are common within the tradition of marxist aesthetics, from Pleckanov to Lukaçs to Hauser or Read. For a comprehensive discussion of the various types of studying the relationship between discursive and non-discursive practices, see Stefan Morawski, *Inquiry into the Fundamentals of Aesthetics*, pp 295–308, ch 8: 'Art and Society'.
28. Rudolf and Margot Wittkower, *Born under Saturn*, Weidenfeld and Nicolson, London, 1963, p 31.
29. Louis Althusser, *Lenin and Philosophy*, Monthly Review Press, NY, 1971, p 222.